NATIONAL INSTITUTE FOR SOCIAL WORK TRAINING

SERIES NO. 20

HOMELESS NEAR A THOUSAND HOMES

Publications by the
National Institute for Social Work Training
Mary Ward House, London, W.C.1

HOMELESS NEAR
A THOUSAND HOMES

A Study of Families without Homes
in South Wales and the West of England

by

BRYAN ⎣GLASTONBURY

FOREWORD BY
JOHN GREVE

*Professor of Social Administration in
The University of Southampton*

London
GEORGE ALLEN & UNWIN LTD
RUSKIN HOUSE   MUSEUM STREET

ISBN 0 04 301033 4 cloth
0 04 301042 3 paper

PRINTED IN GREAT BRITAIN
in 11 point Fournier type
by Cox & Wyman Ltd, Fakenham

The illustrations used in this book are true, but all the names of people and sometimes of places have been changed.

ACKNOWLEDGEMENTS

The title is taken from the poem 'Guilt and Sorrow' by William Wordsworth:

> And homeless near a thousand homes I stood,
> And near a thousand tables pined and wanted food.

This study began in 1966 with the encouragement and co-operation of Mr W. D. Davies and Mr I. R. Jenkins, Children's Officer and Director of Welfare Services for Glamorgan County Council. It has benefited throughout by the advice of Mr S. G. Wilkinson, Principal Assistant Children's Officer for Glamorgan. In 1969 a grant was received from the Department of Health and Social Security to enable the project to be extended into other areas—the County Boroughs of Cardiff, Swansea and Bristol and County Councils of Gloucestershire and Somerset as well as Glamorgan. Councillors and officials of these local authorities, staff of Department of Health and Social Security Offices and members of many other agencies, statutory and voluntary, gave their support generously.

Nine part-time researchers joined the project—Mrs Brenda Masterman, Mrs Suzanne Young, Miss Mary Sharp, Mrs Margaret Lowe, Mrs Stella Thompson, Mrs Christine Jones, Mrs Lilian Daniels, Mrs Peggy Simons and Mrs Jane Meager. Their primary task was obtaining information for family case histories, but some of them helped in writing up the study. Mrs Christine Jones contributed extensively to the first part of Chapter 5 and the middle section of Appendix I; Mrs Brenda Masterman to the last sections of Chapters 7 and Appendix I; Mrs Suzanne Young to the first part of Appendix I and Miss Mary Sharp to the penultimate section of Chapter 7. Mrs Rita Austin and Mrs Mary Viner helped to prepare and programme the statistical findings for computation. Miss Deirdre Hogarth was secretary to the project, bringing order to the chaos, and was assisted in typing drafts by Mrs Denise Johns, Mrs Iris John, Mrs Liz Evans, Mrs Jose Nuttall and Mrs Marion Rees. My tolerant colleagues in the Social Administration Department took over some of my teaching to free me for this work and three of them, Dr Michael Ryan, Mr. A. V. S. Lochhead and Miss Grace Trenchard, made useful comments on the drafts. The Director of Social Administration courses at Swansea—initially Mr. Lochhead and later Mr R. A. B. Leaper—gave the project continued encouragement. Mr Robin Huws Jones of the National Institute for Social Work Training gave detailed and valuable comments.

Lastly, and most importantly, many homeless families allowed us to pester them and to probe the intimate depths of their difficulties.

FOREWORD

BY JOHN GREVE
Professor of Social Administration in The University of Southampton

———————

This book by Bryan Glastonbury is another contribution to the melancholy story of homelessness in contemporary Britain. It describes the experiences of some of the homeless—how they became homeless, the helplessness and bewilderment that are the permanent lot of many, and the misery that is a constant accompaniment. All this experienced acutely by thousands of people on any day of the year—a quarter of a century after the creation of the so-called 'Welfare State'. All this in the midst of a society committed to affluence. And homelessness is no ephemeral phenomenon but a growing feature of our society.

While the national product and, for the majority, personal real incomes rose in the 1960s so did the number of homeless. Government statistics show that during the decade the number of persons in England and Wales who were in local authority 'temporary accommodation' doubled. But there are strong reasons for believing that the official figures understate the incidence of homelessness.

No one knows the true figures of homelessness. Nor, with strikingly few notable exceptions, has much time or effort been expended by the responsible public authorities on discovering the precise causes or measuring the real effects on individual persons and families. But here the initiative taken by the Department of Health and Social Security should be acknowledged, for in 1969 the department commissioned research teams to study homelessness in Greater London and in South Wales and the rest of England, respectively.

A major defect of official statistics is that they refer only to what would be more accurately described as 'homeless families with dependent children'. Thus, homeless adults not accompanied by children or whose children happen to be over 16 years of age are not usually admitted to local authority temporary accommodation. Some local authorities exclude husbands, presumably, like the Poor Law workhouses, on the ground that a family might become too comfortably ensconced in a welfare hostel if it remains united and lose the will to look for its own accommodation. Other local authorities, however, either do not regard this as a great danger or—not surprisingly perhaps for statutory welfare authorities—are enlightened enough to consider the risk preferable to splitting up a family whose stability is already under great strain.

If homeless people of pensionable age are admitted they are not likely to be shown in the statistics. It should also be noted that people without homes who find shelter in accommodation provided by private individuals or voluntary agencies—however insecure, makeshift, or unsuitable it may happen to be—are not recorded in official statistics even if they have to go there because the council's welfare accommodation is already full. In many areas the statistics of homeless reflect the availability of temporary welfare accommodation rather than the dimensions of a social problem.

Another factor masking the truth about homelessness lies in the variety of policies adopted by local authorities. Many of the differences are irrational and unjustified in that they are not determined by objective assessments of needs and resources.

Universality and equality of provision in social services—two of the primary aims of post-Beveridge social policy—are still distant goals as far as implementation is concerned. As regards services for the homeless and potentially homeless, how many local authorities are seriously trying to attain these goals? And how resolutely are the central government deparments trying to ensure that people in urgent need of assistance from the social services are not dealt with on grotesquely unequal terms according to where they happen to live?

Each local authority pursues its policies for the homeless in its own way, resulting in a variety of practices so that homeless people with similar needs are treated differently in different areas. Geography—the arbitrary geography of local government boundaries— is an important factor in determining whether and how a person is helped. As the author comments in Chapter 7: 'Geographical boundaries were strictly observed in the provision of aid . . . it was common practice to press families to go back to the area where they belonged.' Administrative convenience triumphing over social service responsibility? Notwithstanding the progress that has been made in welfare policies since 1948, the ideology of the Laws of Settlement and the Poor Law still colours the attitudes and behaviour of some welfare officials.

The author produces disturbing evidence not only about the

homeless, but also about the public agencies—particularly the welfare and housing departments—on which they must rely most heavily for assistance. The material he produces cannot be dismissed merely as freak results thrown up by one local study, for it repeats in several respects findings of the study of homelessness in Greater London that was made at the same time by another research team.

One seemingly minor but, in reality, not unimportant finding, is the degree to which local authority officials—and in the social services at that—set themselves up to judge morality, and punish the accused by depriving her (usually) and her family of the kind of welfare assistance needed. The employment of moral criteria for judging human needs was encountered by some of the people whose histories were examined in the course of the study (Chapters 5 and 7). This is one of the causes of inequality and injustice in treatment by social services; it conflicts with the aims of social service legislation, and ignores the explicit views and requirements of a number government circulars issued over the past twenty years which have been pointing the way towards more adequate and humane provision in dealing with and preventing homelessness. There is, regrettably, no shortage of evidence from different parts of the country that many local authorities ignore the liberal aims promoted by central government and, consequently, administer services that are not only less effective than they need be, but also less compassionate in their treatment of people in trouble.

The Glastonbury study produces further evidence of conflicting or divergent policies often within the same local authority. Our study in London found comparable situations. The result of this conflict and divergence is that the homeless family caught in the middle is generally worse off. Children's departments are, typically, more sensitive and less judgemental than welfare of housing departments in aiding the homeless. But why should this be if the nature of need is intended to be the criterion that determines the form of assistance that should be provided? It raises the question of what kinds of differences in policies and practices will emerge in the new Social Service Departments, more often than not to be headed by officers from the existing welfare or children's departments. The creation of these departments is a positive expression of the widespread desire to make the personal social services more humane and effective, and the pursuit of these goals—involving a more sensitive and ready adjustment of the services to varied social needs—must override differences in the backgrounds and experience of administrators and social workers alike.

It is curious that in the heyday of cost-benefit analysis and purportedly economy-minded administrators—and all claim to be that, though for a variety of motives—no attempt has been made to calculate the economic costs of homelessness or to work out the comparative social arithmetic of present arrangements as against, say, the development of a comprehensive housing service. Such a service might rehouse a higher proportion of the homeless, linked with the provision of supporting and follow-up social work for the many who need this assistance. In short, an integrated housing service designed to do far more than has been attempted so far to meet the needs of some of the most deprived people in our society. An early-warning system—spotting potential crisis situations before they get out of hand and the family is on the street—would be an essential feature of such a local housing service.

The questions raised in the preceding paragraphs and the proposals made for adjusting services more sensitively to the needs of homeless and potentially homeless people are merely a few of those that spring to mind on reading the pages of Bryan Glastonbury's report. He goes much further in describing conditions and prescribing remedies and his book is commended to officials, politicans, social workers and the public alike, for all have a duty to inform themselves and to determine where they stand on the issues raised.

CONTENTS

INTRODUCTION

Homeless families are the subject of this study, although it is often impossible and undesirable to separate the family from the homeless individual. The basis of statutory provision for families who are homeless in the narrow sense of being literally without a roof over their heads is contained in the National Assistance Act of 1948, Part III, section 21 (1)(b). This requires every local authority to provide 'temporary accommodation for persons who are in urgent need thereof, being need arising in circumstances that could not reasonably have been foreseen', and impresses on local authorities their responsibilities for the welfare of families in these circumstances.[1] The Act offers last-ditch support for families who have not been effectively covered by housing provisions and the growing body of preventive services.

The problem of homeless families is a regular feature of public debate at the present time, primarily because of a steady increase in the number of persons using temporary accommodation hostels. The average occupancy of hostels in England and Wales during 1969 was approximately four times that of twenty years ago. Government response to the situation was first to find out from local authorities what provisions they were making for homeless families.[2] This was followed by a further circular suggesting ways in which local authorities could improve their services,[3] and since that time continuous pressure has been placed on local authorities to implement the spirit rather than the letter of the National Assistance Act.

Undoubtedly, however, the most voluble pressure has come from outside the government. In September 1961, Jeremy Sandford wrote in the *Observer* about the conditions in Newington Lodge, a hostel run by the London County Council. His concern at this stage was with the physical conditions under which homeless families were expected to live. Much more recently, Sandford

---

[1] National Assistance Act 1948, 11 and 12 Geo 6, Ch. 29.
[2] Circular 20/66 (Wales) Welsh Board of Health.
[3] Circular 19/67 (Wales) Welsh Board of Health.

produced the drama/documentary 'Kathy Come Home', backed with a lengthy press campaign. His emphasis in this turned more to the administrative fragmentation of services for homeless families and what he saw as the general mistreatment of families who suffered from the misfortune of losing a house. A well-documented campaign was organized by the Friends of King Hill (King Hill is the hostel provided by Kent County Council) to get two rules rescinded:

(a) exclusion of husbands from the hostel;
(b) the restricting of a family's stay to a maximum of three months even if at the end of this period they have nowhere to go and accommodation was still standing empty at the hostel.

The campaign exposed the harshness of life for the families living at the hostel and the ineffectiveness of provisions for their rehousing. It involved hardships for the participants, including imprisonment for some of the husbands who were attempting to enforce their rights to share the hostel with their wives. 'Our twelve months struggle with and on behalf of the homeless families in Kent has brought about a complete change of attitude on the part of the Kent County Council ... husbands are now allowed to stay with their families and we have accepted the Kent County Council's assurances that in future no family will be evicted from the hostel while accommodation is available, simply for having exceeded a certain length of stay.'[1]

The Shelter organization has added a further dimension to the public debate on homelessness by questioning the definition of that word as used by the Government. It has suggested that, instead of defining homelessness narrowly in terms of persons resident in temporary accommodation hostels at any particular moment, a more realistic definition would include all those housed in grossly unsuitable conditions—those for whom a house cannot be reasonably called a 'home'.

In 1967 and 1968 a pilot survey was conducted in Glamorgan. The objectives were:

1. To try to fit a family's experience of homelessness into the context of its total living pattern. Material for this was obtained by use of case records of social agencies and interviewing

[1] Note of the King Hill campaign—press statement by the Friends of King Hill, August 29, 1966.

families, attempting to cover the family's life over a period of five years prior to the experience of homelessness and from the moment of rehousing up to the time of interview.

2. To attempt to assess the needs of these families and how these needs were being or could be met by local authority social services.

This produced evidence that the picture of homelessness described in London[1] was not necessarily applicable in another area. It therefore seemed justified to expand both the scope and area of this survey. This was done with the aid of a grant from the Department of Health and Social Security in the spring of 1969.

Definition of homelessness
'What do you mean by homelessness?' was a question regularly put to members of the research team. It soon became apparent that this concept was given a variety of definitions by those concerned with the care of homeless families and was a source of confusion and misunderstanding. It is important therefore to state how the term was used in this survey, as well as its use by local authority officials in the survey area.

The local authorities defined a homeless person as someone who had no roof over his head, but two further considerations limited the numbers of people whom they officially accepted as homeless. Firstly the circumstances leading to homelessness were reviewed. Persons losing their homes in overtly emergency situations were clearly acknowledged as both homeless and in need of support. Those losing their homes in non-emergency circumstances were generally assessed according to the extent to which they could be seen as blameworthy for the loss. The decision on blameworthiness was an arbitrary one, and there were large variations between different officers and different local authorities. Throughout the survey area there were examples of refusals or reluctance to acknowledge and provide for 'blameworthy' homelessness. A similar assessment was sometimes made according to the efforts of the homeless people to try to overcome their own problems before asking for help. Secondly, the local authorities tended to categorize homelessness to fit in with the facilities provided under the terms of the National Assistance Act. Men were therefore commonly excluded as, sometimes, were single persons and couples without children,

[1] Cf. John Greve: *London's Homeless*, Codicote Press, 1964.

B

and the frequent chronic nature of homelessness was often overlooked.

In short the local authorities have evolved a narrow working definition of homelessness, given its numerical presentation in the total of people recorded as occupying temporary accommodation hostels on the last day of each year.[1] In contrast, Shelter has given wide publicity to a definition of homelessness in terms of people living in very bad housing conditions, as well as those with no house at all. The research team drew a definition between these two. Homelessness was understood to include all those people who were without a roof over their heads, whether they qualified for temporary accommodation under local provisions through the National Assistance Act, or whether they were part of a number of small groups within the population who were helped by other, mainly voluntary, organizations, or whether they did not receive any kind of servicing at all. There were people who had a roof, but in circumstances that were clearly seen as temporary—a derelict railway carriage, or a caravan only available until the holiday season began, for example—and these were also classed as homeless.

Hypotheses

The research set out to investigate a number of hypotheses. The central one postulated a fundamental difference between London and other large urban conurbations and the remainder of England and Wales, based on the fact that the provinces did not necessarily share the acute and chronic housing shortage of the conventional type of dwellings, which characterized London; nor was there overcrowding in temporary accommodation hostels, so that South Wales and West Country authorities, where the study was set, were not forced to impose any methods of selection of families who could receive attention under the terms of the National Assistance Act. An analysis of families from the Glamorgan pilot survey suggested a further range of ideas which warranted more investigation.[2] These are listed below:

1. It was clear that the picture of homelessness given in national statistics (Ministry of Health Annual Reports) was altogether different from that emerging in the pilot area (Glamorgan). Nationally at that time, the biggest cause of entry to temporary accom-

---

[1] Ministry of Health Annual Report.
[2] The author is indebted to Howard Kent for work on the pilot study.

modation (approximately 60 per cent) was eviction, mostly for rent arrears. The emphasis (e.g. in the Milner-Holland Report)[1] was on high rents in relation to family incomes, and an acute housing shortage. In the pilot study, although poverty showed up quite strongly, eviction for rent arrears occurred in only one of ten families and the housing shortage received no mention. What emerged was that for homeless families their homelessness was one of a wide range of social and individual difficulties, and often not the dominant one. The overlap with those classified as multi-problem families was considerable, and marital breakdown appeared to be central.

2. As might be expected therefore, the motives for using temporary accommodation for both clients and social services were also at variance with national policy. In the pilot survey there were several instances of the hostel being used by mothers to effect either a permanent or temporary separation from their husbands, and social workers in contact with these families openly accepted this situation. To a lesser extent the hostel was used as a lever to get a family rehoused. In general, the hostel in the pilot area was used as a social work rather than a housing aid.

3. In the pilot study the Welfare and to a lesser extent the Children's Department were seeing homelessness as a short-term emergency situation, not part of chronic family difficulties. Several families entered the hostel with no record of prior contact with social workers, and although work with families in the hostel appeared to be intensive, there was a sharp fall-off of contact after the family was rehoused. In two of ten instances the family could not be traced from social work records, and the experienced social worker who conducted the interviews several times commented on the urgent need for follow-up services. To put this in more general terms, just as there were administratively convenient points of referral of a family to a social work agency, which might be quite unrelated to the type of help a family required or the time when it was most needed, so there might be convenient and similarly unrelated points for breaking contact. The pilot study suggested that rehousing may be one such point and movement across a local authority boundary another.

4. The apparent need for a follow-up service has been mentioned. There was a similar need for a wider early warning system. Those involved in the pilot survey felt that where there had been an early warning of the homelessness threat to Welfare and Children's

[1] Report of the Committee on Housing in Greater London, 1965.

Departments, the preventive services had worked effectively (as with referrals of rent arrears cases from Housing Departments). But many of the circumstances leading to homelessness were not covered by such procedure.

The Glamorgan study had strongly suggested that homelessness was a social work rather than a housing issue as far as the local authority social services were concerned. It therefore became important to make further checks to test out recommendations of the Seebohm Committee, which appeared at least on the surface to suggest methods of treatment which were not necessarily appropriate in South Wales.[1] In particular this quotation from the introductory summary to the Seebohm Report was causing concern '. . . we recommend that the responsibility for accommodating homeless families, as distinct from providing limited overnight accommodation, should be placed squarely on housing departments. We suggest that the social workers from the Social Service department might be attached for all or part of their time to housing departments in order to deal with the more difficult social problems among council tenants or people in need of housing.'[2]

Paragraphs 403 to 409 inclusive of the main report also seemed to warrant further assessment from a particularly local viewpoint.

403. *Standards of provision in temporary accommodation.* We endorse the suggestions made in the joint Circular of 31st October 1966 from the Ministry of Health, Home Office and Ministry of Housing and Local Government about the arrangements in temporary accommodation. Two points are particularly important for the preservation of families:

(a) they should not, in any circumstances, be split up on reception into temporary accommodation. It is in just such predicaments that they need the mutual support of all their members. Domestic friction is an important factor in precipitating homelessness; we should not by public policy help to make this a permanent separation of husband and wife.

(b) Many of the homeless families will come from poor, overcrowded or hopeless housing conditions. If they have to face in temporary accommodation incessant noise, communal

---

[1] Report of the Committee on Local Authority and Allied Personal Social Services, H.M.S.O. Cmnd. 3703.

[2] Report of the Committee on Local Authority and Allied Personal Social Services, H.M.S.O. Cmnd. 3703: Introduction Summary Part 4, paragraph 14.

cooking, crowding, poor facilities and lack of privacy, they are less likely to respond to efforts to help them regain their independence. Privacy at least should be available in even the most temporary accommodation.

404. *Recuperative units*. There is a distinction to be drawn, however, between accommodation for homeless families and special residential care. By the latter we mean provision in rehabilitation or recuperative units of various kinds which take a family (including the husband where there is one) for a temporary period, and provide them with accommodation, respite, support and any necessary training to give them a reasonable chance of being able to manage on their own again, if necessary with help from the personal social services. Provision such as this, even though some of the families concerned may also be homeless, should be the responsibility of the social service department.

405. Some of the families becoming homeless will need social work help and assistance which falls short of admission to a recuperative unit. This should be provided by the social service department on the same basis as for other families living in their own houses.

406. *Measures to avoid homelessness*. As far as local authority housing is concerned, the remedy lies in the hands of individual authorities. Some, including several of those in areas of great housing need, have worked out measures either within their own internal organization (in county boroughs or London boroughs) or with district councils (in administrative counties) which reduce the number of families evicted from council houses to very small proportions. A basic element must be an efficient system of early warning which will enable families in difficulty or potential difficulty to be identified, so that measures can be taken to prevent arrears accumulating to an extent which makes eviction a serious possibility. In the last resort, however, local authorities must face the problem of the bad payer in the light of the repercussions of eviction on the children and on themselves in terms of the further high costs of any alternative.

407. The main problem arises, however, from tenants of privately owned accommodation. It might be met in three main ways. First, if local authorities knew more about the private sector, negotiation and liaison might forestall some evictions, as they do now in some areas. If an advice service existed on the lines we suggest, it could accumulate a wide variety of useful

information in this respect. Second, if local authorities take increased responsibility for housing the most vulnerable families, fewer of them will have to depend on the private sector. These are the families least able to make arrangements and to negotiate with private landlords. Third, the courts and rent tribunals should (as some already do) work in close collaboration with the local authorities. The court officers should be under a duty to inform the local authority as soon as they know of proceedings which might lead to eviction. More effective advice, assistance, and sometimes prevention, would then be possible.

408. The early identification and notification to the housing and social service departments of families at risk of eviction should be regarded everywhere as the immediate and urgent responsibility on any social service agency which is in contact with them. We have in mind in this context, not only the social service and housing departments, but the health and education departments, the Supplementary Benefits Commission, the probation and aftercare service and the prison welfare service (particularly in connection with prisoners' families), voluntary societies, and the hospitals (for example, when an elderly person is living alone and is in danger of losing his accommodation if admitted to hospital).

409. *Co-ordination between neighbouring local authorities on arrangements for homeless families.* There is a need for co-ordinated policy and action between neighbouring local authorities, particularly in the conurbations, over provision for homeless families. The more 'helpful' authorities require protection from their 'less helpful' neighbours; if the treatment of homeless families differs radically from one area to another, families are likely to gravitate to the more generous authority. A central government inspectorate might have an important role to play as an impartial adviser of local authorities on the practices and standards of their own and neighbouring authorities.[1]

Survey area

The time-span of the study was set at approximately six months, and most of the material was collected between May and October 1969. The area covered included six local authorities, three in South Wales, Swansea, Cardiff and Glamorgan, and three in the South West of England, Gloucestershire, Bristol and Somerset. Although

[1] Report of the Committee on Local Authority and Allied Personal Social Services, H.M.S.O. Cmnd. 3703.

selected primarily because they were within reasonable access from Swansea University College, these areas in fact did provide a reasonable cross-section of the range of situations which may be expected outside the metropolis. They cover three county boroughs and three county councils and include some agricultural communities. In addition there were some declining industrial areas of South Wales to compare with a number of rapidly expanding industrial areas both in South Wales and in the West Country. In parts they were not typical of the rest of the country because of their large coastline, bringing with it the possibility of homelessness caused by migration from outside the country.

In range of provisions there was also a lot of variety. In Swansea, as in Cardiff and Bristol, the National Assistance Act had been interpreted in such a way that Welfare Departments provided basic temporary accommodation and utilized the services of a number of other agencies, in particular the Children's Department, to combat any social problems which homeless families might face in addition to the fact of homelessness. In contrast to this, in Glamorgan the servicing of homeless families had been passed very considerably to the Children's Department although the Welfare Department maintained administrative control of the hostel itself. In Gloucestershire the entire provision was made by a Welfare Department with relatively little contact with other agencies, unless the families involved were already on the case loads of these other agencies. In Somerset, the entire provision had for several years been in the hands of the Children's Department and so was operated by a group of people with rather different qualifications from those in Welfare Departments.

Survey programme

The central core of the research was a study of 549 families who had entered temporary accommodation in one of the six local authorities between January 1, 1963 and the middle of 1969. The fact of using the hostel provided an appropriate point of contact with the families. The investigation extended, however, beyond those circumstances where the hostel was used, to include the many other experiences of homelessness amongst these families where local authority help was either not sought or refused. Because the method of sampling still left open the possibility of concealed homelessness, a section is included on 'Hidden Homelessness', which tries to pinpoint areas needing further investigation or new forms of service.

As in the earlier pilot study, the material was obtained from the case files of a number of local authority departments including Housing, Children's, Welfare and usually Health as well. Further facts were taken from the Department of Health and Social Security (Supplementary Benefits Commission), Probation and Aftercare Departments, and from a large number of voluntary organizations. This was followed by interviews with as many of the families as it was possible to locate. As before, one of the objectives was to build up comprehensive case histories covering several years, with emphasis on fitting the experiences of homelessness into their social context and not isolating them. Running parallel with this survey was a programme of interviews with welfare officers, housing officers, social workers and many others involved in housing homeless families, with a view to building up a picture of homelessness from the point of view of both the recipient and the provider of the services.

Certain decisions were made affecting the sources and presentation of material. One was the working definition of homelessness, already given. Another involved deciding what was meant by the term 'family'. Applicants for hostel accommodation ranged from unattached women to three-generation groups with attendant lodgers and domestic pets. There was some question of treating the unattached women as a separate group, but this would have been unrealistic, since for so many of them their isolation was a temporary phase. It was finally decided to include all of them under the umbrella heading of 'family'.

The most difficult decision of all was to determine which particular circumstances could be designated as major causes or effects of homelessness. For many families the occasional loss of a home was an expected routine, sometimes almost incidental to their other difficulties, and they were unable to see it in a context of causes and effects. At the same time, social agency case records could be equally indecisive, since treating homelessness was a part, often a minor one, of a more widely ranging social work objective; the records of the Welfare Departments in South Wales and Bristol, on the other hand, tended to focus on the issues immediately surrounding an entry to temporary accommodation. Where they were available the comments of family members, social workers, case records and other sources were taken into account, but the final assessment of the major causes of a family's homelessness, and their impact, was made by the research team after a detailed family dossier had been assembled.

Structure of the book

Much of the comment in recent years on the plight of homeless people, from government and other sources, has been strongly critical of the type and standard of services provided to cope with this problem. The argument is presented in Chapter 1 that much of the cause of present-day inadequacies can be traced back to the origins of the National Assistance Act. The chapter is historical, looking at significant developments in the Poor Law and in Public Housing in the half-century before 1948, and then at the way services which were developed to cope with those made homeless by bombing in the early 1940s influenced estimates of the extent and nature of post-war homelessness. The chapter goes on to trace the tardy reaction of many local authorities to the unexpected sources and increasing numbers of the homeless in the 1950s and 1960s, leading to the outburst of public concern in the last few years.

The next five chapters are specifically concerned with the survey of homeless families. Chapter 2 provides some basic data in sections on family size and structure, and on income and employment. The chapter acts as an introduction to Chapter 3, which offers a detailed assessment of the causes of homelessness. The causes are grouped under a number of headings—Housing, Material Circumstances, Illness, Family Size and Structure, Family Relationships, Behavioural Difficulties, Community Relations and (in a footnote) Difficulties with Children. The format under each heading is for the presentation of the statistical results of the survey, extensively illustrated from case histories. The reader who wishes to bypass the illustration will always find the statistics at the beginning of each section.

Chapters 4, 5 and 6 are mainly concerned with the housing aspects of homelessness. Chapter 4 begins with a look at each family's housing history for the five years before their last entry into temporary accommodation, particularly focusing on the number of moves each family has made. It goes on to look more closely at the circumstances in which people become homeless, considering whether they were such as could 'reasonably have been foreseen', and what actions were taken to deal with them. Chapter 5 tackles the subject of rehousing. It begins with the results of a survey of local authority housing policies and attitudes towards the homeless, and goes on to a narrative of how these people were rehoused. It finishes with a look at family housing histories in the period since leaving temporary accommodation, making a broad comparison with the earlier history. Chapter 6 takes, for each family, the last house before entering temporary accommodation and the first house afterwards, to provide a comparison of basic conditions. The comparison is made under several headings—Type of Dwelling, Tenancy, Rental, Housing Facilities, and State of Repair—with a view to seeing whether the families had experienced an improvement or deterioration in their conditions.

Chapter 7 uses the results of the survey as well as other sources of information from the survey area, and sets out to give a broadly based view of the impact of our social services on the threat and fact of homelessness. It begins with a section on methods used to prevent people losing their homes, but the bulk of the chapter is concerned with those who actually become homeless. There is a section on the different sorts of temporary accommodation, and the kind of life it offers. A further section looks at the part played by social workers and those (particularly supplementary benefits officers) with access to financial and other forms of material aid. Voluntary organizations have been especially voluble on behalf of homeless families, and the next part examines the practical work that volunteers are doing. A final section of this chapter tackles the problems of relationships between local authorities and between departments within a single local authority in the provision of services for the homeless.

Chapter 8, the final chapter, returns to the initial hypotheses and brings together the conclusions of the study. Some recommendations are made for future services.

During the course of the survey a number of groups were studied who were at risk of becoming homeless but were unlikely to come within the orbit of Welfare Department temporary accommodation. Appendix I reports on them. It begins by looking at old people, particularly those who cannot look after themselves. Then there is a section on homeless children in the care of local authorities, followed by a discussion of other areas where the risk of homelessness was great.

Appendix II provides statistical and other comparisons with a study of homelessness carried out in London, under the direction of Professor John Greve, at the same time as the South Wales and West of England study.

BACKGROUND TO HOMELESSNESS

This chapter begins by looking at three important influences on policy towards the homeless, as it was expressed in the 1948 National Assistance Act. Firstly, the development of relevant aspects of Poor Law policies is discussed. For three centuries before the early 1940s the workhouse was the central provision for homelessness, and many of the local authority staff who established postwar Welfare Departments brought with them years of Poor Law experience. Secondly, housing policies are examined with specific reference to the recognition given to those who, from poverty or other problems, have been classed as unsatisfactory tenants, and to the importance of housing shortages. Thirdly, some attention is paid to the methods employed in helping people made homeless by wartime bombing. With the Poor Law discredited,[1] the experiences of relief services between 1939 and 1945 were in the forefront of plans for dealing with post-war homelessness.

The chapter then proceeds to the passage of the National Assistance Act, and from there traces developments in policy up to the end of the 1960s.

The Poor Law tradition

The relief of the poor, including the homeless, began as a form of charity, with government interest arising very gradually, firstly by authorizing begging, next by encouraging gifts for giving succour to the needy, and then, in 1563, by allowing parishes to introduce a weekly tax for the same purpose. The Elizabethan Poor Law, administered by J.P.s, Overseers of the Poor and vestry officials, established the dual structure of poor relief—domiciliary relief and institutional care.

Domiciliary relief, more commonly called parish or outdoor

---

[1] The National Assistance Act, 1948, opens with the words, 'The existing Poor Law shall cease to have effect'.

relief, was always the dominant and erratic part of the system, because Poor Law administrators experienced great difficulty in implementing a balanced programme of benefits for families who continued to live in the community. Although it was always cheaper to support a family in its own home than to provide it with minimal standards of care in an institution, willingness to give domiciliary benefits tended to increase the demand for relief, and led to accusations of exploitation against people who, it was said, had no real need for funds. Worry about the cost and moral basis of outdoor relief prompted some of the recommendations of the 1834 Royal Commission. The administration of the Poor Law was taken out of the hands of parish officials and passed to a central authority. Outdoor relief to the able-bodied—in effect the poorest unemployed —was prohibited for a time, and the principle of less eligibility set upper limits to the standard of relief. 'The hanger-on', said J. S. Davy, 'should be lower than him on whom he hangs',[1] or, as Thomas Carlyle saw it, 'If paupers are made miserable, paupers will needs decline in multitude. It is a secret known to all rat-catchers.'

The Elizabethan Poor Law authorized the provision of residential accommodation for the impotent poor, but it was not until 1722 that parishes were authorized to open, or pay contractors to open, workhouses for the more generally destitute.[2] The inevitable evils of institutions contracted out to the lowest tender, and run for profit, were ended sixty years later.[3] But primitive living conditions continued into the present century because of the policy of less eligibility, because an uncomfortable way of life deterred people from applying for it, and because the cost of good residential conditions—even for the young, old and chronic sick—always exceeded the funds available.

Although the 1834 Royal Commission Report recommended breaking down the workhouse population into separate categories and housing them separately, the years following 1834 saw the most intensive period of building large general-purpose workhouses. Many of the buildings are still in use, commonly as hospitals, some as temporary accommodation hostels.

The Victorian workhouse kept its doors always open for urgent applicants, and for all others after a short warning. Everyone could

---

[1] J. S. Davy, Principal Officer of the Poor Law Division of the Local Government Board: evidence to the Royal Commission, 1905–9.

[2] 9 Geo. 1 Ch. 7.

[3] 'Gilbert's Act, 1782'—22 Geo. 3 Ch. 83.

come and stay without limit. '. . . life in a workhouse has a decided advantage. There can be no worry about the future. . . . When one gets to the workhouse, the worst has happened and speculation and foreboding are gone. There is nothing left to fear except ill-health and death.'[1] Living conditions conforming to the principle of less eligibility were allied to a privilege-based daily routine not altogether unlike prison.[2] Indeed many workhouses were locked and barred to contain the inmates securely, with hard labour compulsory for the able-bodied. 'You have got to find work which anybody can do, and which nearly everybody dislikes doing (otherwise) you will have your workhouse crowded up with loafers.'[3] But while such a system might have been applicable in a specialized workhouse, it could not survive in general-purpose institutions. 'The presence in a workhouse of the sick, or of any class in whose favour the ordinary discipline must be relaxed, and who receive special indulgences, has an almost inevitable tendency to impair the general discipline of the establishment.'[4] The House has proved 'too bad for the good and too good for the bad'.[5]

For a few years after 1871 the Local Government Board tried to keep the able-bodied under a separate penal regime, but this successfully deterred the genuinely able-bodied, and in practice these 'Test Workhouses' took in homeless old men or those with a variety of mental and physical ailments, and acted as overflows for the general houses. Jack London described the regime of a test workhouse in 1902,[6] and since he gave an unusually detailed customer's-eye view, some long quotations are included. 'I asked them what I might expect in the way of treatment if we succeeded in getting into the Poplar Workhouse, and between them I was supplied with much information. Having taken a cold bath on entering, I would be given for supper six ounces of bread, and "three parts of skilly". "Three parts" means three-quarters of a pint, and "skilly" is a fluid concoction of three quarts of oatmeal stirred into three buckets and a half of hot water. . . .

'And I was informed that I was sent directly to bed. "Call you at half after five in the mornin', an' you get up an' take a 'sluice'—

[1] *Through a Workhouse Window* by R. M. Noordin: Pub. Cecil Palmer 1929, p. 15.
[2] One of the post-1834 reforms ended corporal punishment for able-bodied adult residents of workhouses.
[3] J. S. Davy: evidence to the Royal Commission 1905–9.
[4] Fourth Annual Report of the Local Government Board, 1874–5.
[5] B. and S. Webb: *English Poor Law History*, Part 2, p. 972.
[6] Jack London: *People of the Abyss*, Panther Books, 1963.

if there's any soap. Then breakfast, same as supper, three parts o'
skilly an' a six-ounce loaf. . . .

' "Then you've got to do your task, pick four pounds of oakum,
or clean an' scrub, or break ten to eleven hundredweights of stone;
I don't 'ave to break stones; I'm past sixty, you see. They'll make
you do it, though. You're young an' strong." '

Jack London found that, in London at least, the number of
workhouses was not enough to cope with the level of homelessness.

'After my two unsuccessful attempts to penetrate the White-
chapel casual ward, I started early, and joined the desolate line
before three o' clock in the afternoon. They did not "Let in" till
six, but at that early hour I was number twenty, while the news had
gone forth that only twenty-two were to be admitted. By four
o'clock there were thirty-four in line, the last ten hanging on in the
slender hope of getting in by some kind of miracle. Many more
came, looked at the line, and went away, wise to the bitter fact that
the spike would be "full up".'

The workhouses were full because the alternative was worse.

'Should you rest upon a bench, and your tired eyes close, depend
upon it the policeman would rouse you and gruffly order you to
"move on". You may rest upon the bench, and benches are few and
far between; but if rest means sleep, on you must go, dragging your
tired body through the endless streets. Should you, in desperate
slyness seek some forlorn alley or dark passageway and lie down,
the omnipresent policeman will rout you out just the same. It is his
business to rout you out. It is a law of the powers that be that you
should be routed out. . . . But for old men of sixty, seventy, and
eighty, ill-fed, with neither meat nor blood, to greet the dawn
unrefreshed, and to stagger through the day in mad search for
crusts with relentless night rushing down upon them again, and to
do this five nights and days—O dear, soft people, full of meat and
blood, how can you ever understand?'

The majority report of the 1905–9 Royal Commission argued that
persons needing penal treatment should receive it through the Home
Office, not the Poor Law Division, and put the 'Principle of
Restoration' in place of the 'Principle of Less Eligibility'. Although
there was no rash of legislation following this report, the agreement
to make separate provision for, amongst others, state schools,
hospitals, old-aged pensioners and the unemployed[1] set the tone
for Local Government Board circulars, and was officially acknow-

[1] B. and S. Webb: *English Poor Law History*, Part 2, p. 545.

ledged in section 5 of the Local Government Act, 1929.[1] Ten years later the Minister of Health discussed his duty to see that 'as soon as circumstances permitted, all assistance which could lawfully be provided otherwise than by way of poor relief should be so provided. This policy, commonly referred to as the "break-up" of the Poor Law, takes its origin from the reports of the Royal Commission of 1905–9.'[2] He went on to add, however, that the subsequent period 'has clearly shown that the Poor Law has still an important role to fulfil . . . it still remains the service whose function it is to fill the gaps left by the specialized services with their necessarily limited powers'.[3]

But homelessness was not one of the social needs to be exempted in the Majority Report from the Poor Law stigma, and remained part of a category described by Professor Bernard Bosanquet as 'a failure of social self-maintenance . . . a defect in citizen character, or at least a grave danger to its integrity'.[4] A modified version of less eligibility continued to be practised in poor law institutions through to 1940, until it was overrun by old and handicapped evacuees and by the rush of victims of bombing.

Families have always been accommodated in workhouses, though it is difficult to find references to them as such, and they were broken up on entry and generally segregated except during restricted visiting hours. Separation was initially by sex, but humanitarian views towards the end of the last century favoured a more extensive break-down, to isolate the sick from the able-bodied, the young from the old. When arrangements were made in the present century for married couples to share quarters, they were half-hearted and sometimes frivolous. A guardian of the poor of the Romford Union described it thus: 'In our workhouse we had three different classes of inmate to cater for, I mean outside the hospital and mental cases. The three classes were the young and able-bodied, the able-bodied and the infirm. The men and women being in separate institutions, there were two institutions to keep up. . . . We started a system of "married quarters" which were never a thoroughgoing success. After the one and only couple who lived in them had gone there were no more applications for the vacant quarters. I write this with unholy joy as I am yet unmarried. . . .'[5] Charlie Chaplin, recalling

---

[1] From 1919 the Local Government Board was merged into the new Ministry of Health.
[2] Ministry of Health Annual Report, 1938/9, p. 67.
[3] Ibid., p. 67.
[4] *Sociological Review*, April 1909.
[5] R. M. Noordin: *Through a Workhouse Window*, p. 17.

his days as a child in Lambeth workhouse, wrote of 'the shock of seeing Mother enter the visiting room garbed in workhouse clothes', and the 'forlorn bewilderment' of himself and his brother, separated from their family life.[1]

Local authorities would have found it difficult and costly to provide accommodation for whole family units because of the unsuitability of many of the buildings at their disposal—a reason for separating families which is still used (e.g. by Glamorgan County Council). But to have done so would have run quite contrary to prevailing opinion at the time. The Royal Commission 1905–9 Minority Report for Scotland stated the position concisely, with the full approval of the Webbs.[2] Talking of families which had 'slipped into destitution', the report continued, 'We think that each member of even such a family requires, for restoration, specialized treatment according to his or her need. The infant, the child of school age, the mentally defective, the sick, the infirm, or incapacitated, the boy or girl above school age, and finally the able-bodied and able-minded adult, each requires that something different should be done for him or her, if that individual is to be properly dealt with. The alternative, namely to treat the family as a whole, means to place it in the Mixed General Poorhouse, or merely to give it a dole of Outdoor Relief. This indeed, is today the dominant practice; and as such, has been condemned by Majority and Minority alike.'[3] Thus to many of the progressive and influential reformers in the first forty years of this century the concept of 'family problem' had meaning only as the sum of problems of individual family members. Homelessness was seen as in no sense a catalyst of chronic family destitution, but as a secondary condition following on from a failure in preventive service by such bodies as the Education, Health, Lunacy, Pension and Unemployment Authorities.

The Poor Law Authorities were subjected to a tremendous barrage of criticism for their failure to recognize these individual needs and encourage the growth of suitably specialized services. Indeed, in the first flush of enthusiasm for the new system of separate specialized services, it was argued that the Poor Law should be completely abolished.[4] Later sections of this study will show that

[1] C. Chaplin: *My Autobiography*, p. 25 onwards in the Penguin edition.

[2] Quoted in B. and S. Webb, op. cit., pp. 301/2.

[3] Report of the Royal Commission on the Poor Law, 1905–9; Report for Scotland: H.M.S.O. Cmnd. 4922.

[4] e.g. Minority Report for Scotland—'We see no need for any general Poor Law or "Public Assistance Committee" at all.'

the growth of a fragmented social service structure contributed to the difficulties facing homeless families in the 1960s.

The restructuring of services continued throughout the years prior to 1939, hampered for much of the time by severe restrictions on public spending. Simultaneously the Poor Law authorities' concern grew for those groups left in their care, particularly old people, 'for whose special needs provision can best be made under the wide and flexible powers of the Poor Law acts'.[2] However, a good deal of confusion was caused, and some blame attached (perhaps unjustifiably) to the Poor Law, by the slow growth of other services and their consequent inability to keep up with the demand for help. Education authorities found it difficult at times to remove children from workhouses within the statutory six weeks, and public health hospitals showed reluctance to accept the senile and chronic sick. 'How can the Poor Law authorities make conditions in their institutions inviting to the infirm old, who make up far the greater part of their inmates, when they are constantly having to shelter what they call the "residuals" of the other social services?' asked an *Economist* correspondent.[2] Homeless families formed part of the general confusion, and little was done to try to identify any group for whom homelessness was the main or only problem. Then in July 1939 the Poor Law authorities were made responsible for feeding and sheltering the victims of bombing.

The development of public housing

It is significant that the major responsibility for the care of homeless families has largely remained with health and welfare interests, and only in a few areas have closer links been forged with housing authorities. Early developments in housing policy suggested something different. In 1864 Octavia Hill began her practical demonstration in housing management, and showed that a concern for the welfare of tenants could have a dramatic impact on their standards of tenancy behaviour—'combining good social work with good business.'[3] Her methods were extended through the activities of the Society of Housing Managers. Furthermore, the debate towards the end of the nineteenth century, as to whether local authorities should build houses, showed a close concern for the very poorest elements of the population, in part at least with workhouse

---

[1] Ministry of Health Annual Report, 1936/7.
[2] *The Economist*, April 19, 1947.
[3] *The Social Services of Modern England*: M. P. Hall: RKP: p. 92.

occupants. The authority for municipalities to build houses was motivated by a double failure, of private builders to produce houses at sufficiently low rentals for the working class, and of philanthropists to cope with such a massive need. The emphasis of the debate was clear: that the main task of building rested with private operatives, and that for local authorities to enter into competition would be unfair. The only gap open to the municipality was therefore the poorest section of the community, 'that nethermost unit of the population.'[1] 'Among the slum dwellers there is a certain class which it is above all things desirable to segregate. . . . It is a class which may be made to diminish more quickly if it is put under control and under better conditions. It is, then, for the improvident and semi-vicious class that I ask the Corporation to build. . . . They should be houses which the tenants cannot spoil—four bare walls, say, of concrete, with an indestructible set-in fireplace, and an indestructible bed-frame. So far as possible no wood to hack and burn, no plaster to pull down. . . .'[2]

But could local authorities build houses for letting at a rental which would both be low enough for the very poor and cover the cost of construction? The cost of housing has featured strongly in this century as a factor forcing families to enter a workhouse or hostel. Evidence to the Royal Commission of 1905–9 compares closely with comments in the Milner-Holland Report of 1965. 'Bad housing . . . shameful overcrowding . . . and the life in one room to which the high rents in London condemn such large numbers of the people, allow no training in elementary decency . . . the broad conclusion appears to be incontestable that bad housing conditions largely contribute to pauperism.'[3] '. . . multiple occupation, high prices for land, high rents, an ageing stock of houses and homelessness, all are features of the current situation.'[4] In some urban areas the shortage of accommodation at the turn of the century was desperate. W. C. Steadman, an M.P. and London County Councillor, recalled that 'in some cases, in consequence of the want of house accommodation, working men, in employment, are obliged to take their wives and families into the workhouse, and pay for

[1] Plans of the Glasgow City Engineer, 1890s.

[2] William Smart: Professor of Political Economy in the University of Glasgow; Proceedings of the Philosophical Society of Glasgow, *circa* 1902. This paper discusses the whole question of municipal building.

[3] Evidence of Special Investigators to the Royal Commission, 1905–9: quoted by B. and S. Webb, op. cit., p. 525.

[4] Report of the Committee on Housing in Greater London, 1965.

them until such time as they are able to find accommodation for them outside'.[1]

The Government made promises to tackle housing shortages after the 1914–18 war, but was faced with rapidly rising building costs. As a temporary expedient rents were compulsorily pegged, but a more permanent answer lay in subsidized rents which were gradually made available from the 1920s for a large proportion of the working population. Throughout the inter-war period successive governments stimulated house building, and housing policy for the public sector expanded beyond the limited framework of earlier discussions, with the result that the specific needs of the very poor family, especially the homeless and destitute family, were submerged under the vastly wider building programmes which Housing Departments took on. Over four million houses were built between 1919 and 1939, but while demand was primarily for cheap rented properties, supply concentrated more on the owner-occupier, with two houses built to sell for every one intended for renting. By 1939 most families wanting and able to buy a house had found a new one, and demand had begun to slacken; but this left for the poorer section of the community a supply of rentable property which was usually old, pre-1914, often structurally unsuitable, and in short supply. So, while the overall volume of housing may have been sufficient for the entire population, the allocation was uneven, and the greatest shortages continued to be located amongst the lowest income levels.[2]

Most local authorities were of course putting a high priority on supplying cheap rented property, though the envisaged tenants were not the 'nethermost unit' so much as the mass of reliable, regularly employed workers. Standards of tenancy were and still are set at a high level, as witness the strictness with which problems of rent arrears were treated, and many families who found themselves in hostels were there for failing to maintain such standards. For, as Professor Smart's earlier quotation suggested, there was often a link between the chronically homeless family and the multi-problem family which might require some service in excess of the normal tenancy arrangements. Whereas, however, Professor Smart advocated housing provision for families who were bad tenants as well as poor, the trend grew in the 1930s, and continued after the war, that the unsatisfactory tenant must either be excluded

[1] Fabian Tract No. 103, 1900, p. 5.
[2] Discussed in M. Bowley: *Britain's Housing Shortage*, O.U.P. 1944.

from council property altogether, or relegated to sub-standard dwellings.

This is the origin of the dilemma facing housing officials at the present time. As the size of local authority housing estates increased, the problems of large-scale management came to the forefront, and less individual attention was given to tenants. In particular the methods of rent collection, policies towards the treatment of tenants with rent arrears, and systems of house allocation have often become more standardized, and have deprived the housing authorities of the flexibility to offer the special, sometimes preferential, treatment which welfare workers might feel should be accorded to a minority of families.

Homelessness during the war, 1939–45

During the pre-war planning of emergency services to meet the needs of civilian victims, the care of homeless people was one of the many responsibilities of the Air Raid Precaution Department, set up in 1935.[1] Understaffed and overworked, this department paid little attention to those whose homes might be demolished or badly damaged, concentrating on what were thought to be two more important needs—financial aid for those temporarily unemployed as a result of industrial dislocation, and for those families which for one reason or another would be deprived of the main wage-earner. Remembering the industrial unrest of the First World War, the Government agreed to accept complete responsibility, using national rather than local authority funds, and keeping the administration quite separate from the Poor Law.

Welfare provision for homeless people was taken over in 1938 by the Ministry of Health, acting initially through the Relief in Kind Committee, which saw its task as countering the risk of breakdown in public order which might follow an attempted mass exodus from bombed areas to the country. In the words of Professor Titmuss, 'the needs of the individual were hidden from view by the sheer mass and crudity of the problems that were expected to result from an attack on civilian society. The more menacing the picture became, the less was seen of the simple, domestic needs of each individual and family, dazed by bombs and worried about relations, home, clothes and furniture. The conscious and deliberate recognition of the individual as the focal point of all services for homeless

---

[1] This section is extensively indebted to Titmuss, *Problems of Social Policy*, H.M.S.O., 1950.

people was eventually found to be an indispensable condition of efficiency. But the lesson was only learnt by experience.'[1] The Relief in Kind Committee felt that, while the demand for help would be substantial, most clients would want nothing more than food or shelter for a few hours before returning home, to friends, relatives or billeted accommodation, or moving out into the country. Plans were therefore put forward for emergency feeding centres and temporary shelters, neither of which were expected to offer seating or sleeping facilities.

The administration of this plan was handed over to local authority Poor Law officials, so that, in contrast to the comprehensive guarantee given to the unemployed, the homeless were made subject to the stigma of pauperism and provided for in Poor Law tradition by officers conditioned over the years to the deterrent criteria of public assistance. Titmuss noted that 'for adults, meals (in feeding centres) were to consist of tinned food, bread and margarine, and for children, bread and margarine, jam, biscuits and milk if available. This diet was indistinguishable from that authorized for casual wards.'[2]

The decision to put the burden of provision on rates rather than taxes was felt likely to put enormous strain on those local authorities which became the primary targets for bombs, but this created less immediate controversy than the expected movement of homeless people in search of help across authority boundaries. In June 1939 the Treasury agreed to pay for assistance given to such migrants, and local authorities were required to record all items of expenditure for allocation as 'resident' or 'immigrant'; but the Treasury was reluctant to spend in advance of the bombs or to agree to provisions (e.g. blankets) which would encourage people to stay longer in shelters than was justifiable.

It needs to be stressed that these attitudes and decisions preceded the first bombing, which began in June 1940 and reached a peak in September. Swansea was one of the first cities to receive a major raid, and over a thousand were made homeless. This rapidly exposed the weakness of provisions, showing up the serious shortages of staff and relevant experience amongst Poor Law officials, as well as the impossibility of clearing people from the temporary shelters as quickly as was envisaged. 'Most of the town's main services were paralysed. . . . Evacuation was being conducted at top speed.

[1] Titmuss, op. cit., p. 50.
[2] Ibid., p. 51.

. . . Food was short and prayers were abundant.'[1] In September the arrangements made for London collapsed under the intensity of bombing, and in November the Poor Law provision was replaced by 100 per cent Treasury responsibility, administered by such staff as local authorities were able to improvise.

The details of the breakdown are not relevant in this context, but two factors are. Firstly, the impact on public and government of the Poor Law's failure, which not only reinforced the view in the Labour Movement that it must be altogether abandoned, but also led to much of value in its long history being overlooked in post-war welfare legislation. Secondly, what was built up out of the chaos left by the Poor Law officers incorporated a whole range of new ideas about the treatment of homelessness. Advice and information centres were set up, assistance payments were made at the temporary shelters, and unified administrative arrangements were made covering a number of social service departments. Some boroughs started 'half-way houses' for families proving difficult to rehouse, and all local authorities were encouraged to give the homeless family priority in housing allocation. Social workers were appointed and their value quickly recognized in the organization of services for the homeless. 'Experience has shown that the rehousing of homeless people involves more than securing simply that there is accommodation. . . .'[2]

As the intensity of the bombing raids died down, so government concern moved towards the longer-term implications of homelessness, and the massive building programme which would be necessary in post-war reconstruction. Once more the hard core of homeless families became part of a much larger group, and when the date came to enact the abolition of the workhouse there was little time made available to discuss family destitution.

Part 3, paragraph 21 (1)(b) of the National Assistance Act, 1948[3]
How far did the developments described in the three earlier sections influence the formulation of this part of the Act? What was the

[1] Keith Pryer and Co. Ltd: *Luftwaffe over Swansea.*
[2] Ministry of Health London Region Circular H.P.C.L. 13, December 1940: quoted in Titmuss, op. cit., p. 290.
[3] Several services have changed their name in the period covered by this study. National Assistance has become Supplementary Benefits. The Ministry of Pensions and National Insurance changed to Ministry of Social Security, and then to the department of Health and Social Security. Generally the name used throughout the text is the one current at the time to which the text refers.

interpretation which Parliament intended by the very brief wording and absence of any detailed instructions?

The Act placed the responsibility for administering what was now called 'temporary accommodation' on local authorities. Their capital consisted mainly of a number of old workhouses and a collection of temporary wartime structures. As a generalization it may be said that none of it was particularly suited to its new purpose, but whereas workhouses tended to be centrally placed in urban concentrations, many of the wartime buildings were intentionally erected away from population centres. No provision or encouragement was made at the time of the Act for purpose-built hostels.

Temporary accommodation was to be provided for persons urgently needing it, and in the view of the Minister of Health, Aneurin Bevan, it would be used for such peacetime emergencies as fire and flood, making demands which, like bombing, were sudden, acute and localized.[1] There was a clear reference here to the sort of temporary shelter which was needed during the war, but it is important to note that the time-span involved in the concept of 'temporary' was no longer the few hours envisaged by the Relief in Kind Committee. The Government, towards the end of the war, began planning a number of temporary measures which were expected to help out for the first few years of peace. The most relevant parallel in this context was the Temporary Accommodation Act 1944 which was concerned not with hostels for the homeless, but with the programme for prefabricated houses. While it is risky to make assessments of the Government's use of words, it would seem that 'temporary', in the context of the mid 1940s, meant rather more than the three or six months accepted by many local authorities, and plainly carried the implied addition . . . until a more permanent home is available.

In 1944 the Ministry of Health stated that 'the form of welfare organization adopted may differ according to the circumstances of particular areas, but, whatever arrangements were made, they must be capable of being brought into operation as soon as the need arises and should provide for the comfort and well-being of the homeless to the greatest extent practicable.'[2] This was both a reference to the diversity of welfare provisions made by local authorities, and a testimony to the success of social workers in helping the homeless. Subsection 2 of paragraph 21 of part 2 of the National

[1] e.g. Ministry of Health Report for 1949, pp. 312–13.
[2] Ministry of Health: *The Care of the Homeless*, H.M.S.O., 1944.

Assistance Act returned to this theme: 'In the exercise of their said duty a local authority shall have regard to the welfare of all persons for whom accommodation is provided', and it is important to note that the intention of these words would seem to be to ensure the continuity of the welfare services introduced during the war. But the Act was not specific on this point, and after a short period local authorities reverted to what was, after all, their most durable experience, the administration of the Poor Law. But while there was a return to the Poor Law for guidance on the conduct of hostels, the temporary element, introduced during the war, remained. As early as 1947 worries, as yet rather vague, were expressed about these limitations in the National Assistance Act as compared with its predecessor, and the loss of the all-embracing shelter for those in need of it, with no questions asked.[1]

Perhaps another criticism of the Act concerns the continuation of the gap in policy between Housing and Welfare Departments. As was mentioned earlier, housing managers were often reluctant to take on unsatisfactory tenants, or give homeless families the degree of priority in relation to other prospective tenants which welfare agencies wanted. This placed particular stress on the task of rehousing families from temporary hostels, and there is still no formal machinery for ensuring that such families find a more permanent home.

Paragraph 21 did not then have the solid basis of continuity with the past. It was something of a hotchpotch, taking precedents from widely differing contexts, hastily prepared, and lacking the necessary detail to give local authorities the guidance they needed.

Paragraph 21 in practice
In retrospect it is difficult to see why the Poor Law experience was bypassed in this way, without an alternative to fill the resulting void. Some of the difficulties which have since developed have done so because the Act left local authorities to work out for themselves what they should do, if anything, about preventing eviction, or rehousing, or the conduct of hostels. After a short honeymoon period during which the evicted family was accepted much as the bombed-out families had been, local authorities fell back on Poor Law practice. In part this was inevitable. Although Aneurin Bevan stated 'The workhouse is doomed,'[2] he realized that the process of

---

[1] e.g. *The Economist*, November 8, 1947: 'The New Poor Law'.
[2] Ministry of Health Report for 1949, p. 311.

building new premises would take time. Subsequent shortage of capital for this sort of public building has made the process slower than the most pessimistic estimates, so local authorities continued using old Poor Law institutions as hostels, supplemented by wartime buildings. The hostels were built for communal living with sex segregation, and were often not easily converted into family units.

It had also been part of Poor Law policy to make indoor relief unattractive, as a deterrent to would-be users, and on grounds of less eligibility to see that life was not comfortable. These policies appear again after 1948 in the form of restricted contact between husband and wife, employment as wardens of authoritarian ex-service N.C.O.s, the widespread acceptance that isolated and substandard accommodation was quite in order for such families, and the ultimate threat of removing children into care. If the 'inmates of hostels were to have an incentive to move on and make room for others, they had to be given conditions even viler than those they were likely to get in rented accommodation that they could afford'.[1]

Local authorities were faced with a further problem in that many old workhouses served several purposes and under the new legislation could be administered on a joint user basis by Hospital Board and Health and Welfare Committees. This sometimes involved friction between the hospital and hostel sections, and unnecessary restrictions on the old people and homeless occupying them.[2]

The inadequacy of premises served to emphasize a fundamental misunderstanding of the form homelessness would take. Some quotations from successive Annual Reports of the Ministry of Health illustrate the intentions of the National Assistance Act and the Government's gradual, sometimes reluctant, acceptance that the facts were not always as had been anticipated. Looking forward to the new provisions the report for 1949 says: 'The provision made by local authorities for the temporary accommodation of persons who are in urgent need of it through unforeseen circumstances, such as fire or flood, will vary according to the needs of each area. In a district liable to floods, for example, the authority will usually earmark halls or other buildings, and will keep a reserve of stores and equipment to enable the premises to be brought into use quickly in an emergency.'

[1] S. Alderson: *Britain in the 60s: Housing*, Penguin, pp. 112–13.
[2] For a case study see Dr T. M. Ryan, *Two Former Workhouses*, University College of Swansea.

Although this remained a necessary provision, by the following year, 1950, a new emphasis was already acknowledged. 'It was originally anticipated that the demand for such temporary accommodation would come most frequently from people who found themselves without shelter by reason of fire, flood, or similar calamity. In fact, the majority of those who sought temporary accommodation were families evicted from their homes. This use of temporary accommodation for a purpose for which it was not originally intended gave rise to difficult problems. . . .' Wider recognition followed quickly. In the following year the Minister wrote, of families evicted for rent arrears and other reasons: 'In July, 1950, the associations representing local authorities outside London adopted, and circulated to their members, a memorandum on accommodation for homeless families. The memorandum accepted that the responsibility for such families was a public responsibility of local government and recommended that housing and welfare authorities should co-operate, with a view to finding and carrying out the most practical solution, so as to ensure that homeless families were not left without a shelter of some kind.' In 1956 the Minister reported that 'The main burden of the work by authorities and their officers under Part 3 of the National Assistance Act, 1948, lies, however, in the rehabilitation of problem families who have lost their homes, in order to help them achieve an acceptable standard preparatory to rehousing.' Yet the hope of the mid-1940s, that in future years everyone would have a home of their own except in time of calamity, was still echoed—as in 1959: 'Its (temporary accommodation) primary purpose is to give temporary shelter during unforeseen emergencies such as fire or flood.'

The local authorities in South Wales and the West Country accepted responsibility for these new forms of homelessness, but responded quickly with restrictive regulations for which the government was unprepared and which it was unwilling either to sanction or veto. For example, Aneurin Bevan, the Minister of Health, was asked at the end of 1948 'What instructions he has given to local authorities with regard to the accommodation of homeless families in public assistance institutions; what directions he has issued to separate husbands and families; and if he has laid down any maximum time for this home-splitting arrangement.' The Minister replied: 'I have issued no direction as to the separation of husbands and families, which I deprecate.'[1] The Government was similarly

[1] House of Commons, Written answers No. 70, December 9, 1948.

unprepared for some of the effects of the new regulations. Asked in 1953 how many children had been admitted to care as a result of homelessness, the Government spokesman (Miss Hornsby Smith) replied: 'The information desired by the Hon. Member is not available.'[1]

Despite the Government's reluctance to accept the emerging patterns of homelessness and provide a revised definitive set of provisions to meet them, the Minister of Health was at pains to encourage those local authorities who were showing initiative in tackling the problem. His 1954 report contained a section devoted to 'Prevention of Break-up of Families', in which he commended Bristol as 'one of several authorities employing a health visitor who specializes in working with problem families'. The next year he praised the growing number of authorities who were opening rehabilitative units for homeless families, adding. 'From follow-up inquiries it was found that the rent was being paid regularly and that, almost without exception, good standards of housekeeping were being maintained.' The use of caseworkers was encouraged from the early fifties onwards, and on occasions claims were made of staggeringly high success rates. 'One county borough council . . . found that of 200 families (evicted for rent arrears) visited by one of its psychiatric social workers, 95 per cent afterwards paid their current rent regularly and were able gradually to pay off the arrears.'[2]

The Minister's 1958 report took the form of a ten-year survey of temporary accommodation, in which he was critical of the restrictions imposed by local authorities. 'Some authorities have sought to resolve this dilemma (chronic homelessness) by imposing a fixed limit to the permissible length of stay, but this does not provide a satisfactory solution to the difficulty. . . . Rehabilitative work . . . can be done effectively only where it is possible to give some measure of seclusion to the family as a unit and to enable the mother to do her own catering and housekeeping. It has also been found to be more successful when the father lives with his family in temporary accommodation and can take his share of responsibility.' Thus for over a decade the Government showed awareness of the unsatisfactory nature of many of the provisions for homeless families, but delayed doing more than advise and encourage local authorities to change their methods, with the result that many have preferred to retain parts of the old system. The majority of local authorities did

[1] House of Commons, Written answers No. 61, December 10, 1953.
[2] Ministry of Health Annual Report for 1957.

settle for a time-limit, and many have found that further deterrents must be added if evicted families were not to become a continuing burden. The most common has been the exclusion of husbands, and statistics published annually by the Ministry of Health show that in the early years the proportion of adult men to adult women declined. The number of men per 100 women in temporary accomodation fell from 57 in 1949 to 32 in 1956. By 1960 it had increased to 46, and in 1969 it was 74.

Swansea offers an example of the way provisions have been developed. In common with other authorities, temporary accommodation in Swansea was provided for the mother and children of families evicted for non-payment of rents, 'or for other reasons which could have been reasonably foreseen and avoided'.[1] It was supervised by a health visitor. By 1958 this provision had become a 'thorn in the side'[1] of the authority, and the Council adopted two deterrent clauses:

(a) the maximum period during which persons may remain in temporary accommodation be three months;
(b) that, if on the expiration of that period, no accommodation has been found, the children be taken into care and the mother be admitted on a nightly basis for a maximum period of fourteen days.[1]

Originally temporary accommodation was provided in Mount Pleasant Hospital,[2] but in 1959 it was transferred to Cwmllwyd Hostel, Waunarlwydd,[3] on the outskirts of Swansea. 'The siting of the Hostel, together with the 3-month limit of residence have been effective deterrents . . . another very important factor is that persons in temporary accommodation at Cwmllwyd no longer receive the full range of services as was the case in Block V, Mount Pleasant Hospital.'[1]

In 1965 the Medical Officer of Health was able to report that 'Temporary accommodation which was once a thorn in the side of the authority no longer presents problems at least of a major category, and it is with some satisfaction that we examine the year's activities.' The number of hostel residents on December 31, 1964, was seven, compared with sixty-four a decade earlier—a decrease

---

[1] Quotations are from the Annual Reports of the Medical Officer of Health, County Borough of Swansea.
[2] The old workhouse, partly used as a hospital.
[3] A disused isolation hospital.

attributed to the three-month time-limit, the stringency of conditions for entry, and the isolated location of Cwmllwyd. Temporary accommodation no longer presented problems for the Medical Officer of Health, but it seemed likely that the burden of caring for the homeless had merely been shifted to other departments, whose only means of coping was to devote the services of scarce staff to a time-consuming search for lodgings.

It was circumstances such as these that stimulated the growing intensity of both statutory and voluntary activity mentioned at the beginning of the Introduction.[1]

[1] See pp. 15–17 above.

2

PEOPLE USING TEMPORARY ACCOMMODATION

This chapter contains basic statistical information about the survey sample, with sections on 'Family Size and Structure' and 'Income and Employment'.

In the survey two of the families came from outside the area and returned there after a short stay in the hostel. The breakdown of the remaining 547 families is given in Table I which relates the local authority area into whose temporary accommodation they went and the year of entry into the hostel. The total represents a random sample of approximately 50 per cent of all families using hostels during the survey period. There was considerable variation between different local authorities. The samples from Glamorgan and Swansea are approaching 100 per cent. Those from Cardiff, Bristol and Gloucestershire are much lower, between 18 per cent and 25 per cent. The seven families taken from Somerset are a token number, since the main interest there was not so much in families coming to the hostel as in the effectiveness of the County Council's preventive measures.

Information on 340 of the families (62 per cent) was obtained from case files and discussions with appropriate officials only. Information on the remaining 209 families (38 per cent) came from the same source and from an interview with the family itself.

Family size and structure
In the sample mean family size was 4·7 persons and the number of children per family 2·8. These figures were calculated at a time just before the family became homeless, and were therefore not affected by any regulations which might prevent certain family members from entering temporary accommodation hostels; 493 (89·8 per cent) of these families included children. In 13 families the children were cared for by their father or someone else acting *in loco parentis*,

TABLE I

FAMILIES ENTERING TEMPORARY ACCOMMODATION BY AREA AND YEAR OF MOST RECENT ENTRY

Year of most recent entry	AREA						TOTALS BY YEAR	
	Glamorgan	Swansea	Cardiff	Bristol	Gloucester- shire	Somerset	No.	Percentage
1963	1	17	0	0	5	0	23	4·2
1964	15	27	7	7	12	1	69	12·6
1965	29	20	10	19	9	1	88	16·0
1966	41	24	8	28	5	2	108	19·7
1967	31	23	13	24	10	1	102	18·6
1968	34	25	16	12	7	2	96	17·5
1969	18	21	18	3	1	0	61	11·1
Totals of sample { number	169	157	72	93	49	7	547	100
percentage	30·8	28·6	13·1	16·9	8·9	1·3	100	

but the remaining 480 had their mothers with them. In 335 of the families there was a father or father figure as well, either living there permanently or reasonably regularly. This leaves 145 wholly

TABLE II

FAMILY SIZE—NUMBER OF CHILDREN

	All families* with children		Families with† mother and father		Families with‡ 1 parent only	
	No.	%	No.	%	No.	%
1 child	96	19·5	54	16·1	40	26·7
2 children	120	24·3	72	21·5	45	30·0
3 children	87	17·6	59	17·6	27	18·0
4 children	92	18·7	71	21·2	20	13·3
5 children	49	9·9	40	11·9	9	6·0
6 children	25	5·1	19	5·7	6	4·0
7 children	19	3·9	15	4·5	3	2·0
8 children or more	5	1·0	5	1·5	0	—
Total	493	100	335	100	150	100

For the purpose of this table:

* This is the total of the other two columns plus 8 families with children but no parent—generally the children being cared for by a relative.

† There were 335 families with both parents present and children *at home*, immediately prior to homelessness.

‡ There were 150 families with one parent only (145 mothers, 5 fathers) and children at home, immediately prior to homelessness.

The mid-family in rank order has 3 children where both parents are present and 2 if only one parent is present. The difference is largely explained by the number of children in care from single-parent families.

fatherless families and a further 4 couples and 52 unsupported women without children. A tenth of the families included a third generation, almost always maternal grandparents, and a further 7 per cent housed a relative or lodger.

Table II shows the dispersion of family sizes, and distinguishes between families in which there was both a mother and a father and families where the children were supported by a mother only. This includes only children in the last family home before the hostel. In addition there may have been children in care, staying with friends and relatives, in hospital, in an approved or special residential school, or grown up and who had left home.

Young families were particularly vulnerable to the risk of homelessness. At a time of entering temporary accommodation 17·5 per cent of mothers in the sample were under 21; a further 45·4 per cent were under 31; 27·5 per cent under 41 and 9·5 per cent older. The fathers were a little older, the corresponding percentages being 7, 40, 40, and 13 respectively.

Youthfulness is equally apparent amongst the children. A fifth of them were still 'in nappies'—under 2 that is. A further 30 per cent were between 2 and 5, so exactly half of the children were of pre-school age. Most families had children in this age-group, at home, and thereby limiting the earning capacity of the mother. As will become apparent later, this was a significant factor, in view of the importance of rent arrears and other financial difficulties as reasons for homelessness. 32·4 per cent of the children were in primary school and 12·8 per cent in secondary school. This left less than 5 per cent beyond the secondary school limit, and since very few of these were continuing in education, this can be assumed as the total of children still at home who might possibly be making a financial contribution towards the family budget.

Instability was another very noticeable feature of these families. In the five years before the families went into temporary accommodation, 11 of them had lost a parent through death, 13 had lost a father ostensibly because his work took him a long way away (predominantly servicemen), 43 fathers had been sentenced to spells in prison, and 39 parents, not all fathers, had disappeared for reasons which could not be discovered. It is perhaps significant that 32 of the prison sentences and 25 of the disappearances came within twelve months of the families' experience of homelessness. More numerous still was the number of marriages that split up; 105 couples separated in the twelve months before going into temporary accommodation, adding to the 83 who had already separated at an earlier date. There were 47 more, either while the family was in temporary accommodation or very shortly afterwards. A majority of families did not go to a Court for formal ratification of their separation.

Another indication of the extent of marital trouble was that, of the families remaining physically together at the time they came into temporary accommodation, 103 were nevertheless reckoned to be in serious difficulties. Bringing all these factors together, the overall picture emerges that two-thirds of the entire sample were either actually or at risk of becoming fatherless at the time they went into the hostel. This figure would be quite a lot higher were it not for the fact that many of the women had formed a stable family unit with another man, after their first marriage had broken down. The word 'separation' has been used in the previous paragraphs to indicate not only a clear and permanent break between a couple, whether legally married or just living together, but also where one parent has established a pattern of sporadic comings and goings. The evidence shows clearly that virtually all the marriages which broke up did so as a prolonged and gradual process. Homelessness, which may happen once or several times, appeared very much as an integral part of the course of a marriage breakdown.

Family instability was not confined to parents only. There were 139 children in local authority care at the time the families went into temporary accommodation, and this had increased to 185 at the time of rehousing. These figures represent 9 per cent and 12 per cent respectively of the total number of children in the sample. Children were also lodged with friends and relatives at times of housing difficulty, before the family went into the hostel (94 children), while the family was in the hostel itself (138), and to a lesser extent after the family left the hostel (76); 47 children were away at special residential schools. As might be expected, there was correlation between large family size and the likelihood of children being separated from their mothers.

Not altogether surprisingly the high rate of family breakdown has led to a number of irregularities in family structure. In 83 families one of the adults was not a parent to any or some of the children. Generally speaking, what this meant was that the mother had children by more than one man. There were also 41 families in which there were three adults who could put forward claims as being currently involved as parents.

The rate of family breakdown declined following entry into the hostel as compared with the pre-hostel period, and there was no clear difference between circumstances in which husbands were separated from or living with their wives in the hostel. 5 per cent of couples where the husband was not allowed into the hostel separated afterwards, and 3 per cent separated where the husband was permitted into the hostel. The difference is not statistically significant. As will be suggested later, the evidence indicates a causal relationship in the other direction—that homelessness results from a family breakdown and not vice versa. However, there was a close correlation between entry to a hostel and the permanent ending of extended family units—that is units which contain three generations. Of 71 families which included grandparents before becoming homeless, 42 had lost them by the time they were re-housed. Some of these can be explained by a normal process of family break-up, but some appeared to be due to the failure of local authorities to provide for this type of family.

Income and employment

The range of jobs done by the adult male in homeless families generally placed the family towards the lower end of the Registrar General's Classification of Occupations; 85 per cent of families came into social class 4 or 5. Three men had undertaken white-collar jobs, and 19 had qualifications which enabled them to do skilled work. The remainder, when they were employed, did semi-skilled or unskilled work. The same picture applied to the few women workers.

Detailed information on income and employment was only obtain-ed from 365 families, and it covered the twelve-month period before entry into temporary accommodation; 124 (34 per cent) of these families were able to rely on the earnings of a full-time male worker, and a further 33 (9 per cent) on a full-time woman worker; 77 families (21 per cent) had received some wages during the year, either from part-time jobs or from intermittent work; 131 (36 per cent) had received no wages. Over half of the families were there-fore dependent wholly or partly on social security benefits (exclud-ing family allowances) for their livelihood; 210 families (58 per cent) had received supplementary benefits during the year, 138 of them regularly; 106 (29 per cent) had drawn from a contributory scheme, primarily sickness pay and unemployment pay; 58 families (16 per cent) had received a maternity grant or allowance. By any means of assessment this was an extremely high level of dependence on the social security services.

There were some additional sources of income and fringe benefits to take into account—over one-third of the families received something from these sources; 17 (5 per cent) had regular payments (mostly occupational pensions) while another 57 (16 per cent) had, during the year, received lump sums either from the Supplementary Benefits Commission or from the local authority;

22 families had some free meals, and 8 free board and lodging as part of employment—these were mostly linked with tied housing; 49 (13 per cent) had been given help in kind, mainly clothing, and mainly from voluntary social services.

Focusing on the 157 families who were dependent on regular wages, an attempt was made to find out their average weekly earnings. There was no reliable information for 42 of these, so figures given in the remainder of this paragraph refer to a total of 115 families. From the beginning it was apparent that, although employment might be regular, the level of wages fluctuated considerably from week to week. The families were therefore asked to provide information on the average weekly pay packet, in a good week and in a bad week. Table III shows the number of families in different income groupings (that is income after the deduction of tax, etc.), and a further column showing groupings in terms of the sum handed over to the housewife for housekeeping. The table shows the gradual move of families from concentration at the upper end of the scale in a good week, to the centre of the scale in a bad week, to the lower end of the scale when housekeeping money was handed over. The mid-family (58th) in rank order comes in the £12 10s–£15 group in a good week, in the £10–£12 10s group in a bad week, and in the £7 10s–£10 group for housekeeping. Average wages in a good week were approximately £15 and in a bad week £12, a fluctuation of £3.[1] The money paid over to the housewife did not fluctuate quite so widely week by week and averaged £10 (this is calculated as good week + bad week, divided by 2). Averaging over the whole year, the typical housewife in the group could expect to receive £3 10s less than the total sum in the weekly pay packet. The housekeeping figures are slightly distorted by a small number of families in which the wife herself was the wage-earner and there was therefore no process of handing over money from the earner to the housekeeper; but the effect of this was small, no more than reducing the average of housekeeping from £10 to £9 15s.

A little over half of the wives complained that there were diffi-culties in extracting the housekeeping money from their husbands. Most of them felt that the wage-earner was often reluctant to hand over the money, or could not be relied on to provide a reasonably stable amount each week. In some cases the earner had regularly

[1] There were no significant differences in earning patterns between large and small families.

spent a large part of his wage before reaching home, or, having handed over the money, subsequently asked for some of it back.

The overall picture, then, was of families living on social security benefits, low and unstable wages, or a combination of the two. Poverty therefore becomes an important factor. Indeed the researchers assessed that poverty was a serious family problem for over a fifth of the families, and for 82 of them (15 per cent of the total sample of 549 families) was perhaps the most serious difficulty they

TABLE III

WEEKLY EARNINGS

	NUMBER OF FAMILIES		
	Good week	*Bad week*	*Handed to housewife*
Weekly earnings:			
Up to £5	5	11	22
£5 to £7 10s	5	10	15
£7 10s to £10	7	16	25
£10 to £12 10s	25	31	21
£12 10s to £15	17	20	15
£15 to £17 10s	7	10	8
£17 10s to £20	23	5	4
Over £20	26	12	5
Total	115	115	115

faced; 105 families themselves felt that the low level of earnings or social security benefits, or, less frequently, the irregularity of earnings, was a major cause of the loss of their home; 57 of them were further hampered by hire-purchase commitments undertaken when the family was in rather better financial circumstances, and there was a similar level of concern about the growing expense connected with children's education. The cost of school uniforms, school outings, material for classes, and fares to get to school was most frequently mentioned; 25 families felt that their own mismanagement of money had contributed substantially to the loss of their home. The survey checked only on some of the more publicized aspects of mismanagement—excessive smoking, drinking and gambling; 11 adults in the total sample smoked more than 300 cigarettes a week, 17 went drinking more than three times a week, and one spent more than 30s a week on gambling.

3

THE CAUSES OF HOMELESSNESS

The causes of homelessness need to be assessed on two levels—the immediate factor which sparks off the experience of homelessness, and the underlying range of family problems in which the origins of homelessness are to be found.

The immediate reason for entering temporary accommodation
Table IV shows the reasons for entering temporary accommodation, in total and by the local authority into whose hostel the families went. The overall total exceeds the number of families in the sample because in some instances there was more than one immediate reason for entering the hostel.

Rent arrears at 42·8 per cent were numerically the most important factor, though it should be remembered that the existence of rent arrears did not necessarily imply formal eviction procedure. Only about half of the cases of rent arrears got as far as a Court Possession Order; in most of the remaining instances the existence of rent arrears combined with some other factor as a reason for the family becoming homeless. The mothers and children of broken marriages and new arrivals to the area were the next biggest groups using the hostels, often coming for shelter in genuinely emergency circumstances.

Comparing these figures with national statistics is difficult. In the first place the survey sample covered an intake of families into temporary accommodation from 1963 to 1969 inclusive. During that time the method of recording admissions to temporary accommodation by the Ministry of Health, and later the Department of Health and Social Security, changed considerably. The latest available national figures, those for the quarter ending September 30, 1969 for England and Wales, show that the major comparable percentages are as follows: evictions for rent arrears, from private and council housing, 18 per cent; marital disputes 18 per cent; new

TABLE IV

REASONS FOR ENTERING TEMPORARY ACCOMMODATION 1963–1969

	Glamorgan	Swansea	Cardiff	Bristol	Gloucestershire	Somerset	Total No.	Percentage of 549
Mortgage/rent arrears:								
Council property	23	15	12	0	7	0	57	10·4
Private property	41	59	28	21	26	4	179	32·4
Illegal tenancy (incl. squatters)	7	6	7	1	4	0	25	4·5
Tied cottage/landlord's convenience	10	22	13	5	7	2	59	10·7
Overcrowding	25	14	3	11	6	0	59	10·7
Fire, flood, etc.	4	10	2	1	3	0	20	3·6
New arrival to the area	18	31	9	21	6	0	85	15·5
Marriage breakdown	60	33	10	35	5	0	143	26·0
Family split/non-marital	12	9	10	9	1	1	42	7·6
Illegal possession	3	6	3	0	2	0	14	2·5

arrivals to the area 13 per cent. The whole picture, however, is somewhat distorted by the large number of 'other reasons' which make up 22 per cent of the total. Going back five years to the end of 1964, the numbers recorded as in temporary accommodation on the last day of that year were 12,967, of whom 6,307, nearly a half, are recorded as 'evicted'. At this time there were only two recorded reasons for entry, 'evicted' and 'other'.

The impression given is that there are a good many similarities between the sample figures and the latest national figures. Both show a slight predominance of, broadly speaking, housing issues (arrears, illegal tenancies, overcrowding, termination of contracts, etc.). 'Social reasons' are, however, also very prominent and become more so when we move on to the underlying causes of homelessness.

Underlying causes of homelessness
The assessment of the underlying causes of homelessness is inevitably less precise than that for the immediate reasons for entry into a temporary accommodation hostel. The research has attempted, firstly, to categorize a number of characteristics (sixty-two in all)[1] which might contribute to family difficulties. This material was assembled from case records, discussions with social workers and other local authority officials who had been in contact with families, and interviews. The next and more difficult stage was to decide which of these characteristics, or combinations of them, contributed towards the family's loss of its home. Three groupings were used— characteristics which were assessed as of major importance to the family's loss of its home, characteristics which had secondary or peripheral relevance, and those which appeared to have no connection at all. In addition an attempt was made to date the emergence of the characteristics, partly in relation to the experience or experiences of homelessness, and partly to provide some idea of the time span over which these difficulties were present. Figures are based on a sample of 547.

Housing. The reasons for entering temporary accommodation, or the situation as it was presented to the local authority by the family making application to go into the hostel, contained a very substan-

[1] Twenty-three of the sixty-two characteristics were concerned with children—the ten classifications of need for special education, four groupings of mental illness as defined in the 1959 Mental Health Act, and nine items concerned with children's behaviour or their treatment by their parents. None of these were shown to be related to homelessness, and so they have been left out.

tial emphasis on housing issues. As was seen in the previous section, the existence of rent arrears was the largest single factor, while the flow of persons from other areas who could not immediately find housing, families from overcrowded circumstances, families from tied housing, and families whose homes have been damaged or destroyed were all important. The stress tended to be on that element in the families' overall circumstances which was relevant to obtaining a Possession Order from the Court, or was cited by the local authority as an appropriate reason for offering hostel accommodation. In asking the question why—why rent arrears? why did the family move? why was the family living in overcrowded conditions? why was the family pushed out of tied housing?—a substantially different picture emerged.

Six families were made homeless by fire, four by flooding, four as a result of a slum-clearance programme and seven because their houses became unfit or unsafe for habitation. These were the only families who were made homeless under the kind of conditions that were envisaged in the 1948 National Assistance Act. Thirty-two families got out of their home because it was needed by the landlord. For these families, 9·7 per cent of the sample, their homelessness was in no way connected with any needs or difficulties within the family itself.

The figures following show the incidence and importance of rent/mortgage arrears, overcrowding/illegal tenancy, and poor housing conditions as causes of the loss of a home.

TABLE V

HOUSING ISSUES

	No. of families in which characteristic occurs		Assessed as major cause of homelessness		Subsidiary causes	Not Related
	No.	%	No.	%	No.	No.
Rent/mortgage arrears	126	23·1	89	16·3	28	9
Overcrowding/illegal tenancy	107	19·6	80	14·6	22	5
Poor housing conditions	89	16·3	47	8·6	35	7

In making comparisons between reasons for entering the hostel and causes of losing the family home, it needs to be borne in mind that, whereas most families were recorded as having only one 'reason', they generally had several 'causes'. Taking only those problems assessed as major causes of homelessness, rent and mortgage arrears became less important. Overcrowding and illegal tenancy, however, became rather more important, and poor housing conditions, which would not be accepted as grounds for offering hostel accommodation, were nevertheless the cause of much concern to the families.

Where a family was faced with housing difficulties it was rare for these not to be somehow linked up with the experience of home-lessness. Sometimes these appeared to be the only causes, as was often suggested in newspaper reports: 'A young mother living on a caravan site is to be evicted next Monday for rent arrears. She is among folk on the site who have refused to pay rent as a protest against conditions—and she, her husband and two children have nowhere to go.'[1] Or in some case histories: 'The Cullen family had lived in London for sixteen years. They were found by the police on ——— station having been evicted from their house when it was condemned. They have come to South Wales in search of work and accommodation. The Cullens had not lived in their London house long enough to be eligible for rehousing.' Many of these migrant families got similarly brief descriptions in the records. 'Parents and one young child arrived destitute at the Salvation Army hostel. Previously living with paternal grandparents but left because of gross overcrowding.' 'This young family consisting of husband, wife and baby daughter originated from the South of England. Recently married they were unable to find housing and have travelled down to Gloucestershire in hope of better conditions.'

It is a mistake, however, to take the absence of any further information as an indication that there were no more major causes of homelessness. In virtually all the examples that were followed up, a much more complex picture gradually emerged. For example, there was a Bristol family, written up rather critically as a case of chronic rent arrears, where the husband was nevertheless in a job which gave him a large wage. Shortly after eviction he became an in-patient in a psychiatric hospital, and a long history of sporadic treatment for mental illness became known. In another instance a Welfare Department was called in by the police to deal with a case of a wife complaining that her landlord had removed all her furniture, and was holding it at his own home. Since the woman's

[1] *South Wales Echo*, December, 1969.

husband was in hospital, action was taken rapidly to deal with the situation, only for it to be discovered that the woman had shortly afterwards followed her furniture and was now living with the landlord.

It was not quite clear whether local authorities dealt more generously with homeless families who were able to furnish 'housing' reasons for the loss of their home, or whether families have gained the feeling that they will get better treatment if they can provide such reasons. Whichever applies, there were a number of instances in which completely fabricated excuses were given. A woman called Mavis, obviously pregnant, and with a toddler in a push-chair, arrived at the Central Police Station. She said she had been evicted from premises in Sheffield because, as soon as the landlord had noticed that she was pregnant, he reminded her of a rule that only one child per family was allowed. She therefore had to leave the dwelling and came South to join her sister, who was only willing to put her up for a short while. Inquiries in Yorkshire showed that there had been no such eviction, but that the woman had two children living with relatives, that her husband was fed up with her behaviour and did not want her back, and that the woman had a long record of wandering around the country. Perhaps less deceptive, but more frequent, was the extent to which a housing factor was extracted from a multi-problem situation and used as a convenient label for the official statistics. The Watt family had a long-standing record of serious illness, unemployment, and recurring homelessness. On one occasion they came in contact with the local authority and were recorded as 'evicted from private property for rent arrears'. Marriage troubles which did not lead to a physical split-up of the family, or where the split did not coincide with the hostel entry, were commonly concealed under some other heading, particularly rent arrears.

Material Circumstances. Such things as rent arrears and poor housing conditions were usually linked with a more general poverty in the families' material living standards. Table VI lists five items with a bearing on these standards.

Only one of these has an entirely factual basis. Unemployment and irregular employment are a measurement of work patterns, and hence the frequency of earnings entering the household, over a twelve-month period prior to homelessness. The remainder involve an assessment by the researcher. Income levels are given in Chapter

TABLE VI

FAMILIES' MATERIAL CIRCUMSTANCES

	No. of families in which characteristics occur		Assessed as major cause of homelessness		Subsidiary cause	Not Related
	No.	%	No.	%	No.	No.
Unemployment/Irregular employment	266	48·5	64	11·7	71	131
Severe poverty	188	34·3	66	12·1	48	74
Debt (excluding rent arrears)	46	8·4	17	3·1	13	16
Inadequate domestic facilities	27	4·9	11	2·0	10	6
Inadequate/Insufficient clothing	9	1·7	1	0·2	7	1

2, and severe poverty here refers to instances in which a low income had a major impact on the family's living standards. This was not a straightforward measurement of income levels, because it took into account such factors as the difficulty of shopping economically (where, for example, the nearest shopping centre was a costly bus-ride away), unavoidable extra expenses (such as court fines and school uniforms), and repayments of long-standing debts (often the enormous hire-purchase interest rates of a door-to-door salesman). Nevertheless over 80 per cent of those families listed in Table VI as suffering from severe poverty had per capita incomes of less than £2 10s a week, at the time they entered temporary accommodation.

There is a large overlap between the categories of 'severe poverty' and 'debt'. Not all families incurring debts are recorded, only those where the debt was large enough or had been unpaid long enough to provoke official action, such as a court order for payment, or where the debt payment took up more than a quarter of the family's income.

Inadequate domestic facilities and clothing are a subjective judgement by the researcher or social worker visiting the family.

Unemployment as the sole and immediate cause of homelessness only occurred in limited circumstances—generally where a man was working for an employer who had provided him with tied housing, such as the National Coal Board or a farmer. Mr Johnson's family, for example, entered the hostel after leaving N.C.B. housing. Mr Johnson had become redundant when his pit closed, and had been given plenty of time in which to leave his house. But he was unable to find a new job in the vicinity, and found it difficult to envisage his ability to pay the substantially increased rent that would be necessary, once he left the seclusion and reduced rent of his N.C.B. house.

More commonly unemployment, which may in itself be in a sequence with such things as illness or marriage problems, was likely to result in poverty, which would then lead to the risk of homelessness. The Rowe family's problems originated from the time when Mr Rowe was discharged from the army on medical grounds. Since then they have never had a permanent home, as Mr Rowe has moved around from farm job to farm job, and therefore from tied cottage to tied cottage. The family's weekly wage, just before they finally called on the Welfare Department for help, was little more than £10 with a free cottage and some other fringe benefits in the form of free milk, etc. But too often Mr Rowe's illness had kept him away from work and reduced his earnings, and more recently his wife had also had a chronic sickness, so that Mr Rowe was forced to take time off to look after the six children. Mr Lord had a similar employment pattern, though without any record of illness. 'Completely inadequate' and similar phrases were liberally sprinkled through his case history, and he seemed unable to keep a job for more than a few weeks at a time. The work he was able to obtain for these brief periods was always unskilled, usually casual, and brought in an average of £12 a week. He had a wife and five children to support, three of them pre-school age. The Lords were rated by local authority officials as 'nice' and 'deserving', and as such have been given a good deal of assistance, including a job by the Chairman of the Housing Committee. Mr Lord was desperately keen to work, and all attempts to explain his inability to keep a job in terms of some form of mental illness failed, so the continual process of unemployment, poverty and homelessness, first noted by the social services over five years before, was still present.

The severest poverty affected those who were not only unemployed but also unable to receive social security benefits. The biggest hole in the supplementary benefits net was for people of no fixed abode, and almost by definition a homeless person or family was in that category on occasions. The nomadic homeless might be crafty enough to exploit the system by obtaining temporary addresses and hence supplementary benefits from a number of different areas within a short period of time. But more commonly those wandering groups found that they were unable to get any money. Diana, for example, made her first approach to the local authority for temporary accommodation five years ago. She explained, and it was subsequently validated, that her parents had deserted her and she had been brought up by her grandmother, who had just died. She was reported as 'mentally confused and distressed', admitted to a psychiatric unit, and given electro-convulsive therapy. After this she took to wandering around the country taking jobs here and there and living on a casual basis with a number of men, including married men. This went on for three years, and her history included being the victim of an indecent assault, having a baby (now adopted), and finally being thrown out of lodgings by a man who took away her last penny. She applied to the Supplementary Benefits Commission for a grant but, since she was of no fixed abode, she did not get one. Eventually she spent a short stay in a temporary accommodation hostel, so qualifying for a small supplementary benefits payment, and has vanished without trace during the last two years. There were a sufficient number of similar, though perhaps less cruel, examples, to make clear the unfairness of dismissing calls of help from people with no fixed abode on the grounds that they were simply spongers on the Welfare State. Families who made their own arrangements to cope with their homelessness, and did so by sharing with friends or relatives, were continually at risk. Sharing with another family usually resulted in overcrowding and was often illegal, so there was the choice of giving the address and risking everyone being evicted for overcrowding or for illegal sub-tenancy, or offering no address and thereby losing supplementary benefits.

Debts were closely linked with rent arrears. When there was not enough money to go round the majority of families seemed prepared to allow debt to accrue in sectors where its impact would be most imperceptibly or slowly felt—and rent for the house was an obvious choice. Occasionally a family was found which had not only substantial rent arrears, but debts as well; or a family with a clear record of rent payments, but an enormous volume of debts to local grocers and other shops. Families who acquired a sudden extra financial burden were often placed in this kind of difficulty.

For example, a family suddenly finding that a fall in wage made it difficult to keep up with existing commitments, especially hire purchase; or a family suddenly faced with a Court fine. Mrs Thomas and her seven children came into the hostel several years ago after her marriage had broken down. The Welfare officer who dealt with her was not at all happy about her ability to care for the children, but gave her the benefit of the doubt and helped in getting her rehoused in a council house with a high rent. For four years nothing was heard of her, and her rent was paid with the greatest of regularity, until quite suddenly she reappeared with a request for help in paying off debts. Her debts were the equivalent of three months of the family income, and she had been subjected to twenty-two Court Orders for debt repayment.

The inadequacy of domestic facilities was often used as a basis for complaining about housing conditions, but families rarely continued complaining if to do so risked losing their tenancy. Protest action did, however, have more serious results than was sometimes envisaged. Mrs Murphy was one of three mothers who stated to a local reporter, 'We originally signed a petition about the site conditions and the repairs needed to our caravans. We decided not to pay rent until repairs were done. I was without heating for my children. They were dressed in hats and coats inside the caravan. Why should I pay for conditions like that?'[1] The report went on to mention that Mrs Murphy was to be evicted. Returning to Mrs Thomas and her seven children, one of the complaints held against her by the Welfare Department was that she had been evicted from some particularly poor accommodation for refusing to pay the rent, on the grounds that the housing had no internal water, no source of hot water, no bath, and was extremely damp. Another family received a warning from the eldest son's headmaster that he must have much improved clothing if he wished to stay at the school. Several weeks' rent was spent on this, and the family were evicted for arrears.

Illness. Table VII gives details of various forms of mental and physical illness amongst the families. The first four items in the list are taken from the categorization of mental illness in the 1959 Mental Health Act. It was not always easy to fit a person into one of these categories, and where there was a difficulty the researcher tended to use the 'other mental disorder' grouping. 'Stress/suicidal'

[1] *South Wales Echo*, December, 1969.

refers to at least one attempted suicide or nervous breakdown in the history of the person concerned. The death of a parent or child is entered only if it happened within twelve months before the experience of homelessness. Frequent physical illness covered a longer period, but must have been confirmed by a doctor or social worker as present in the months shortly before homelessness.

TABLE VII

ILLNESS

	No. of families in which characteristic occurs		Assessed as major cause of homelessness		Subsidiary cause	Not related
	No.	%	No.	%	No.	No.
Mental subnormality	20	3·6	12	2·2	7	I
Severe subnormality	I	0·2	0	—	I	0
Psychopathic disorder	9	1·6	6	1·1	I	2
Other mental disorder	57	10·4	33	6·0	15	9
Stress/suicidal	35	6·5	12	2·2	18	5
Physically handicapped	10	1·8	3	0·5	4	3
Disabling accident	13	2·4	9	1·6	2	2
Death of parent	8	1·5	3	0·5	4	I
Death of child	9	1·6	I	0·2	7	I
Frequent physical illness	53	9·6	22	4·0	24	7
		39·2		18·3		

The total impact of illness was substantial, though the figure of 18·8 per cent is slightly inflated by a small quantity of double counting. Illness, especially mental illness, was particularly frequent amongst single homeless people. Social workers' reports were liberally sprinkled with opinions that a particular client was in need of psychiatric attention, though they occasionally went on to record that the local psychiatric hospital did not agree. Carol, a spinster just into her forties and registered blind, was picked up by the police 'in a drowsy condition due to sleeping tablets'. She was seen by a doctor who diagnosed physical illness, and recommended surgery. A welfare officer, backed up by a mental welfare officer, considered her 'in need of care and attention due to mental retardation'. When she was seen by the local psychiatric hospital however, she was returned as 'not suitable for psychiatric treatment'.

Cathy, another spinster, a little older, was a known alcoholic and prostitute who had been in and out of the temporary accommodation hostel, as well as psychiatric wards. She had also spent time in prison and a number of voluntary institutions. She circulated around a large dockland area, and the high spots of her life occurred when a boat came in and she was able to earn some money. For the rest she lived as and where she could. The hospital had become fed up with her reluctance to co-operate in treatment, classified her as a psychopath, and said there was nothing else they could do. The Welfare Department tried to find a place for her in a home for people suffering from nervous disorders, and succeeded, but Cathy refused to sign to be admitted as a voluntary patient.

When mental illness hits a family, its impact can be wholly devastating. Mrs Millings's entire life history provided such an example. She had a very unhappy childhood. 'I never got on with my mother; she never liked me or wanted me. I lived with my father in the back of the house, and my mother lived with my sister in the front. They never got on, but it's funny he never spoke to her until the day she died, from the day I got married. My mother wanted me to turn out bad.' When she was 16 Mrs Millings tried to take her own life, and began to receive regular treatment under a psychiatrist. She became pregnant and married, in that order, when she was 18. Asked about her husband, she said, 'Oh, him! I only married him to get away from my mother.' She complained bitterly of parental discipline. Married life began in a council house but was never very satisfactory. Mrs Millings complained that her husband drank and gambled too much, got into trouble with the police, and eventually deserted her. At around this time both Mrs Millings and her young daughter made suicide attempts, and underwent further psychiatric treatment. Mrs Millings received a conviction for shop-lifting, and was later registered as a drug addict.

The family's housing history over this period showed the same gradual deterioration. After their spell in a council house the family moved into private rented accommodation, but following Mr Millings's desertion the family got into serious debt and was evicted. There then followed a number of years when Mrs Millings was unwilling to make contact with the Welfare Department, and preferred that she and her children should shuffle around between friends, relatives, and some particularly squalid lodgings, finishing up in a derelict caravan. For long periods the children were not living in the same house as their mother. She finally went into temporary accommodation from the caravan, and while there her children were taken into care, subsequently to be farmed out to the various relatives with whom they had, in any event, spent many of their early years.

At this point there was an upward swing in Mrs Millings's history. Looking at it retrospectively, a turning-point seems to have been her entry to a psychiatric hospital. Even though after leaving hospital she lived rough for a while, sleeping on buses or in public lavatories, eventually she obtained a flat for herself, and later her children joined her. From there she was rehoused by the local authority and with a good deal of social work support managed to look after her family.

Commonly there was a straightforward relationship between illness, unemployment, poverty and homelessness. The housing history of the Earl family is an example. 'Mr Earl again lost his job and hence his home because he stayed away during the haymaking to look after his children, as his wife was in hospital.' Later on, the record continued, 'The family were in temporary accommodation for four months during which time they did not pay the rent because Mr Earl was out of work through illness. They broke open the electricity meter and Mrs Earl received a suspended sentence for selling a rented TV set.' The social worker's summary read: 'This family has always suffered from poverty and as far as I can make out, illness. The one bright spot in their lives was when they were in temporary accommodation in a three bedroomed council house. The woman said she wished she could live there always.'

Homelessness rarely seemed to follow a short spell of illness where there was complete recovery. Rather it was a side effect of persistent or recurring bouts of illness, either in one member of the family or at different times affecting several members. Mr Earl's welfare was disrupted not only by his wife's chronic ailments, but by his own occasional illnesses, which might well have been the result of exhaustion. Mrs Broughton's problem was a little different. She was faced with a husband who was mentally unstable and intermittently left the household, taking as much money as he could raise and going off to live by himself. No one knew what he got up to on his times away from the home. But he also had chronic lung congestion, and returned to the home when the state of his physical health had deteriorated so much that he felt he could no longer look after himself. His wife was therefore faced with the problem of caring for him while he was ill, and having him away from the home when he was fit. In this instance the illness was recorded as a subsidiary cause of homelessness. The Broughtons had for many years lived in derelict accommodation, and went to temporary accommodation when their house was condemned as unfit to live in. While Mr Broughton's illness undoubtedly contributed to the poverty of the family's circumstances, the basic cause of homelessness in this instance was seen as poor housing conditions.

Family size and structure. Only two items are taken into account here—the problems of caring for children with only one parent, almost always the mother, and the difficulties implicit in having a large number of children. Table VIII gives the relevant figures:

TABLE VIII

FAMILY SIZE AND STRUCTURE

	No. of families involved		Assessed as a primary cause		Subsidiary cause	Not related
	No.	%	No.	%	No.	No.
Single-parent family	150	27·4	106	19·4	36	8
Large family (5 or more children at home)	98	17·9	32	5·8	60	6

Further relevant figures are given in Table II of Chapter 2, where it is shown that there was only a little overlap between large families and single-parent families. Looking at families containing a mother, father, and children, 79 out of 335 (23·6 per cent) have 5 children or more, whereas of the single-parent families only 18 out of 150 (12 per cent) have 5 or more children.

It was clear that for a family to have more than the normal number of children, or to be fatherless, placed it very much at risk of becoming homeless. For the unsupported mother, the experience of homelessness often stemmed from the straightforward reaction of the housing authority or the landlord. Referring back to Mrs Murphy's newspaper interview, she said: 'Children are like dogs. They are not allowed. You ask for rooms and mention that you've got children, and you've had it. They don't want to know.'[1] Survey

[1] *South Wales Echo*, December, 1969.

evidence gave some support to Mrs Murphy's assertion, though only in relation to private landlords. A typical example was the unmarried mother who had just been discharged from hospital after the birth of her third child. One child was being fostered permanently, and the second being cared for by the woman's landlady during the mother's confinement. But when the woman returned to her digs the landlady handed her the child and locked her out. In another instance Mrs Wallace was married, but legally separated from her husband, and looked after her five children, all of primary school age-range. She first contacted the Welfare Department when she felt that she was no longer able to manage on her national assistance of less than £9 (excluding family allowances). She was visited in her private rented housing by a welfare officer who found that she kept the premises neatly and paid the rent regularly. This was considered grounds for not offering help to Mrs Wallace, but just a year later she was evicted, illegally, because the landlord was fed up with her children.

The most severe difficulties, where an unsupported mother had to cope with a large number of children, could prevent the initial establishment of anything which would normally be called 'a family home'. For example, Gloria left her parents' home fourteen years ago, and has had six illegitimate children since then. She has been chronically homeless, made frequent use of the temporary accommodation hostel, spent several periods in hospital, and for the rest got rooms as and when she could. The fathers of several of the children were men who had offered her temporary shelter. After one of these incidents she was admitted to hospital with a haemorrhage, thought by the doctor to be the result of a rather crudely attempted abortion, and when she returned her man refused to take her back. The impact on the children has been such that they have spent relatively little time with their mother, have been in and out of care, and have stayed for short periods with a number of neighbours. At the time of writing Gloria has been lost to the sight of the social services.

These examples focus on the twin problems of getting a home and coping within a domestic context. Housing issues were particularly relevant for this group of families. A woman at the head of household was generally reckoned to be uncreditworthy and therefore at serious risk of getting into rent arrears. For this reason she might well have difficulty in getting the tenancy of a dwelling, whether from a private or council landlord, and if her husband left her she might not find it easy to get the tenancy of their property transferred to her name. For the very large family there were serious shortages of dwellings, except for the old-fashioned, often unmodernized, and generally unsuitable buildings. This was one of the few sectors where there was a genuine housing shortage.

The task of coping with a large number of children could be made easier by a more active policy on the part of the social work services. Whereas there were many examples of frequent and generous use of material aid, both cash and kind, it was rare to find the family receiving regular day-to-day domestic help. An unsupported father could expect to receive the aid of the Home Help Service, but an unsupported mother or a couple with a large number of children could not. A number of the examples already quoted show that there were circumstances, such as illness, when the loss of the job or the loss of the home could have been avoided by the rapid and temporary provision of a home help. Another characteristic attitude of the social services was their reluctance to accept a situation which was not clear, in the sense that the family structure and/or size was not static. Mrs Street's children were taken into care not because she was unable to look after them, but because the Children's Department was unable to cope with a situation in which her husband was sometimes in the house and sometimes not, and in which there was regular adultery on both sides. Mrs Street was in effect given an ultimatum—either to break away completely from her husband, or to lose her children. Mrs Johns was subjected to the same kinds of pressure. She owned her own house, albeit a very sub-standard one. She had seven children and a very unsatisfactory relationship with her husband, from whom she was legally separated, but who occasionally turned up to the house and caused a certain amount of trouble. The solution suggested by the social worker was for the wife to apply a notice to quit to her husband. When she argued that she was unable to do such a thing against her husband, the record described her as having 'sado-masochistic tendencies'!

Family Relationships. The substantial impact of difficulties in family relationships on the process of losing the family home is illustrated by the figures in Table IX.

There is some overlap of categories here, particularly between marital breakdown and domestic violence. Sixty-two families were assessed as having both marriage breakdown and domestic violence as a major cause of homelessness. The overall picture still remains,

TABLE IX

FAMILY RELATIONSHIPS

	No. of families involved		Assessed as a primary cause		Subsidiary cause	Not related
	No.	%	No.	%	No.	No.
Marital breakdown	255	46·6	202	36·9	38	15
Domestic violence	116	21·2	75	13·7	29	12
Family disputes (not marital)	91	16·6	71	13·0	19	1
Mismanagement of children	22	4·0	3	0·5	14	5
Child cruelty/neglect	32	5·9	6	1·1	24	2
Poor parent-child relationship	18	3·3	3	0·5	12	3
Families with children in care	102	18·6	4	0·7	89	9

however, that about half of all the families in the survey lost their homes, wholly or partly, because family members could not get on with each other. Perhaps it is relevant at this point to add further that marriage breakdown does not overlap with earlier figures for single-parent families (Table VIII). In the case of single-parent families what is being stressed is the difficulty that accrues from a family being managed by only one parent. On the other hand marital breakdown as a cause of homelessness is concerned with the actual event of breakdown in which the couple split up either permanently or temporarily. The loss of the family home is linked directly with the specific emotional and physical upheaval of the split.

The separation of a family, and the wife's entry into temporary accommodation, might be the signal for a final and complete split within the family. Two of the six local authorities covered by the survey openly used the hostel as a place in which the wife, often with the support of the social worker, could think through the marriage situation and decide what action should be taken in the best interests of herself and her children. If it was felt that separation should lead to divorce and an entirely different domestic arrangement, then this could be arranged from the hostel. Encouragement to make separation permanent sometimes became quite strong. Mrs Willard, for example, was offered help with rehousing, virtually the promise of a house, if she would formalize the separation from her husband.

More commonly the hostel was used following temporary marriage breakdowns, resulting in some kind of reconciliation. It might be a completely isolated incident, where the wife left the family home with her children, spent a few days in the hostel, and then returned to her husband, with no further difficulties being presented. This was not necessarily to suggest that the couple completely overcame their marriage problems; merely that any further developments were not recorded by the local authority. A typical example would be Mr and Mrs Frances. They were unknown to the social work services, and there was no record of any previous difficulties of any kind. Late one Saturday night Mrs Frances and her three children, accompanied by a neighbour, came to the local police station and reported that Mr Frances had thrown them out. The neighbour added that Mr Frances was very quarrelsome, particularly when he had had a drop to drink. The police sergeant called on Mr Frances and found him, as described by the neighbour, in a drunken and aggressive mood. He refused adamantly to have his family back, on the grounds that his wife nagged him too much. The police had no option therefore but to call in the duty welfare officer, who, on the advice of the police sergeant, left Mr Frances alone, and offered the wife and children hostel accommodation. The following morning a very repentant Mr Frances came, apologized to his wife, and took the family back home.

The gradual and final break-up of the marriage may be dotted with entries into temporary accommodation, or sporadic short separations between husband and wife. Two and a half years passed from the first time Mrs Levine came to the notice of the N.S.P.C.C. until her final split from her husband. During that time she twice entered the hostel and three times went for refuge to relatives. Throughout this time the case history mentioned gradual deterioration in the marriage, as well as in Mrs Levine's mental and physical health. The N.S.P.C.C. officer, and later a child-care officer, ensured that throughout these sporadic separations Mrs Levine was not parted from her children, but they were unable to guide her about the case for or against taking divorce action. Eventually Mrs Levine divorced her husband, on the recommendation of and with some pressure from her solicitor. The grounds were adultery and sexual malpractice which amounted to cruelty.

A large number of the situations recorded as marriage break-downs never led to total separation. Rather, the entire marital history was characterized by perpetual ups and downs. Hannah came into temporary accommodation as a single woman with an illegitimate month-old baby. A few weeks after entering the hostel she found herself a residential job as a housekeeper to a relatively wealthy man. Not long afterwards she married her employer. This was several years ago, and since then the marriage has gone through a continuous tempestuous process, with several months of relative tranquillity followed by an upheaval and the wife's entry with her children to the hostel. Her husband was occasionally violent, and Hannah came to the hostel for a few days to allow him to cool off. She then went back home. She said that she had completely lost count of the number of occasions on which she had used the hostel, and the Welfare Department were accustomed and prepared for her to use this service, and had assured themselves that it was maintaining some stability in her marriage. The Platts were in a similar situation. They both married very young, and through the ten years of their married life had faced a conflict between, on the one hand, their strong attraction to each other, and on the other hand the complete contrast in cultural backgrounds in which they grew up. Mrs Platt did not have a happy childhood. Her parents separated when she was in primary school, and she lived with her father, never seeing her mother again. She had been conceived before her parents were married, and as a child had often had this fact thrown up at her. A wish to get away from this background was part of her motivation in marrying. Her husband grew up outside Britain, in a culture in which woman held a very lowly position, and in which adultery was a man's prerogative and certainly of no great consequence. Twice Mr Platt threw his wife and child out on to the street, and they went into a temporary accommodation hostel. A social worker (woman) began visiting the family after the second reconciliation, but dropped out after Mr Platt was extremely unpleasant to her. When, therefore, Mrs Platt tried again for hostel accommodation she was refused, and at a still later date, when sent along by a probation officer, she was refused again. She spent altogether a further eight months separated from her husband, living with friends, but then, as the divorce hearing was approaching, she was reconciled. Since that time the marriage has become much more stable.

Other sorts of family dispute commonly involved the extended family. Mr and Mrs Hall, for example, an elderly couple, offered to share their home with their daughter when she got married. Shortly afterwards their house needed some major repairs, and their son-in-law offered to pay for these on condition that the tenancy of the house was transferred into his name. This was done in good faith, but a little while afterwards, when the first grandchild had been born, the Halls were evicted on the grounds that there was no longer any space for them in the home. Another instance involved Judy, a young girl, from a family of fifteen. She had an affair with, and a baby by, a young soldier whom she expected to marry, only to find he was already married with children. She lived in succession with two married sisters, but both times the man in the household found the situation unacceptable and she spent periods in temporary accommodation. Judy got a lot of help from her welfare officer and a sympathetic housing manager, and was shortly rehoused in a council flat.

Already a number of examples have been given where children have been taken into the care of the local authority. As the figures in Table IX suggest, this was rarely connected in any causal sense with homelessness, but was rather the result of a period of homelessness or general family disruption.

Behavioural difficulties. Table X lists nine items, and except for the first one, conviction for crime, they all need some explanation. A specific measurement of heavy drinking and gambling is given in Chapter 2, page 53. The substantially higher figures given here are reached by the addition of references made to drunkenness or excessive gambling by a member of the family, and recorded in the family's case history. An entry under the heading 'sexual misbehaviour' is also strongly characterized by the extent to which the family felt that this was a particular problem for them. Certainly not all infidelities have been recorded. The remaining five items are based to some extent on the opinions of members of families themselves, but predominantly on the views of welfare officers and other social workers who have been in contact with each family.

There are a lot of multiple entries in this Table (that is, families appear under more than one item), so that nothing of value is achieved by adding each column. Behavioural difficulties rarely occurred in isolation from each other. Nevertheless, in the eyes of family members, and to an even greater extent of social workers,

TABLE X

BEHAVIOURAL DIFFICULTIES

	No. of families involved		Assessed as a primary cause		Subsidiary cause	Not related
	No.	%	No.	%	No.	No.
Conviction for crime	117	21·4	31	5·7	72	14
Drunkenness	67	12·2	38	6·9	29	0
Excessive gambling	21	3·8	7	1·3	14	0
Sexual misbehaviour	70	12·8	33	6·0	26	11
Workshy	53	9·7	29	5·3	24	0
Poor domestic management	68	12·4	29	5·3	28	11
Misuse of resources	56	10·2	33	6·0	19	4
Domestic filth	34	6·2	8	1·5	24	2
Poor personal hygiene	26	4·8	5	0·9	13	8

these sorts of difficulties were very important as causes of homelessness.

The Price family was an example of this, as a few quotations from their case history will show. 'First child born 3 weeks after marriage ... mother always had to cope with father's bouts of brutality and irregular housekeeping money ... father excessive drinker and gambler, inadequate, irresponsible and workshy ... mother immature and hopeless with money ... father several convictions for housebreaking ... family muddles along.'

The effects of criminal conviction could be severe. Mrs Harry had five young children to care for and another due in one month, when her husband received his prison sentence. Often, however, the Court showed leniency to families in this kind of situation. There were instances of prison sentences being given, but only after a series of offences, and it was rare for a Court to impose a heavy fine on a poor family. The probation order, and more recently the suspended sentence, featured regularly. Mr Howell was himself written up as 'inadequate', and had a poor work record. He never managed to obtain a job with a reasonably high wage, and this meant his large family lived in poor housing and with a low standard of living. Possibly in order to supplement the family income, but almost certainly with other more deep-seated reasons, Mrs Howell had a very long record of larcenies. These stretched over fifteen years and more than twenty convictions. While in temporary accommodation she twice stole money from an electricity meter, and sold someone else's television set. She was on probation at the time she got married, and continued on probation. She has never been imprisoned or fined.

There was only a little evidence that chronic alcoholism or cost of drink were contributory causes of homelessness. Much more frequently a bout of drunkenness, sometimes an isolated incident, sometimes part of a regular pattern, would spark off problems which were latent in the domestic situation. It was a time when a person's (virtually always a man's) long-standing discontent with his family position would be bolstered and perhaps exaggerated. Given the additional courage from the drink, he would throw out his wife and children, or take some other action which he would almost invariably regret on becoming sober again. Drunkenness itself often had provoking factors, as with a man whose behaviour, when drunk, was seriously exacerbated by some brain damage.

In a few instances drunkenness was a man's reaction to his wife's adultery. He might also react violently by beating up his wife, or the man with whom she was having an affair. Adultery by a man rarely brought more than prolonged complaint from his wife. Adultery, or the strong suspicion of it, was in fact a common feature of families in the survey, but rarely severe enough in itself to be a major cause of homelessness. Rather, the forms of sexual misbehaviour which did contribute substantially towards the loss of a home were of a much less usual nature. Myra was 13 when she first came to the notice of the local authority. She arrived late one night in a terribly distressed state at the police station claiming that she had been assaulted by her father. She was taken to a children's home and since that time has been in care. When her allegations were investigated, a picture of sexual behaviour was uncovered in which the young girl was expected to help stimulate her father so that he could achieve intercourse with his wife. The father lost the tenancy of his house following the publicity of his Court appearance.

In another example, a woman went to the local Children's Department, and a record of her first interview mentions allegations of 'excessive sexual demands' and 'unnatural practices'. The 'excessive demands' were for intercourse five or six times a day, and 'unnatural practices' of a homosexual nature. When questioned, the husband acknowledged the demand he made on his wife, and admitted that he was also a promiscuously active homosexual. These circumstances caused a great deal of soul-searching for a number of social workers, before the wife was advised and agreed to leave the house with her children and go into temporary accommodation.

The man mentioned in the last paragraph was recorded by his employers as workshy, on the ground that he regularly took an hour or so off from his work during the day. Evidence suggested that diagnosis of workshyness was often the result of an absence of some important information. Yet even where all the information was available, there may still be a dilemma as to what sort of diagnosis should be made. Mr and Mrs Martin had a depressing housing history since they were married ten years ago. During this time they had four houses, two on mortgage, two rented, and were evicted from all of them, each time for substantial arrears. In between they stayed four times with relatives, and the wife and four children made three visits to the temporary accommodation hostel. The presenting problem was Mr Martin's chronically poor employment record. He has nominally been with one employer for a large part of his married life, but has a record of absenteeism which shows him to have been absent for rather longer than he was actually at work. Mrs Martin saw the issue as that of a good man hampered by a record of accidents, and she had a lot of evidence to support her view. Mr Martin hurt himself falling off a ladder and out of an upstairs window. He had also been involved in several pit accidents, and had spent a period in a miner's rehabilitation unit. The welfare officer had a different interpretation of the situation. He saw Mr Martin as workshy and given to 'spending all his time in clubs'. He had the view, supported by the man's boss, that Mr Martin had exaggerated the severity of some of his accidents, and possibly brought some of them on himself. For this reason the Welfare Department have not been keen to help the Martins. They have always been left to find their own housing, without any help from the local authority, and when Mrs Martin made her last application to go into the hostel, she was seriously criticized by the welfare officer for not going to stay with relatives in England. These particular relatives lived on an Army base, and the welfare officer was fully aware that, had she gone to stay with them, Mrs Martin would have placed her relatives in a position of breaking military regulations.

Such things as poor domestic management or misuse of resources were equally difficult to establish with any objectivity. The case of Mr and Mrs Leach would illustrate the point. They married in the early fifties, and since that time Mr Leach has been regularly em-

ployed, albeit on a below-average wage. At the time they last became homeless, three years ago, Mr Leach was earning £16 a week
and there were then four children. Mr Leach was not a heavy spender,
and over the years had regularly handed over most of his wages to
his wife. The family's housing history quite belied the pattern of
family stability which Mr Leach's employment might suggest. The
family had been evicted from both council and private housing for
rent arrears, and from two private houses because of the state of
domestic squalor. The temporary accommodation hostel has been
used twice, relatives on several occasions, and for a while the family
lived in a cellar. The reaction of the social services has varied. On
occasions Mr and Mrs Leach have been given substantial sums to
pay rent arrears, while on other occasions the family has been refused
entry to the temporary accommodation hostel on the grounds that
their financial circumstances (i.e. Mr Leach's wages) simply did not
justify entry. Although Mrs Leach has no flamboyant idiosyncrasies
in the way she spends her money, nevertheless the debts always
seemed to pile up. At this point the reader has as much basic information as the welfare officer, and can make up his own mind as to
the validity of that officer's eventual diagnosis of 'mismanagement'.

Several of the illustrations in this chapter have traced the family
history back to the parent's own formative years. In fact unfortunate
childhood experiences of the parents featured frequently, and sometimes tended to establish themselves as patterns of behaviour which
have to be worked out in adult life. For example, one young couple
with three children both came from homes in which their own
parents had separated. The husband showed signs of mental
instability, and both were recorded in case histories as being
'chronically insecure'. It was an unhappy marriage, and the wife
and children eventually entered a temporary accommodation hostel
following an incident of violence by the father. Yet the shock of
seeing his wife and children move into the hostel caused such distress that he had to be taken into hospital. The history of another
young family with four children described the husband as 'completely ruined by an over-indulgent mother', and the wife as
having 'had a very deprived childhood and wants to give her
children everything. She has to organize everything and cope herself as she feels her husband is a liar and a very weak character.'

Sometimes a way of life could be handed down from generation
to generation, like the man from the Midlands who was threatened
with homelessness. He suffered from chronic illness and had been

discharged from the armed forces on medical grounds. Eventually
he felt that he and his wife could no longer cope with their house
and children. Since he himself had been brought up in care in South
Wales, his action was to travel down with his children and hand
them over to his own Childrens' Department. In another example,
a girl called Jean had repeated her own babyhood. An illegitimate
child, whose mother had deserted her when she was only a few days
old, she had herself given birth to three illegitimate children and in
turn deserted them.

Community Relations. Only two items are listed here and neither is
numerically important.

TABLE XI

COMMUNITY RELATIONS

	No. of families involved		*Assessed as a primary cause*		*Subsidiary cause*	*Not related*
	No.	%	No.	%	No.	No.
Failure to use social services	23	4·2	3	0·5	12	8
Complaints from neighbours	14	2·5	5	0·9	9	0

Because of the source from which the survey sample was taken,
families who wholly failed to use the statutory social services would
simply not appear. However, in the next chapter, which deals with
the narrative aspects of the family's housing history, there will be
a good deal of evidence to show how far families who were threatened with homelessness depended on their own resources rather
than making use of the Government or local authority social service.
Those who appear in Table XI come into two groupings. Firstly,
families that have at one stage or another made use of the services
of a welfare officer or other social worker, but have subsequently
asked for the worker to stop visiting. Mrs Platt, whose story is told
earlier in this chapter, welcomed a visiting social worker, but her
husband did not, was rude and ordered the worker to stop coming.
Secondly, families who were not receiving their full entitlements
from the social security provisions, either because they were un-
aware of their rights, or because they were being incorrectly

assessed by a supplementary benefits officer. The Williams family are an example of the former.

Mr and Mrs Williams were in their fifties but had no children. Both were reported as 'simple souls', but the husband had managed to work regularly and with the help of a mentally ill wife ran the house 'efficiently and hygienically'. However, as Mrs Williams's illness became more serious, her husband decided that he would have to give up his work and stay at home to look after her. Because he had no work he had no income, and made no approach to the Department of Health and Social Security or any other agency for money. The Williams's began to use up their savings to buy food and, to start with, to pay the rent. Eventually they were unable to continue with rent payments, and a notice to quit was issued from the local authority. Mr Williams decided to cash an endowment insurance policy to pay off his arrears, but this took time, and before he could obtain the money the wheels in the Housing Department had continued rolling and a Possession Order was granted. It was not until the family were on the verge of being evicted that the full story came out, and at this stage it was so late that the housing manager felt he could not overrule the Possession Order, and the family had to move into a hostel.

Mrs Huggin's difficulties illustrate the problem of supplementary benefits assessments. She was thrown out of her house with her children, one of whom, a chronically sickly baby, subsequently died of pneumonia. She had no money and appealed to the Supplementary Benefits Commission for help with burial costs. She was offered a small sum, sufficient for a pauper's grave, which would have meant that there could be no headstone, and Mrs Huggin might never have known where her baby was actually buried. Later on it was discovered that a grant for a normal burial was perfectly within the discretionary powers of the supplementary benefits officer. There were a number of disputes between social workers and supplementary benefits officers, almost all of them about the discretionary nature of grant-giving powers, or the secrecy of the 'A code'.

Many families had strong and often extreme views as to the part played by their neighbours in the development of problems. But few seemed able or prepared to identify the complaints of neighbours as a specific cause of the loss of the family home. Indeed, complaints needed to be very numerous or from an influential person if they were likely to be successful. In one example Mr and

Mrs Burge brought their six children to a new housing estate, and shortly made it clear to the entire neighbourhood that they had many of the usual social problems which would have them categorized as 'a multi-problem family'. Within a few months they were not so much evicted as moved on (to sub-standard housing) following complaints from a local councillor, who sat on the housing committee and happened to live at the far end of the same street.

The patterns of causes

An attempt was made to link those factors assessed as causes of homelessness with the experience of homelessness itself, by trying to date the emergence of the causal factors. This proved extremely difficult, partly because many of the factors were undateable, partly because the experience of homelessness was equally undateable. The homelessness may have been a single isolated incident, involving no longer than one night in a hostel, or it may have been a chronic state lasting for ten years or more. All that can be said, in a most tentative way, is that a third of the difficulties can be dated as coming within the twelve months immediately prior to entry into temporary accommodation, and a further half, perhaps slightly over, to the four years immediately preceding that.

Another tentative suggestion is that whereas some characteristics have a fairly immediate, explosive impact on homelessness, others might be said to have a more insidious and gradual effect. Those with immediate impact include criminal conviction, marriage breakdown, other domestic quarrels, overcrowding, illegal tenancy, and physical violence. Those items with the slower impact included sexual irregularities, unemployment, poor domestic management, misuse of resources, rent/mortgage arrears, poverty, poor housing conditions, severe debts, large family size, and the loss of a parent.

The majority of families (62·6 per cent) were assessed as having one or two major causes of homelessness; 27·2 per cent had three or four major causes, 6·3 per cent had five or six major causes, 2·6 per cent had seven or eight major causes, and the remaining 1·3 per cent had more than eight major causes. The case histories in the earlier part of this chapter will have given the reader some idea of how various social problems are linked in individual families. What follows is an attempt to rationalize the interrelationship of these difficulties in a general way. Table XII is a two-dimensional chart of relationships between 18 variables. Sixteen of the eighteen items listed are taken direct from Tables V–XI, and take in all those providing 5 per cent or more of entries assessed as a major cause of homelessness. Two items are composites. Mental disorder includes subnormality, severe subnormality, psychopathic disorder, other mental disorder, and stress/suicidal. Physical handicap/illness includes physical handicap, disabling accident, and frequent physical illness. In both instances overlapping within the composite item has been eliminated.

The column headed 'No. of families' shows the number of families in which the particular characteristic was assessed as a major cause of homelessness. The main chart shows, for each relationship of two variables, the number of families in which they appeared together as major causes of homelessness. The column headed 'Overlap factor' is calculated by adding, separately for each item, the number of occasions on which it overlaps with the seventeen remaining items. Dividing the total by the number of families listed for the item provides the overlap factor. It shows a measure of the link, for each item, with other major causes amongst the 18 listed in the chart. A low factor indicates the likelihood of a cause occurring in some degree of isolation, while a high factor suggests a multi-causal situation.

The figures indicate that the items most likely to be sufficient in themselves as causes of homelessness were those connected with the breakdown of a family. Marriage break and family dispute have the same overlap factor (1·6), though the pattern of connections for the two items is rather different. Family disputes link up most commonly with sexual misbehaviour, poor housing conditions, and mental disorder. Marriage breakdown links most closely with domestic violence—sixty-two out of a total of seventy-five occurrences of domestic violence were within the context of a marriage breakdown. Other noticeable connections were with drunkenness and overcrowding. There were 100 families assessed as having a marriage breakdown or other form of domestic dispute as the sole cause of homelessness, and the proportion of single-parent families having no cause of homelessness beyond the problems of the single parent was slightly higher.

At the other end of the scale poor domestic management, misuse of resources, drunkenness, and poverty were likely to appear in a multi-causal situation, with three or more other factors. Circumstances specifically concerned with housing or housing management (rent and mortgage arrears, overcrowding and poor housing conditions) came in the middle of the scale, though there were

TABLE XII

TWO-DIMENSIONAL CHART OF RELATIONSHIPS BETWEEN 18 VARIABLES

	No. of families	Overlap factor	Physical handicap/illness	Workshy	Poor domestic management	Criminal conviction	Large family	Sexual misbehaviour	Misuse of resources	Drunkenness	Poor housing conditions	Mental disorder	Unemployment	Poverty	Family dispute (non-marital)	Domestic violence	Overcrowding	Rent/mortgage arrears	Single-parent family
Physical handicap/illness	28	2·9																	
Workshy	29	2·5	2																
Poor domestic management	29	3·8	2	3															
Criminal conviction	31	2·6	2	3	2														
Large family	32	2·3	4	5	3	3													
Sexual misbehaviour	33	2·6	1	2	2	1	6												
Misuse of resources	33	3·2	3	0	3	2	3	0											
Drunkenness	38	3·2	5	6	7	3	1	4	7										
Poor housing conditions	47	2·7	4	3	5	4	3	2	8	4									
Mental disorder	52	2·1	6	3	5	4	2	4	4	5	2								
Unemployment	64	2·3	11	12	6	5	7	2	1	7	9	6							
Poverty	61	3·1	10	9	10	5	14	7	10	6	19	8	22						
Family dispute (non-marital)	71	1·6	0	0	1	3	0	10	1	2	6	6	2	5					
Domestic violence	75	2·2	1	2	9	7	0	10	5	20	5	9	4	9	2				
Overcrowding	80	2·3	5	5	8	5	7	5	8	2	19	9	9	19	18	7			
Rent/mortgage arrears	89	2·5	15	8	15	11	4	4	21	10	10	9	25	20	5	5	18		
Single-parent family	106	1·2	2	0	4	13	8	4	4	4	6	6	4	8	25	8	9	15	
Marriage breakdown	202	1·6	7	10	10	9	5	17	11	29	19	20	17	25	25	62	30	24	3

forty-two families with exclusively housing causes for their loss of home.

Once all the material had been collected for each family, an attempt was made to determine what was the dominant family problem or problems. This included trying to assess the importance to the overall family situation of its experiences of homelessness. These assessments are inevitably subjective.

The experiences of homelessness were reckoned to be a major contributory factor to family problems in nearly a third (31·9 per cent) of all the families. For 19·3 per cent the homelessness difficulty was of a chronic nature, and for 12·6 per cent acute. For the remaining two-thirds of families their experience of homelessness and entry into the temporary accommodation hostel was thought to be of secondary or peripheral relevance to the total scale and extent of family problems.

The most frequently assessed dominant family problem was marital conflict, at 35 per cent of the total of all families. The absence of the father was rated as of crucial importance in 14·2 per cent of the families, and nearly a third (32·3 per cent) were reckoned to be suffering seriously from 'inadequate member of family'. This is a rather vague classification, and refers to a general malfunctioning in the way family members get on with each other and with the community at large.

Poverty was assessed as a dominant factor for 15 per cent of the families, illness for 10·6 per cent, and unemployment for 10·4 per cent. A new item which comes in here is the clients' satisfaction with their treatment. The information on this was based entirely on comments from the families themselves and so only applies to the 209 families who were interviewed; 64 families complained that they had been inadequately provided for in a material way—that is through help with rent arrears, clothing, etc. A further 94 were dissatisfied with the standard of service provided by the local authority, generally by the welfare officer or the child-care officer. In particular they were concerned with the lack of help families got with rehousing. More information on the quality and quantity of servicing will be given in Chapter 7, including some examples of the circumstances in which family members felt justified in making complaints, and the viewpoint of the social workers involved.

4

THE PROCESS OF BECOMING HOMELESS

Chapter 3 attempted to analyse the reasons and causes of homelessness, and Chapter 7 will look at the impact of the social services. This chapter focuses on the same basic situation, but from the viewpoint of the family itself. It is divided into three sections. The first looks at families' housing histories, aiming to put the experience of homelessness into chronological context, and to discover something of the stability or instability of each family's housing experiences. The second part takes a family-eye view of the events immediately preceding the latest entry to the temporary accommodation hostel, and what the family did to try to prevent or cope with the loss of its home. The third part tackles the question of motivation for becoming homeless, and looks at the relationship between a homeless family and the community in the period before homelessness.

Housing history
Each family's housing history was traced for a five-year period before the latest entry into the temporary accommodation hostel. Three specific measurements were made—the number of dwellings each family had occupied during those five years, the number of times the family or part of it had gone into temporary accommodation, and the number of times the family or part of it had stayed with friends or relatives. Table XIII shows these measurements expressed as percentages of the total sample.

Since the sample was taken from families who had been into temporary accommodation, by definition every family had made at least one entry.

If we look at this five-year period before the family entered the hostel, the significant feature was the family's reluctance to make use of temporary accommodation. What shows up is that, when a family was faced with homelessness, it would make arrangements to

TABLE XIII

HOUSING IN 5 YEARS PRIOR TO THE LATEST ENTRY TO TEMPORARY ACCOMMODATION

No.	Entries to T.A. (inc. latest)	Single occupant	DWELLINGS No.	Shared
	%	%		%
1	77·8	28·0	None	37·0
2	13·3	21·0	1–2	43·1
3	5·6	12·0	3–4	12·8
4	1·6	15·4	5–6	3·5
5	0·9	8·4	7–8	1·5
Over 5	0·9	15·2	Over 9	2·0

share with relatives and friends, or find some other dwelling. Many families would only seek help from welfare services when they had spent several years going through the range of possible alternatives which they could organize themselves. Perhaps it is relevant to point out here that the level of entry into the hostel was not determined by the availability of space. The hostels were rarely full, and there was only a little evidence that the occasional genuine applicant was turned away. Generally speaking, the local authorities exercised a deterrent approach to the use of temporary accommodation, in the sense that a family which was effectively without a roof over its head would be helped, but the family reporting the threat of homelessness would be sent away to try for itself to work out some alternative arrangements. This, and the reputation gained by some of the hostels, had an influence on many of the families.

Sharing a dwelling was virtually always a response to homelessness, whereas moving from one dwelling to another for a family's sole occupation may have been a perfectly normal removal. While no attempt was made in the survey to assess the extent of routine removals, the overall impression given in the housing histories was that these formed a relatively small part of the total removals. Excepting therefore that there may be a slight over-statement of the position, if we look at the average family's housing pattern in the five years immediately prior to its only or latest hostel entry, the ratio between hostel entries, entries to shared dwellings, and removals to separate dwellings was 1:2·7:5·0. The suggestion is, then, that the average family would share a home on three occasions, and move to a separate home on up to five occasions, for every one entry into the hostel provided by the local authority.

While this gives some idea of the housing pattern of families in the five years before they enter the hostel, if an attempt is to be made to assess the total number of homeless families, the latest entry into temporary accommodation must be taken into the calculations. The picture which then emerged was that, for every one family moving into a temporary accommodation hostel, there would be two moving in to share with friends or relatives, and three searching successfully for some alternative accommodation of their own. Put in other words, of every six homeless families, only one would overcome its immediate difficulties by entering temporary accommodation. Statistically, therefore, the figures for families in temporary accommodation on a particular date are likely to represent no more than one-sixth of all homeless families.

These averages represent a fairly narrow spread. There was a small number of families with a very stable housing record. For most of them homelessness resulted from a solitary, usually temporary, domestic upheaval. At the other extreme there was an equally small number of nomadic families and individuals who had moved around more or less continuously over the five years. What emerged from the central body of families was a positive correlation between using the hostel more than once and sharing, but a negative correlation between frequent removals to separate dwellings and the other two variables. That is, the variables do not so much complement each other as appear as alternatives. One group of families avoided sharing altogether, whether in a house or the hostel, and these were predominantly the complete families, in the sense of both parents being present. The other group tried to minimize the number of permanent removals by making temporary use of sharing, and these were predominantly the families or parts of families made homeless through a marital breakdown, or other domestic dispute—families that have not necessarily lost their home. Perhaps a few examples will make the position clearer.

The word 'dwelling' has been used in this chapter to cover a wide range of housing, from a modern centrally heated house at one extreme to something as grim as a derelict railway carriage with broken windows and holes in the roof at the other. The prospect of stability in housing depended very much on what type of housing it was. There could be no stability in derelict accommodation without any of the basic sanitary services. Even if the family could stick it for a long time, there were a number of agencies, including the local authority Health Department and the N.S.P.C.C., who were particularly active in removing families from such premises without having any duty to find a better place for them to live. Caravans were generally looked upon as offering only a brief shelter. Mrs Nicholson, for example, lost her house when her husband deserted, and she and her three children moved firstly to temporary accommodation, and were then rehoused in a caravan. In view of this rehousing the welfare officer's report anticipated (correctly) the family's return to the hostel.

The chances of stability were scarcely much greater in good-quality high-rental housing. Though the rents in South Wales and the West might be considerably lower in the private sector than in London and other big cities, there was still a good deal of housing which, for a large family, was very expensive. Despite rent subsidies,[1] there were examples of large families being placed in such dwellings, without the prospect of being able to keep up with the rents. The immediate reason for Mrs Davies's eviction from her home was rent arrears, although this was very much tied up with the breakdown of her marriage. On her own admission Mrs Davies was not efficient in handling money, and this was reflected in the case history, which asked the question whether she would ever be able to avoid debts and rent arrears without a great deal of support. Nevertheless, after a long stay in temporary accommodation, and under pressure from a welfare officer to move on, she and her children were rehoused at a rental which was nearly 30s more than her earlier rent. Not surprisingly she was immediately in rent-arrears trouble again, found this was a considerable emotional strain, and moved out of her own accord into a caravan.

Stability, then, was generally confined to those living in low-rental, often sub-standard properties. This did not mean that the threat of homelessness was absent—one family was evicted on its 31st notice to quit. It meant, rather, that the demand for sub-standard property was lower, and both public and private landlords were prepared to tolerate lower standards of tenancy behaviour and longer-drawn-out arrears. But there were examples where the family home was never threatened. Mrs Price would not have had to come into temporary accommodation had her neighbours not

[1] These subsidies consisted of rent rebates and subsidies operating in some local authority Housing Departments and contributions towards the rent from the Supplementary Benefits Commission.

been afraid of her husband's violence, too afraid to offer her overnight accommodation when her husband threw her out. Mr Price was, however, extremely upset and apologetic the following day, and his devoted wife, as always, went back to him. There was no threat to their home, and in a long-term sense there was no threat to the stability of their marriage.

There were a few nomadic families and individuals who never had a home, but the majority of wanderers had stable housing periods before and after a phase of mobility. Mr Watkins's first marriage ended in divorce, and the social worker involved at that stage commented that he had 'an inability to relate'. He married again ten years ago, a much younger woman, and has had two children by her. His health was not standing up very well, and when the building in which the family had rented rooms was sold for property development, and the family given notice to quit, the impact was serious. Despite a long stay for the whole family in temporary accommodation, Mr Watkins was too upset to set about finding a new home, and the family spent the next ten months wandering through the South of England and South Wales, staying with relatives, sleeping rough, and stopping in the temporary accommodation hostels of four different local authorities. It came to an end when both children fell ill, and Mr Watkins was sufficiently shaken out of his depression to find a flat for the family.

The Binns family stayed in the same area but in many other respects had a similar sort of housing record. They began their married life living with Mrs Binns's parents, but following the birth of children there was conflict and this arrangement broke up. The family then moved to a caravan, but a complaint was made to the N.S.P.C.C. on the grounds that three children rendered it overcrowded. The N.S.P.C.C. called in the medical officer of health, who felt that the family should leave. At this stage the family went into temporary accommodation, but left it to 'squat' in a near-derelict vacant warehouse. Mr Binns then found what was described as a 'Shelter hidden-homeless type of house', and the family has lived in it for the last four years, while waiting for local authority housing. The house was damp, falling down, overcrowded and without a lavatory. In contrast Mr Fox was prepared to move with his family, but not to endure the indignity of pleading with relatives to share their housing, or to go into a hostel. Mr Fox was discharged from the Army with no trade to follow, and took to agricultural work as a task which he felt required no specific skills. His own views, however, were not shared by the succession of farmers for whom he worked, who found him uniformly unsuitable for the work, and therefore deprived him of the tied cottage which went with the job. He went with his wife and six children to temporary accommodation, because, much to his surprise, he was offered not a hostel but a four-bedroomed house. From temporary accommodation the family was housed by the local council, but both in the Welfare Department and the Housing Department property Mr Fox has found it difficult to pay the rents. These were, of course, much higher than for any of the earlier tied cottages.

Losing the family home
Although the family may spend many years under a close and direct threat of homelessness, the actual incident of losing a home could be more narrowly identified in time. At one end of the scale were the emergencies envisaged in the National Assistance Act of 1948, when the trouble was a landslide, flood, fire or some other kind of immediate natural disaster, and the family had little opportunity to acclimatize itself to the fact of being homeless. But they could at least expect immediate support from the police, fire service, and any appropriate local authority social service. Glamorgan County Council Welfare Department, for example, always has at hand 'A Scheme for the Provision of Temporary Accommodation for Persons rendered Homeless by reason of Fire, Flooding or other Emergency'. This document lists a mass of relevant telephone numbers, forty-one premises in the county (mostly Church or Chapel halls) which are already designated as emergency reception areas, and general guide-lines as to how emergencies should be approached.

There is no such procedure to help with the much more likely cause of emergency homelessness—marriage breakdown. Mrs Phillips's experience is perhaps typical. She was quite shattered one night when her husband returned from an evening at the local club to announce that he had invited a woman to share the house. Mrs Phillips had suspected for some time that her husband might have been having an affair, and this confirmed her suspicions. Furthermore, her husband went on, the other woman was waiting outside in his car, and he intended to bring her into the house in a very few minutes. Mrs Phillips was thrown into complete panic, took her two young children from their cot, bundled them into the pram and rushed off, despite the late hour, to her neighbour's. There she found a roof for the night, and in the morning went off with her troubles to the local police sergeant, who in turn brought in the welfare officer. In a physical sense this was every bit as much of an emergency as a fire or flood. Emotionally, for Mrs Phillips, the situation was more desperate than a fire. She had not only lost her home, but found the whole fabric of her life collapsing around her. She had never been through such an experience before, and had none of the resilience of, for example, Hannah (see Chapter 3), for whom such things were a regular and recurring part of her family life, without any permanent threat to family unity; 223 families (40·7 per cent) became homeless in this sort of emergency, and a large majority of them were marriage breaks of one sort or another.

At the other end of the scale were families who received a good deal of warning that they might lose their homes. A family being evicted for rent arrears from a council property could expect up to six months to do whatever was possible to avoid eviction, or to prepare for the removal, and families in private accommodation could expect some warning as well, albeit very much less; 111 (20·3 per cent) were the subject of an early warning to the Welfare Department (and also to the Children's Department and the Supplementary Benefits Commission). This in no sense indicates the level of activity of early-warning systems, because it fails to account for incidents where an early warning prevented the need for the family to go into the temporary accommodation hostel. It does, however, point to a substantial block of families (39 per cent) whose homelessness was neither an emergency measure nor the subject of early warnings. These were predominantly families coming from the private sector of housing, and the weakness of preventive measures in this sector is again taken up in Chapter 7.

When a family was given some time to prepare for the loss of its home, it could and often did make early contact with the local authority. Generally speaking, it was to the housing manager that the family first went, hoping for rehousing or, at the very least, for some advancement on the waiting-list. It was rare to find the housing manager taking any action on the immediate issue of homelessness, without first consulting with the Welfare Department or Children's Department. Indeed, housing departments rarely did more than put the family through a few formalities, such as adding its name to the waiting-list, without firm prodding from one of the social service agencies. Whether a family got any immediate help from a social worker or welfare officer depended very much on the circumstances.

All the local authorities in the survey area accepted the responsibility of trying to prevent eviction from council property. But if the family reported that they were to become homeless from private property, then they were likely to be told to go away and do whatever they could on their own accord, and return only when they had an immediate need for hostel accommodation. Again it must be stressed that this assertion is based on information about families who subsequently became homeless, rather than families who were successfully helped to save their homes. Family attitudes to the social services were inevitably coloured by the success of the attention they received. Mrs Lord, for example, commented, 'I didn't get as much help as some people, like when my husband was ill and had to stay off work. They didn't help me look after the children. The Children's Department don't help. We have not been given clothes like some people. The welfare man told me to go along to the Rent Tribunal, and that did get my rent down.' Mr Cox commented, 'The welfare officer was all right. He helped me to find a council house. Before we lost our home he brought some furniture and some toys and clothes for the children. But if the landlord won't play what can he do? We just got kicked out.'

In the event families did try very hard to combat the threat of homelessness. A minority (42·8 per cent) became immediately dependent on the local authority, and went directly to the temporary accommodation hostel without having any alternative. Many of these were the sort of emergencies where the family simply had no time to do anything else. The remaining 57·2 per cent only came to the hostel after making one or more successful efforts themselves to find a temporary lodging.[1] The Brown family was a straightforward example. Mr and Mrs Brown had six children when Mr Brown was discharged from the Army. Some time before that he had contacted his local council, but, for reasons which were never unravelled, he was not put on the housing list and there was no house for the family when he left Army quarters. Mr Brown did not use the temporary accommodation hostel straight away because he did not like the local authority social services. A child care officer's report described him as 'aggressively critical and tends to ignore any

---

[1] This should not be seen to conflict with the ratio of homeless families entering temporary accommodation to those finding alternative shelter (p. 84). Although the families in the survey had all used temporary accommodation at some stage, the figures on p. 84 cover many experiences of homelessness over a five-year period, which were overcome without using the local authority hostel. The figures on this page concern only the occasion when the family did use temporary accommodation.

approach'. Mr Brown took his entire family to stay with his parents, but the over-crowding was acute and after two weeks he had to call in the welfare officer and agreed to his wife and children moving into a hostel.

Reluctance to use hostel accommodation, rather than ignorance of the hostel's existence, was generally the reason for finding alternatives. Ivy Wilson, for example, had been in the hostel before. She had found the discipline there not at all to her liking, and particularly resented what she felt was the over-familiarity of the warden in examining her every morning to see if she was properly washed. The warden had changed, but Ivy was not to be convinced that the regime had undergone similar reformation. Ivy was described as 'not very bright', and after her last spell in the hostel had taken her three children to live with her mother. She was separated from her husband. She became homeless again when her mother, the tenant of their privately rented house, became so incontinent that she had to move into an old people's home. First of all Ivy was referred to a caravan site by a local voluntary organization. This ended at the beginning of the holiday season when she either had to get out or pay a very much higher rent. She stayed with friends for a couple of weeks, until her provocative flirtatiousness with the friend's husband got her thrown out. From there she went to an empty and largely derelict farmhouse. She was allowed to stay there for several months, because no one from the local authority much liked the idea of tramping up the two miles of muddy track to find out what circumstances she and her children were living in. But eventually a public health inspector did call, immediately condemned the premises, and Ivy finally agreed to another stay in the hostel.

Attitudes and motives
The analysis of circumstances leading families into a temporary accommodation hostel suggested that 223 of them were emergencies. A few more families, making 236 altogether, felt themselves that circumstances were such that their entry into the hostel was an emergency measure. Another 98 families, in their application for hostel accommodation, argued, and their arguments were accepted by Welfare Department, that although their homelessness was not an emergency, nevertheless they had no choice in the matter. Another 186 families broke up, either because the marriage was in trouble or for some other domestic reason, and homelessness repre-

sented a need for a second dwelling for what was previously one family unit. This left a few families who could have had some ulterior motive for wishing to use the hostel. The objective in making this point is to dispel any idea that families have used temporary accommodation with the specific idea of pressurizing the local authority Housing Department into providing a house. Only 12 families were aware of the possibilities of queue-jumping in this way.

The local authority Welfare and Children's Services were a little more conscious of the rehousing possibilities that accrue from a careful use of temporary accommodation. It was an admitted intention of the social service agency for 27 families. It was a hope in the case of Mr Brown, whose difficulties were mentioned earlier in this chapter. Since there had been some oversight in the failure to put him on his local authority housing list, when his family had gone into temporary accommodation, the welfare officer felt fully justified in putting a great deal of pressure on the housing manager. The family were rehoused by the local authority, although Mr Brown was very much dissatisfied with the standard of the house he received. Mrs Harris was treated in a similar way. She had spent several years with her children in a remote farm cottage with structurally unsafe bedrooms, and with access only across fields. She was persuaded to move out and take a place in a hostel on the promise of rehousing in a local authority house. The Children's Department had made this promise without previously contacting the Housing Department, but fortunately the housing manager was prepared to co-operate.

For 408 entrants, the local authority Welfare Department felt that they were coping with an emergency, and had no option open to them. For a further 71 there was felt to be no choice between taking the family in or turning it away, and eventually the families were accepted, but purely as a means of providing them with a temporary roof over their heads. In addition to the 27 families helped for reasons of rehousing, there were 45 who went into the hostel as part of a longer-term process of treatment. These were predominantly part of an attempt at marital conciliation. Only one of the local authorities studied maintained a residential unit which was equipped for rehabilitative work. In this instance entire families were taken in, and stayed for as long as the children's officer considered appropriate. In another authority, the hostel regulations excluded men, and the Children's Department made use of this regulation to work with the wife in the guaranteed absence of her husband.

The fact that the local authority's involvement in the care of homeless families was relatively limited must be taken in part as a comment on the importance of help from each family's local community. There were very few case histories which did not mention at some point help offered by relatives, friends and neighbours. The homeless families themselves, however, showed a rather ambiguous attitude towards such help. While generally being prepared to accept it, they did so with, seemingly, some reluctance, and many families were not prepared to acknowledge it. Focusing on the 209 families that were interviewed, only 50 (23·9 per cent) claimed to have been helped in preventing the loss of their home by a relative or a friend. In contrast 122 (58·4 per cent) acknowledged help from the local authority, and 11 (5·3 per cent) from a voluntary organization. Fifty-one families (24·4 per cent) claimed not to have been offered any help at all, and a further 69 (33·0 per cent) felt that the help they were offered was of no use to them.

Besides being asked about the sources of help in facing the family problems, including the threat of homelessness, families were questioned about the type of help that might be available to them. Table XIV lists as numbers and percentages the responses to these questions.

TABLE XIV

HELP AVAILABLE FROM NEIGHBOURS, FRIENDS AND REL-
ATIVES IN TACKLING GENERAL DIFFICULTIES CONNECTED
WITH HOMELESSNESS (SAMPLE—209 INTERVIEWED
FAMILIES)

	No.	%
Nothing	74	35·4
Tiding over with food /money	64	30·6
Help with shopping	89	42·6
Help with cooking	62	29·7
Help with washing/ironing	53	25·4
Caring for children	107	51·2
Cleaning/decorating	40	19·1
Advice	35	16·7

The Table shows that there was a substantial block of families claiming no help of any sort (74). As this figure suggests, there was not an even spread of different forms of assistance. Rather, the picture tended to be that a family would have a lot of help in a variety of ways, or would receive very little help at all.

The ambiguity of families' attitudes was mentioned earlier on, and this is illustrated by comparison of family case histories with their own comments on community support. Several times Mr Leach's family moved in with relatives, and when they were living on their own the family was able to obtain help of every form listed in Table XIV above, except for cooking. Nevertheless, Mr Leach said, 'I would kill myself before they'd go through that again. People wouldn't leave us alone.' Mrs Platt, who had willingly sent her children to a neighbour for daily care, later said, 'This is not a nice place for the children to grow up in—I don't let them out of the front.'

Family attitudes were not always, however, unjustifiably critical, and commonly complaints were backed up by a social worker. Speaking of the Fox family, for example, one worker said: 'The family is not liked by the long-standing residents in the Close. They don't like all the young children around, because their own children have grown up and left home. They complain about the noise the children make.' In a domestic or marital dispute the neighbourhood attitude would often involve taking sides, supporting one part of the family against the other. Mrs Lee said, 'The neighbours thought my husband's behaviour shocking. They all wanted to help me.'

Each of the families was asked also about their general feeling towards the attitudes of the neighbourhood. Forty-seven (22·5 per cent) in a sense avoided the question by responding that they themselves preferred isolation from their neighbourhood, and therefore had no feelings one way or another about community attitudes. For example, one of the middle-class wives said, 'I inflict isolation on myself. All the neighbours are business people like my husband, but I think they look down on us a bit. I don't go in much for coffee mornings and bridge parties.' For the remainder the answers were fairly evenly distributed. Seventy-six (36·4 per cent) felt the basic attitude of the community to be supportive, while 55 (26·1 per cent) thought the community to be unsupportive. Sixty-seven families (32·1 per cent) said that they were made to feel welcome within their community, whereas a rather larger number, 80 (38·3 per cent), felt ignored or disapproved of by their neighbours. There were a few more specific complaints, such as that neighbours disapproved of families living on social security, of fatherless families, and of families with a large number of children. There were 12 families who felt that the neighbours never took the trouble to find out what their problems were. Over all however, the part played by the neighbourhood in a family's homelessness experience was likely to be substantial. Despite a family's tendency to feel some resentment about a neighbourhood which it has now left or from which it has been evicted, it has nevertheless almost certainly had a good deal of help from neighbours, and possibly stayed for short periods in neighbours' houses.

5

REHOUSING

Rehousing from temporary accommodation presented a major difficulty both for the families themselves and for local authority officials, except for most of the 19 per cent of families who returned to the same house from which they initially became homeless. This chapter has two sections. The first takes a broadly based look at the policies and practices of housing departments in the Administrative County of Glamorgan, seeing how they relate to the risks of losing a home as well as the chances of being rehoused. This needs to be placed in an appropriate context. The evidence of the survey suggests a growing reluctance on the part of local authorities to evict families, but this was matched by an equally strong antipathy to rehousing families who have unsatisfactory past records, whether rent arrears have been paid off or not. Only a minority of the homeless families in the survey came within the orbit of local authority housing. Twenty-eight per cent had occupied a council house in the twelve months before entering temporary accommodation, and 42 per cent were rehoused by the local authority.

The second section looks more specifically at the rehousing difficulties and experiences of the families in the survey. It looks at the immediate process of becoming rehoused, as well as the longer-term housing developments since the family left temporary accommodation.

Housing attitudes and policies
The Administrative County of Glamorgan is divided into 23 housing authorities. The population of the area in the Registrar General's estimate on June 30, 1967 was 737,620. During the average year from 40 to 50 families were admitted to the temporary accommodation hostel at Rhoose and a further 10–15 families to the temporary accommodation in Llonwono, Mountain Ash. A further small number of families were admitted to the intermediate

G

accommodation run by Port Talbot and the Rhondda, and also to the two houses owned by the County Children's Department.

During the period from 1962 tp 1968 the population of the Administrative County of Glamorgan declined by 10,250 (mostly because of the transfer of some 28,169 people to Cardiff C.B.). The number of council houses has increased by 10,990; or, to put it another way, there are now 16 more council houses per 1,000 of the population. Table XV gives details.

TABLE XV

	Population		No. of houses	No. per 1,000
30.6.61	747,870	31.3.62	48,403	65
30.6.62	748,700	31.3.63	49,525	66
30.6.63	752,250	31.3.64	51,390	68
30.6.64	755,480	31.3.65	53,409	71
30.6.65	761,260	31.3.66	55,599	73
30.6.66	764,000	31.3.67	58,241	76
30.6.67	737,620*	31.3.68	59,393	81

*Following a reduction of 28,160 transferred from Cardiff R.D.C. to C.B.

The number of people in local authority housing varied tremendously from one area to the next depending on the demands of the area, its political make up, the physical geography and the social patterns within each area. In 1962 the figure varied from 26 per 1,000 persons in the Rhondda to 130 in Port Talbot, and in 1968 they varied from 30 per 1,000 in Gower to 142 per 1,000 in Port Talbot. At the same time the total number of properties in the area was also increasing, so that local authority provision was not made at the expense of the total provision of accommodation. On April 1, 1962, 215,709 domestic properties were assessed for rating purposes, and this number had increased to 231,459 by the April 1, 1968.

As one would expect with so many housing authorities, there was no general pattern to housing or rehousing in Glamorgan. There were 23 authorities, 23 different methods of rehousing people and wide variations in the time spent on the waiting-list. There was no relationship between the number of council houses per 1,000 of population and speed of housing. The main differences occurred between the housing position in the urban and rural parts of Glamorgan, between the valley and the vale.

The valleys, particularly in east and central Glamorgan, are dominated by older terraced properties, often built by the mine-owners, without the basic amenities considered necessary for modern living, i.e. hot water, a fixed bath and an inside lavatory. According to the 1966 sample census only 34·2 per cent of the houses in the Rhondda had these basic amenities; in Aberdare the figure was 46·7 per cent; in Mountain Ash 38·3 per cent; in Gelligaer 50·8 per cent; and in Pontypridd 54 per cent. In the Western Glamorgan Valleys, Maesteg had 50·2 per cent of its houses with basic amenities and Ogmore and Garw 41·5 per cent. If one compares these figures with those of some of the vale areas, which have never been 'industrial', one can appreciate the difficulties many valley author-ities have to cope with. In Penarth 70 per cent of the properties have basic amenities, in Penybont 82·7 per cent and in Llwchr 60·5 per cent. The only heavily industrialized area of Glamorgan with a high percentage of houses with basic amenities is Port Talbot (75·4 per cent), but the industry there is of a much more recent origin. The figure for the whole of the Administrative County of Glamorgan is 61·5 per cent; thus, in 1966, 38·5 per cent of dwellings in the county lacked exclusive use of basic amenities.

Some of the problems these outworn houses pose were illustrated by the Treasurer of Glyncorrwg, which is situated in a West Glam-organ valley to the north of Port Talbot. The population, estimated in 1967 at 9,940, relied on the three coal mines in the area for employ-ment, but two of these have now been closed, and the only alternative employment to be attracted to the area employed mainly women. Much of the property consisted of old terraced houses which London property companies had bought up for their rental value. These companies had not made any improvements to the houses, and the property has since changed hands so frequently that the local authority has been unable to collect rates. Eventually some of the houses became very poor, and the local authority was unable to trace the owners. They were slowly being demolished by the local authority who were accepting £1 each week from the tenants in lieu of accumulated rates. The area is very depressed, and houses which did come on the market sold for £200 or less if they were in poor condition. This was in many ways typical of pockets in other areas of the valleys. There was accommodation to spare, which was cheap to buy, but it was in depressed, unattractive areas, some distance from employment. This was to some extent because of the closure of the mines, a problem of which the National Coal

Board were very conscious. They are the largest private landlords in South Wales and are torn between the facts that people expect them to make money and that they are also expected to be good landlords. Only 40 per cent of their tenancies were occupied by 'active miners' (this includes widows and sick miners), so that the National Coal Board was naturally loath to spend money on old property in which none of its employees lived. They would like to dispose of the property but find people reluctant to buy it.

The reverse of this situation occurred in many of the coastal and vale areas. These are attractive areas and often draw commuters to the large industrial centres in Cardiff, Port Talbot and Swansea. There is little old 'industrial' property; most of the old property falls into the 'cottage' class, and is deemed highly desirable. Housing was expensive to buy or rent. This was partly because these are seaside areas and partly because the R.A.F. at St Athan were willing to pay high rents to obtain accommodation for servicemen. From what the housing managers said it would be virtually impossible for a poor family with children to find private accommodation in areas such as Porthcawl, Bridgend, Cowbridge U.D.C., Cardiff R.D.C., Penarth and Barry, unless they were willing to accept a caravan or a very sub-standard flat. There were big variations in the number of council dwellings per 1,000 population in these areas, but most of them still used either a residential qualification, a compulsory period on the waiting-list, or found that it took some time to rehouse people.

Some people lived in caravans and were the subject of the most varied rules and regulations, dependent on the area they lived in. Most of them either lived in a caravan when first married, as they had nowhere else to go, or they drifted there later in the marriage as a desperate measure when all else had failed. Many caravan-dwellers in the valleys appeared to be women with young children, separated from their husbands, and unable to find alternative accommodation. If they moved into a caravan in Porthcawl they would not be rehoused at all; in Cardiff R.D.C. they must wait five years; in Penybont twelve months; in Aberdare 'until they have shown they want to settle in Aberdare'; in Llantrisant fairly quickly; and in Gelligaer no one was to be rehoused until the site was closed. There were other areas with variable policies towards caravan-dwellers. Scarcely anyone had a good word for them. They were a 'nuisance', a 'problem', a 'headache' to housing managers.

As the provision of accommodation for homeless people was the function of the Welfare Department, and the Children's Department were also very much involved in the prevention of homelessness, there was constant reference to 'the county' and use of the phrase 'that's a county responsibility'. Once a family went into the temporary accommodation at Rhoose it became a 'county responsibility' and the district authority could forget it. Disputes between 'the county' and district councils were common.

All twenty-three authorities in Glamorgan notified the Children's and Welfare Departments in advance of taking out a possession order against a family. The value of this varied tremendously, as some local authorities issued as few as ten notices to quit per month, whereas others issued fifty or more in some months, and it was obviously impossible to follow up every one. All the authorities claimed that co-operation between themselves and county departments was good, but they seemed to have different views of its usefulness. Some housing managers felt that the Children's Department helped persistent 'deadlegs' and people who were constantly in arrears and not worth helping. Again, the co-operation reached different points; some authorities, Rhondda and Maesteg for example, would accept rent arrears up to the day the possession order expired; others, particularly Penybont and Llantrisant, were very loath to accept any money once a possession order had been granted.

All authorities were obviously concerned that they should not have large amounts of arrears and a large number of unsatisfactory tenants. This often brought clashes with their social policy (if they had one) of rehousing known problem families who would probably not pay their rent regularly. The Children's and Welfare Departments felt that some authorities paid no more than lip-service to rehousing problems. One family had been refused rehousing when their house burnt down because the mother was felt to be immoral. In another case a young family was living with maternal grandparents in desperately overcrowded conditions. Both the maternal grandparents and the families were known as problems, and the husband was constantly in and out of prison. The mother eventually became so depressed by her surroundings that she was admitted to hospital and the children came into care. They were eventually reunited in the temporary accommodation. This was at a time when, according to the housing manager, subject to a one-year qualification, any family in real need would be rehoused.

The haunting spectre of unsatisfactory tenants and mounting arrears must have dominated the dreams of many housing managers. Llantrisant and Llantwit Fadre have used an 'Organization and Methods' team to discover the most economical way of collecting arrears, and to advise on the maximum number of notices to quit or possession orders to issue. At January 31, 1968 the arrears for each authority varied from £49 for Llwchr U.D.C. to £11,652 for Caerphilly U.D.C. Llwchr had 2,042 houses and Caerphilly 3,771. Both these authorities were very reluctant to evict tenants and took a good deal of care to prevent arrears piling up. In Llwchr people were invited to appear before the Housing Committee once they were four weeks overdue with their rent, and they were served with a notice to quit at this point. This policy was said to work in most cases, although people occasionally have to be brought back two or three times, but no one had been evicted for arrears for the past two years.

Caerphilly U.D.C. first sent a letter to people who were in arrears and asked their rent collector to call. If this failed it was followed by a further letter, a notice to quit and a possession order. The housing manager stated that the authority were loath to evict anyone—'to evict is an admission of our failure as an authority'.

At least part of Caerphilly U.D.C.'s problems with arrears would seem to have been caused by their estate at Nansbury Park, where the inclusive rents went up to £5 and over. The estate is new and the houses all conform to Parker Morris standards. The problem which was occurring with these houses in Caerphilly was mirrored in new estates in other parts of the county, particularly in Pontypridd. These houses cost about £5 each per week, plus approximately 30s for the central heating. The problems which this produced were fairly obvious in an area where wage levels were low. The average person with a regular wage of £20+ tended to buy his own property, and Lansbury Park seemed to attract people with unstable work records, or in jobs where wages fluctuated widely. Many of the inhabitants of Caerphilly seemed convinced that 'people who live in Lansbury Park are all on social security because they pay the rent and it's the only way you can afford to live there'. This tempting hypothesis was manifestly untrue. The housing manager tried to ensure that anyone who had a house on Lansbury Park had a sufficiently large income, and the Supplementary Benefits Commission did not pay the full rent to those in receipt of benefit. Whatever the intricacies of this particular situation, the fact remained that it was often very difficult to meet the rents of these houses and that a few weeks arrears could soon amount to a daunting sum.

The actual allocation of houses was subject to tremendous variation. Some authorities used points lists, others allocated on 'general needs', others on the length of time families had been on the waiting-list, and yet others on the advice of local councillors working on a ward basis. Some, but not all, insisted on basic residential qualifications or a minimum number of years on the waiting-list. A family living in Penybont could be rehoused fairly speedily, but for one living just over the border in Port Talbot there were certain residential qualifications; whereas if one lived in Porthcawl the hope of being rehoused at all seemed remote. But of course the urgency of people's needs did not vary much because they lived ten yards on one or other side of a boundary line. All authorities said that they would give special consideration to someone in 'genuine need', but it was difficult to know exactly what was meant by this. There seemed to be a basic, though unacknowledged, division between the 'deserving' and the 'undeserving', motivated by the reluctance to take on potentially bad tenants. On the other hand there was one medical officer of health who had overall control of housing, and a policy to provide local authority housing for anyone who might need it and to provide it when they first marry, 'to give them a good start'. Although his authority have not reached this stage yet they did know what they are working towards.

Aberdare joined with Mountain Ash and Pontypridd in their own scheme to prevent families being broken up by admission to the temporary accommodation hostel. They therefore set up their own unit to deal with homeless families in the old isolation hospital at Mountain Ash, which was turned into two houses, and the matron's house into two others. Each house was rather large and unfurnished but had coal fires and hot water. Families were admitted for a maximum period of six months, and might be rehoused at the end of this if they did not accumulate any arrears and were otherwise satisfactory tenants. Not every one was rehoused if they had a previous history of local authority arrears, but the authorities involved felt that the families had time to sort themselves out. The only other authorities to provide intermediate accommodation were Port Talbot with three houses and the Rhondda, which has six. These houses were supposed to be occupied for a period of six months, but people frequently stayed for much longer if they were deemed unsuitable for rehousing in modern houses.

It would seem that, in general, accommodation was fairly easy to obtain in Glamorgan. A modern semi-detached house would cost between £3,000 and £7,000 depending on the area, and, in the valleys, there was a great deal of older property available at a fairly reasonable price, but in poor condition and too far from places of employment. Local authority housing, with one or two exceptions, was usually available in a maximum of three years and often much more quickly in cases of genuine need. However, families still slipped through the net and progressed to temporary accommodation or intermediate accommodation, even in areas like Caerphilly, which could rehouse very quickly. Obviously the simple provision of houses is not the answer to this problem. The attitudes of housing managers are of crucial importance, as is the need for social work agencies to work much more closely with housing authorities to help tenants in difficulties.

Rehousing history
Since the survey was concerned with families entering a temporary accommodation unit at any time between the beginning of 1963 and mid-1969, it was possible to trace, for many of them, their subsequent housing records. Much the same sort of questions were asked, and information sought, as was given in Chapter 4 about the process of becoming homeless. Information in this section relates to the 209 families who were interviewed.

Forty families left the hostel for the same house from which they had arrived. Mostly, as has already been suggested, these were cases involved in domestic crises of different sorts, and the loss of the house was never threatened. There were, however, a few more serious upheavals which did put the tenancy of the house at risk. These were likely to occur when the official tenant left the household, and the landlord was approached for a transfer in tenancy. Such transfers were never merely a formality, mainly because they involved a change of tenancy from a man to a woman, and hence from a potentially better wage-earner and rent-payer to a potentially worse one. Landlords used the opportunity to tie up any loose ends that there might be. Mrs Hive presented a typical example. She lost her husband (the tenant of her council house), when he was sentenced to prison for housebreaking. Mrs Hive came into temporary accommodation more for a rest than anything else, while the county Children's Department pressed the local housing manager to transfer the tenancy into her name. This he did, but only after unnecessary delay, and after extracting £24 rent arrears from the Children's Department. Just occasionally the landlord used the opportunity to end the tenancy altogether. Mrs Law was refused the tenancy of her house, and was evicted with her children, after her husband had deserted, on the basis of an assessment by the housing manager (no doubt perfectly correct) that she would be unable to keep up with the rent. Her husband's activities resulted in a second tenancy becoming vacant. Having deserted his wife in preference for another woman, a tenant of the same housing authority, he became the cause of her eviction, because of the immorality of her conduct in taking him in.

Thirty-seven families (17·7 per cent) left temporary accommodation for intermediate, half-way, or some other sort of housing specifically set aside for homeless people. What such a designation might mean was very dependent on the local authority area in which context it was set. For the entire Hancock family it involved two days in an emergency hostel, followed by removal to a rehabilitation unit. Successfully meeting a number of tenancy standards in this unit was, for the Hancocks, the precursor to the promise of a house and a job elsewhere in the county. With such a carrot being dangled and a good deal of social work support, the family made rapid strides towards the kind of standards which any local authority housing manager expects of his tenants, and was eventually re-housed and re-employed. For another family, the Baileys, inter-mediate housing was a nearly new three-bedroomed bungalow, under the management of the Welfare Department. This again, in a sense, was a prize for good behaviour in the hostel. There were regular visits from the welfare officer, rather than a specific re-habilitative programme, but again a successful stay was some assur-ance of obtaining a house from a local authority housing manager. Much more common, however, was the position typified by Mrs Garnett and her children. She had been widowed for several years and although there were a number of factors in the family finding itself homeless, the whole situation was underpinned by chronic poverty. Even had the offer been made, she would have felt unable to accept the tenancy of a good standard house and the high rent it would have involved. Instead she jumped at the opportunity of an intermediate house, which for her meant the most sub-standard of properties held by the local authority. There was no social work linked with the tenancy, but no time limit either. Twice the family has been overtaken by the needs of redevelopment, and twice it has been removed to the remaining most sub-standard housing.

In view of the extent of social problems that many homeless families experienced, the question of servicing becomes very important. This will be taken up at more length in Chapter 7, but a few basic facts are appropriate at this point. 101 families (48·3 per cent) received some follow-up after rehousing from a social worker or welfare officer, and for 19 of them there was, in addition, a continuance of a rent guarantee. What is significant is the very high correlation between social work follow-up and rehousing in council property, or, to reverse the picture, between the absence of follow-up and rehousing in private property. A pilot study of the general public's use of the personal social services, undertaken in part of the survey area, suggested that a council house tenant would receive approximately four times as much attention as a private tenant.[1] The experience of homeless families have reinforced that finding.

Ten families found that they had to enter into special tenancy agreements in order to be rehoused. Although statistically this was not important, it appeared to represent a growing tendency, particularly on the part of local authority Housing Departments. Always the issues involved were those illustrated in the following comment from a housing manager: 'As a housing manager, responsible for large housing estates, I have to care for a lot of bricks and mortar. But my job is more than that. I have to pay attention to the ordinary standards of decent people. We don't want these dead-legs. They muck up the books and make life a misery for ordinary folk.' Mrs Royal's history illustrates such attitudes. Her husband could never resettle after he left the Army, and eventually abandoned her and the children, leaving behind a fairly substantial volume of debts and rent arrears. The family was evicted, briefly, but later allowed to return to the house, and the rent arrears were written off. As far as the housing manager was concerned, everything proceeded quietly and smoothly for three years, until Mr Royal reappeared and wanted to join his wife again. She wanted him back as well. The housing manager reacted by placing a new contract in front of Mrs Royal with the alternative of signing it or being evicted for the original rent arrears. The agreement Mrs Royal finally had to sign

---

[1] University College of Swansea, Social Administration Department, unpublished survey. The assertion made in the pilot study was based on a sample of private and council tenants which had been balanced for socio–economic status.

was to the effect that her tenancy would become null and void, 'in the event of your husband ever living in the house under any guise whatsoever'.

Mrs Harrison found herself in a similarly difficult situation. She had four children, two older ones from the time when she was living with her husband, and two by a co-habitee. The two elder children were nearly grown up and on the verge of leaving the family home. The others were in primary school. Mrs Harrison and her family first became homeless when they were evicted from council property for rent arrears at a time when her husband was the official tenant. This was early in the 1950s, and those arrears were never paid off. The Harrisons' housing history for the next ten years was a dismal succession of sub-standard rooms, caravans, and shared dwellings. The local authority were next brought into the picture when a domestic upset led to a temporary split between Mrs Harrison and the co-habitee, causing the landlord, who lived on the same premises, to issue an instant eviction order. Mrs Harrison and her four children went into temporary accommodation, and for over a year the Children's and Welfare Departments tried to persuade the housing manager to rehouse them. Eventually he agreed, but on two specific conditions, which he said should be written into the tenancy contract. The first of these was that Mr Harrison, who had in any event totally vanished, should not be allowed into the property until he had paid off the arrears of the distant past; and the second was that the co-habitee should not be allowed in under any circumstances. By this time there had been a reconciliation between Mrs Harrison and the co-habitee, so that the offer of a tenancy was in effect conditional upon breaking up a family unit. The child care officer and the welfare officer argued at great length on this matter, stressing its harmful impact on the children. The housing manager adamantly maintained that 'my first responsibility is to the legitimate children'.

Twenty-nine families (13·9 per cent) were faced with a complete refusal by the housing manager of their local authority to rehouse them, and a further 48 (23·0 per cent) experienced a good deal of reluctance, sufficient to deter many of them from continuing with their application. Occasionally, in the very small housing administrative units, there were genuinely no vacant tenancies. But in the vast majority of instances the housing manager's attitude was determined by his knowledge of the unsatisfactory past records of the applicant families. With one or two exceptions, housing

managers did not feel it to be in the best interests of their departments to take on such bad business, nor was there any feeling of
obligation to help the rest of the local authority agencies in providing an effective social service. In short, so far as rehousing was concerned, there were a few difficulties over the shortage of tenancies,
and a great many difficulties resulting from the attitudes of housing
managers.

Many families, migrants in particular, knew they did not qualify
for local authority housing, and therefore did not apply; 88 of the
interviewed families were rehoused by their local authorities, and
this represented two-thirds of all those who were serious applicants.
There were another 7 families who acknowledged some valuable
help and advice from the housing manager. This left 99 families to
be rehoused in the private sector.[1] For a very high proportion of
them, 73 (73·7 per cent), this represented a continuation of temporary housing and hence chronic homelessness. They left temporary
accommodation for holiday caravan sites, to share again with
friends and relatives, or to go into condemned property. Some of
this was a response to pressure imposed by hostel time-limit
regulations, or frequent reminders from a welfare officer. Equally
frequently it represented the family's own reluctance to stay any
longer in the hostel.

Families were asked what sort of help they had received in finding
somewhere to live after the hostel. Nearly half of them replied that
they had no help at all, and did the job themselves. Table XVI lists
different sources of outside help. The figures give the number of
families acknowledging help, and are in no way a measurement of
the type or quality.

As with the question of help at the time the family was becoming
homeless, there is again some suggestion of ambiguous attitudes.
Table XVI includes references to families who, at a different point
in the interview, disclaimed receiving any help. It has proved
extremely difficult to judge with any accuracy the impact of the
social services on each family during its entire experience of homelessness. The difficulties were by no means entirely methodological
(that is, concerned with establishing the appropriate means of
measuring the part played by the social services). In addition to the

---

[1] This figure was arrived at by deducting from the total of 209 interviewed families,
18 who returned to the council house from which they were made homeless, 22 who
returned to the same private dwellings and 70 who were freshly housed by the local
authority.

TABLE XVI

SOURCES OF HELP ACKNOWLEDGED BY FAMILIES IN
REHOUSING

Help from	No.	%
Welfare officer	95	56·2
Housing officer	77	45·6
Child-care officer	73	43·2
Friend/relative	47	27·8
Local Councillor	26	15·4
Supplementary benefits officer	20	11·8
Voluntary worker	18	10·7

absence of consistency within the views of the families themselves, there were discrepancies between family attitudes and information, and material given in relevant case histories. Mr and Mrs Jones provided examples of such a conflict. Mrs Jones went into the hostel with her two children after a prolonged quarrel with her husband. The breakdown of marriage was a feature (in the event temporary) of a wider upheaval stemming from the death of a young baby in the family. Mr Jones felt that his wife had been neglectful and that, if she had been more attentive to the children, the baby might not have died (from pneumonia). Mrs Jones found the distress over the loss of her baby very great, and the husband's subsequent harassment made it difficult for her to re-establish her balance. She sought the hostel as a temporary refuge. Contact with the social services at this time was almost entirely through a child care officer. Mrs Jones grew to rest heavily on her support, and subsequently was grateful for the help given. Mr Jones accused the child-care officer of refusing to take seriously the allegations of neglect, and in this he was strongly supported by an N.S.P.C.C. officer who had been visiting the family, infrequently, for a number of years. The child-care officer had meanwhile recorded that in her view the basic cause of the baby's death had been excessive dampness in the house, and her children's officer had written to the medical officer of health about this.

When Mr and Mrs Jones and some officials were interviewed, about a year later, there were a number of versions of the circumstances leading to the family's reunion and rehousing by the local authority. The child-care officer has recorded a great deal of effort to sort out some of the difficulties of the marriage, and was justified in taking some credit for the reconciliation. Mrs Jones commented that it was only a matter of time anyway, because her husband liked her too much in bed. Mr Jones, who was present for his wife's previous assessment, had nothing to say and no complaints. The N.S.P.C.C. officer felt that the difficulties of the marriage had not been properly evaluated, and that there would be further trouble. Letters on the Children's Department file suggested that the children's officer, the director of welfare services and the medical officer of health had been instrumental in getting the family properly housed. Mr Jones denied that he had any help with rehousing, and claimed that it was a visit that he and the N.S.P.C.C. officer had made to the housing manager that had 'clinched the deal'. The N.S.P.C.C. officer backed up this story, adding that his assistance had been given on the understanding, accepted by both Mr and Mrs Jones, that in future she would take heed of his guidance on the upbringing of the children.

It must be a matter of conjecture which version actually represents what really happened. The written records, perhaps, have an initial advantage, in that they were made nearer the time of the event, whereas memories had been distorted by the passing months. However, so many inaccuracies were discovered in the files, and inconsistencies between files of different departments, that these had also to be treated as suspect.

The longer-term housing history of the families is partly enumerated in Table XVII. This shows the number of dwellings they have had for their own use and shared in the period since the family's last stay in temporary accommodation. The samples are made up predominantly by families who were interviewed, with a smaller number for whom there were comprehensive written housing records.

In terms of frequency of moves, the picture shown after a family has left temporary accommodation suggests a good deal more housing stability than the period before entering the hostel. This is noticeable in the number of dwellings each family had for its sole use. Comparisons between housing histories before[1] and after entering the hostel are slightly distorted by the different periods covered—five years before the hostel and shorter periods afterwards. Nevertheless it is significant that, whereas only 28 per cent of families had a single home throughout the earlier period, this increased to over a half after the hostel. Another sign of greater

[1] Table XIII, p. 85.

TABLE XVII

HOUSING HISTORY SINCE LAST DEPARTURE FROM
TEMPORARY ACCOMMODATION

Family departed up to 1 year *(Sample 80)*	*Dwellings for* *family's sole use*		*Shared Dwellings*	
	No.	%	No.	%
No sharing	—	—	60	75·0
1 tenancy/sharing	50	62·5	11	13·8
2 tenancies/sharing	25	31·3	4	5·0
3 tenancies/sharing	3	3·8	4	5·0
4 or more tenancies/sharing	2	2·5	1	1·3
Sample departed one or two years *(Sample 116)*				
No sharing	—	—	95	81·9
1 tenancy/sharing	69	59·5	10	8·6
2 tenancies/sharing	33	28·4	9	7·8
3 tenancies/sharing	9	7·8	0	—
4 or more tenancies/sharing	5	4·3	2	1·7
Sample departed three or four years *(Sample 82)*				
No sharing	—	—	70	85·4
1 tenancy/sharing	41	50·0	2	2·4
2 tenancies/sharing	27	32·9	6	7·3
3 tenancies/sharing	10	12·2	2	2·4
4 or more tenancies/sharing	4	4·9	2	2·4

stability after the hostel is the decline from 39 per cent to less than 5 per cent in families moving house four or more times.

Stability was equally pronounced in the infrequency with which the family was obliged to share. This fell from 63 per cent in the pre-hostel period to 25 per cent or less afterwards. A further feature was that the number of occasions the families shared did not increase with time in the post-hostel periods, which suggests that more of the sharing was done in the first months after leaving temporary accommodation. The next chapter will consider whether the increasing stability of housing was matched by improvements in housing conditions.

6

HOUSING STANDARDS BEFORE AND AFTER

This chapter has two primary aims—to give some idea of the standards of housing that homeless families experienced, and to examine whether, after the involvement of the local authority, any change in those standards occurred. It looks at the last dwelling occupied by the family before they went into temporary accommodation, and the first dwelling after leaving the hostel.[1]

Type of dwelling. The types of dwellings occupied by each family before and after temporary accommodation are given in Table XVIII. The table expresses the distribution of housing as percentages throughout the survey area. It also compares the position in South Wales with that in the West of England, and in county boroughs with county councils.

The categories of housing are self-explanatory, except possibly 'rooms'. What distinguished rooms from a flat was that, while the latter was likely to be at least partly self-contained, rooms were not. They were, structurally and functionally, an integral part of a larger dwelling, and involved sharing certain facilities, such as bathroom and kitchen, and generally having access to the street only through the other part of the dwelling. The distinction was not, however, a clear one, and there was some confusion, possibly with a social class basis. In working-class circles what would be referred to as 'rooms' might well be designated a 'flat' by a higher social stratum.

One family in ten came into the category of 'other', and a few illustrations might clarify the sort of dwelling involved. Ron and Norma—no one ever knew them by their surname—lived in a sort of attic in what was once a church. It had been de-consecrated and largely destroyed by local teenagers. Lead had been taken from

[1] Facts were obtained on dwellings before the families entered the hostel from four-fifths of the total sample, and on dwellings after the hostel from three-quarters. Sample size for the entire survey area therefore ranges from 390 to 450 in this chapter. Where a single table involves figures based on differing size sample, percentages have been used rather than the actual numbers of families.

TABLE XVIII

TYPE OF DWELLING IMMEDIATELY BEFORE AND AFTER TEMPORARY ACCOMMODATION

(Percentages of Total in Each Column)

	All survey areas		South Wales only		West of England only		County Boroughs only		County Councils only	
	Before	After	Before	After	Before	After	Before	After	Before	After
Detached house	2·5	1·5	1·7	1·7	4·7	0·9	2·0	1·5	3·4	1·4
Semi-detached house	28·0	24·4	30·2	22·6	22·1	28·2	27·0	22·4	29·9	27·3
Bungalow	0·9	1·2	0·9	1·7	1·1	—	—	1·5	2·6	0·7
Flat	14·3	20·9	12·8	18·4	18·6	26·4	14·2	23·4	14·5	17·3
Terraced house	19·3	19·8	19·1	22·2	19·8	14·5	19·1	19·0	19·7	20·9
Rooms	13·1	12·5	15·7	12·8	5·8	11·8	19·6	17·6	1·7	5·0
Caravan	11·8	9·9	11·9	10·7	11·6	8·2	5·4	5·9	23·1	15·8
Other (e.g. railway carriage, voluntary hostel, derelict warehouse)	10·0	9·9	7·7	9·8	16·3	10·0	12·7	8·8	5·1	11·5

H

the roof, the rotting timbers had fallen in, floor boards had been burned, and there were bits of broken statues scattered around. A tottering staircase led to what might once have been a belfry, and as this was slightly less badly damaged than the rest of the building, Ron and Norma bedded down here, on the floor, amongst masses of broken glass. Mr George, aged about 60, and his grown-up son, both alcoholics, possibly meths-drinkers, lived in a voluntary hostel. The hostel was old and in poor condition, and when a new one was built to replace it the less deserving or desirable residents were told there would be no place for them. Mrs Tyler was a widow whose husband had been killed in a surface pit accident, after he had spent his whole life on a little local railway hauling coal from his pit to the nearest goods yard. Mrs Tyler felt that the National Coal Board owed her a livelihood, and when she was moved out of her terraced house, to make way for a redevelopment scheme, she took her son to one of a cluster of railway carriages which had for several years been parked on a siding near the pit.

The type of housing available to the homeless families was consistent with that for people at the lower end of the economic and social scale. Few of them had the more expensive type of dwelling, and most of the detached houses were poorly equipped tied farm cottages. Nearly a half of the families lived in a semi-detached or terraced house. Although there were exceptions, the remaining half of the sample, lived in housing—flats, rooms, caravans and 'others' —which could be described as less spacious and less suitable as a permanent home.

There was little change before and after temporary accommodation, except for a 14 per cent to 21 per cent increase in the use of flats, matched by a small decrease in the number of families housed in semi-detached dwellings and caravans. South Wales followed the same general trend, but with a more pronounced fall in tenancies of semi-detached houses and rooms. To balance this, more families went to live in terraced houses, flats and 'others'. In the West of England there was a decline in the occupancy of terraced houses, caravans and 'others', with a rising use of semi-detached houses, flats and rooms. Comparing county boroughs with county councils showed some major variations in the distribution of housing. In particular, nearly a fifth of families in the county boroughs lived in rooms, while only 5 per cent occupied caravans. In the counties the position was reversed, with very few families living in rooms and a large number in caravans. After temporary accommodation more of the county borough families went into flats, coming mainly from semi-detached houses, but also from rooms and 'others'. In the counties flats, rooms and 'others' were in greater use, mostly to take families who had previously lived in caravans.

The overall result of rehousing from temporary accommodation was that the number of families in flats, rooms, caravans and 'others' slightly increased from just below to just above half. Although later parts of the chapter will show some improvement in the quality of housing, the type of dwellings available does not hint at greater long-term housing security for these families in the future. Whereas many of the families rehoused in a terraced or semi-detached dwelling aimed at and succeeded in settling down,[1] the strong feeling amongst those who went into other types of home was that they were a stand-by until something more suitable came along.

Tenancy of Dwellings. Families tended to be classified as homeless at the time they went into temporary accommodation, but as Table XIX shows, one-quarter of the sample had no tenancy of a dwelling before they became officially homeless; 25·7 per cent of the families were sharing with someone else immediately before entering temporary accommodation, 28 per cent were housed by the local authority, and 30·4 per cent were tenants of a private landlord. A higher proportion of families were housed by local authorities in South Wales than in the West of England. The picture of rehousing from temporary accommodation changed considerably from the earlier period. The amount of sharing declined substantially, although one family in nine still left temporary accommodation to share with someone else. In South Wales this was one family in seven. The fall in sharing is largely accounted for by an increase in the allocation of council houses, up from 28 per cent to 41·2 per cent. In terms of the local authorities' willingness to take responsibility for housing homeless families, the West of England shows a rather better record than South Wales. Though the West of England started from a substantially lower proportion of families entering temporary accommodation from council property, the numbers rehoused more than doubled. In South Wales, however, it increased by no more than one-sixth, and the proportion housed by local authorities in the West of England jumped well ahead of the South Wales figure.

[1] Chapter 5, Table XVII supports this.

TABLE XIX

TENANCY OF DWELLING IMMEDIATELY BEFORE AND AFTER TEMPORARY ACCOMMODATION

(Percentages of Total in Each Column)

	All survey areas		South Wales only		West of England only		County Boroughs only		County Councils only	
	Before	After	Before	After	Before	After	Before	After	Before	After
Owner occupier	9·8	7·9	9·1	9·2	11·8	5·0	10·0	8·6	9·6	7·0
Council landlord	28·0	41·2	30·4	37·5	21·8	49·6	31·2	37·3	23·6	46·8
Private landlord	30·4	34·8	29·4	34·2	32·8	36·1	34·4	35·6	24·7	33·5
Family not tenant (sharing)	25·7	11·8	26·9	14·0	22·7	6·7	20·8	12·4	32·6	10·8
Service tenancy/tied cottage	6·1	4·3	4·2	5·1	10·9	2·5	3·6	6·0	9·6	1·9

In county council areas there was a high level of sharing before temporary accommodation, 32·6 per cent as compared with 20·8 per cent in the county boroughs. After the families had left the hostel the figures fell to 10·8 per cent and 12·4 per cent respectively, and the counties had succeeded in overcoming two-thirds of the sharing. Much of the change can be attributed to the number of families rehoused by local authorities, which doubled from 23·6 per cent to 46·8 per cent. In contrast the county borough housing departments only increased their portion from 31·2 per cent to 37·3 per cent. In the counties there was also a noticeable fall in the number of service tenancies and tied cottages.

Rents. Average rents in the last house before temporary accommodation were approximately £2 10s per week. They tended to be rather lower in South Wales than in the West of England, and there was a solid block of low-rental property in the county council areas. Table XX gives details.

Rents after rehousing were a little higher, at £3 per week average, about 10s more than the family's previous level. Part of this increase was caused by the inevitable rise in rents over the period of time, but the bulk did represent a transfer to genuinely higher-rental property. In view of the incidence of poverty, debt, and rent arrears as causes of homelessness, this tendency to rehouse in higher-rental property could be expected to bring about a number of difficult situations.

The Tulk family provides an example of the way gradually increasing rents can exacerbate family difficulties. Mr and Mrs Tulk had four children and a chronic history of frequent removals interspersed with periods of homelessness. At the root of their difficulties was Mr Tulk's chest trouble, which has given him a record of unemployment and left the family in poverty. They first came to the notice of the Welfare Department fourteen years ago when the family was evicted from a council flat for non-payment of rent. After their first stay in a hostel they moved to a privately rented flat, and followed this with a series of caravans, three in all. This led on to another flat, with eviction for rent arrears, and a further caravan. Again they were evicted for rent arrears, and made a second visit to the hostel. The pattern continued in this way, with the rent arrears and evictions always coinciding with Mr Tulk's bouts of illness and unemployment. The family made its latest entry into temporary accommodation from furnished rooms, where the

TABLE XX

RENTAL/MORTGAGE OF DWELLING IMMEDIATELY BEFORE AND AFTER TEMPORARY ACCOMMODATION
(Percentage of Total in Each Column)

	All survey areas		South Wales only		West of England only		County Boroughs only		County Councils only	
	Before	After	Before	After	Before	After	Before	After	Before	After
Weekly rent up to £1	9·0	2·4	9·2	3·5	8·6	—	8·6	3·1	9·7	1·2
Weekly rent £1 to £2	20·2	15·6	19·2	14·7	22·4	17·4	16·4	13·7	26·4	18·5
Weekly rent £2 to £3	33·5	35·4	36·2	36·4	27·6	33·3	35·3	35·1	30·6	35·8
Weekly rent £3 to £4	22·3	29·7	20·8	28·0	25·9	33·3	27·6	29·0	13·9	30·9
Weekly rent £4 to £5	10·6	11·8	10·8	11·2	10·3	13·0	10·3	13·0	11·1	9·9
Weekly rent over £5	4·3	5·2	3·8	6·3	5·2	2·9	1·7	6·1	8·3	3·7
Rent considered by family to be 'worth it'	56·7	65·3	59·3	65·2	51·8	67·2	64·4	67·0	44·4	64·2
Rent considered by family to be 'not worth it'	43·3	34·1	40·7	34·8	48·2	32·8	35·6	33·0	55·6	35·8

rent was £1 19s per week for one room and a kitchenette, and where they had accumulated arrears of £15. They were moved from the temporary accommodation hostel to a temporary accommodation bungalow, and made to pay a rent of £2 12s a week as part of an effort to help the family learn to pay higher rents from the weekly housekeeping money. Unfortunately the welfare officer did not take into account the effects of Mr Tulk's illness, and when the family were eventually rehoused in a property costing £3 14s a week, they only managed to keep it for a few months. After all the hopes built up during the stay in temporary accommodation had been shattered, Mrs Tulk was unable to face the situation any longer and deserted the family. Inevitably the children came into care, and Mr Tulk eventually spent a long stay in hospital.

The Tulk family were, however, in a minority. A feature of the housing history of many families after they left the hostel was higher rents but greater stability of tenancy. This cannot be explained by rent subsidies or rebates, because the rent figures given here have such items deducted. The explanation lies in the continuing help given by social workers, the understanding and tolerance of some landlords, sometimes higher family incomes, and the family's increased ability to look after itself.

Despite the general increase in rent, a larger proportion of families were satisfied that the rent they were having to pay was worth it in the new house than in the old one. After rehousing, two-thirds of the families were prepared to say that their rent was fair, an increase of over 10 per cent over the pre-temporary accommodation position. A rather different picture of content or discontent with the rent level is seen if a comparison is made between the rents of council and private properties. Table XXI provides figures.

The table shows that, whereas in council property the number of contented rent-payers increased from 69 per cent to 78 per cent before temporary accommodation as compared with after, in private tenancies it fell a little. Families housed by the local authority were a good deal more satisfied that they were receiving a fair assessment of rent than those paying rent to a private landlord. The reason for this is to be found within Table XXI, which shows that council house rents were on average well below those of private property. The former rose from less than £2 10s, on average, before temporary accommodation, to about £2 15s afterwards. Private rents started higher at £3 7s and increased to £4 4s.

TABLE XXI

RENTS OF COUNCIL AND PRIVATE TENANCIES IMMEDIATELY
BEFORE AND AFTER TEMPORARY ACCOMMODATION
(Percentages of Total in Each Column)

| | COUNCIL | | PRIVATE | |
	Before	After	Before	After
Weekly rent up to £1	8·1	1·6	4·3	1·6
Weekly rent £1 to £2	14·9	14·2	18·6	12·5
Weekly rent £2 to £3	45·9	44·9	21·4	20·3
Weekly rent £3 to £4	23·0	32·3	31·4	31·3
Weekly rent £4 to £5	6·8	6·3	14·3	23·4
Weekly rent over £5	1·4	0·8	10·0	10·9
Rent considered by family to be 'worth it'	68·9	78·1	41·0	37·3
Rent considered 'not worth it'	31·1	21·9	59·0	62·7

Housing Facilities. These were assessed in terms of the number of
rooms available for each family, their use, and the basic amenities of
the dwelling. The overall impression was one of improvement in
each family's housing conditions. For example the number of
families with three- or four-bedroomed houses increased from
42 per cent to 48 per cent, while the number of families having to
use certain rooms for a variety of purposes (e.g. a joint bedroom
cum living-room) fell from 29 per cent to 15 per cent. Table XXII
gives what might be considered a more sensitive assessment in
terms of the availability of certain rooms. It compares the situation
before and after residence in temporary accommodation for the
family kitchen and bathroom.

The table shows that in the last dwelling before temporary
accommodation only a little over half the families had sole use of a
kitchen. Nearly a third had to share a kitchen, and one-seventh had
no kitchen at all. After temporary accommodation three-quarters of
the families found themselves with a kitchen for their exclusive use.
Only a fifth had to share a kitchen, and the numbers with no kitchen
at all had more than halved. The sub-sampling produces some strong
contrasts, showing that both before and after temporary accommodation families in South Wales were less well off in terms of
kitchen facilities than those in the West of England. The same
contrast appears as between county boroughs and county councils,
with the latter in a more favourable position.

TABLE XXII

HOUSING FACILITIES: ROOMS (EXCLUDING CARAVANS) IMMEDIATELY BEFORE AND AFTER
TEMPORARY ACCOMMODATION

(Percentage of Totals in Each Column)

	All survey areas		South Wales only		West of England only		County Boroughs only		County Councils only	
	Before	After	Before	After	Before	After	Before	After	Before	After
No kitchen	13·9	5·9	14·5	8·9	12·9	4·4	14·0	11·8	13·8	—
Shared kitchen	29·8	18·7	32·6	24·4	22·9	10·5	33·9	24·4	21·8	11·0
Sole use of kitchen	56·3	75·4	52·9	66·7	64·2	85·1	52·1	63·8	64·4	89·0
No bathroom	33·3	22·6	35·8	25·0	29·9	24·3	33·3	30·6	33·4	18·3
Shared bathroom	22·7	17·2	24·1	20·8	16·4	8·1	26·7	17·8	14·9	8·5
Sole use of bathroom	44·0	60·2	40·1	54·2	53·7	67·6	40·0	50·6	51·7	73·2

TABLE XXIII

HOUSING AMENITIES: LAVATORIES IN DWELLINGS IMMEDIATELY BEFORE AND AFTER

TEMPORARY ACCOMMODATION

(Percentage of Totals in Each Column)

	All survey areas		South Wales only		West of England only		County Boroughs only		County Councils only	
	Before	After	Before	After	Before	After	Before	After	Before	After
Flush lavatory inside	63·4	62·6	59·5	56·4	72·9	76·0	69·7	65·0	53·8	58·9
Flush lavatory outside	33·2	33·2	37·5	39·3	22·9	20·0	29·0	31·5	39·8	35·7
Non-flushing type lavatory	3·4	4·2	3·0	4·3	4·3	4·0	1·4	3·5	6·5	5·3
Lavatory for sole use	60·5	70·2	59·6	67·1	62·7	76·9	57·6	64·7	65·4	80·0
Lavatory shared	39·5	29·8	40·4	32·9	37·3	23·1	42·4	35·3	34·6	20·0

Before entering temporary accommodation a third of the families had no bathroom at all. Just over a fifth shared a bathroom, and the remainder had a bathroom for their sole use. After leaving temporary accommodation there was a substantial increase to 60 per cent in the number of families with sole use of a bathroom, with a corresponding decline in those who had to share or who had no bathroom. Nevertheless there was still over a fifth of the families with no bathroom at all. Again, dwellings in the West of England were better than those in South Wales, while county council areas continued to show better standards than county boroughs. These assessments for kitchens and bathrooms are not necessarily a comment on the local authority, since the calculations include private as well as public housing.

Table XXIII provides similar figures for lavatories. It shows that both before and after temporary accommodation one-third of families had an outside flush lavatory and most of the rest an inside one. Very few families had an earth closet or other type of non-flushing lavatory. There was a significantly larger proportion of inside flush lavatories in the West of England dwellings than in those in South Wales.

Although there was no improvement in the siting of lavatories before and after temporary accommodation, there was a noticeable reduction in sharing. This fell from 40 per cent to 30 per cent of the number of families in the sample, and again was particularly noticeable in the West of England; here the fall was from 37 per cent to 23 per cent, as compared with South Wales where it was from 40 per cent to 33 per cent. Families were noticeably less likely to have to share lavatories in county council areas than in county boroughs.

Two further measurements were made, of hot-water supplies and cooking facilities. In the last house before temporary accommodation 24 per cent of families had a method of water-heating powered by gas or electricity. This included such things as an immersion heater, a gas heater and a gas or electric boiler. After temporary accommodation the percentage increased to 31 per cent. Forty-four per cent of families had water-heating linked with an open fire or solid fuel boiler. For the vast majority this was a back boiler, but for a few it meant central heating. This group increased very slightly to 46 per cent after temporary accommodation. Thirty-two per cent before and 22 per cent afterwards were left with no methods of heating hot water other than in pots on a cooker or on an open fire.

TABLE XXIV

HOUSING: STATE OF REPAIR IMMEDIATELY BEFORE AND AFTER TEMPORARY ACCOMMODATION

(Percentages of the Relevant Sample Size)

	All survey areas		South Wales only		West of England only		County Boroughs only		County Councils only	
	Before	After	Before	After	Before	After	Before	After	Before	After
Structural faults	25·0	21·8	26·2	27·3	22·6	10·3	23·1	16·9	26·4	28·9
Bad interior decoration	23·4	24·8	23·1	27·3	24·2	19·1	24·0	28·5	21·9	18·4
Wet walls	30·1	33·5	27·7	36·7	37·1	26·5	28·1	31·5	34·2	36·8
Paper peeling off	14·1	13·1	10·8	12·9	21·0	13·2	11·6	10·0	17·8	18·4
Plaster breaking off	12·0	8·7	13·1	10·1	9·7	5·9	9·9	9·2	15·1	7·9
Safe for children	67·4	74·9	69·2	75·2	63·9	74·2	70·5	75·7	62·3	74·6
Unsafe for children	32·6	25·1	30·8	24·8	36·1	25·8	29·5	24·3	37·7	25·4

It would have been surprising if the majority of families had not had a normal gas or electric cooker. However, before temporary accommodation one family in eleven did not, and were forced to do their cooking on an open fire or a paraffin stove. Even after temporary accommodation this proportion, although reduced, was still one family in sixteen.

Housing: state of repair. No objective assessment was made of the state of the family's dwelling, but the families were asked about any problems they might have. The figures given in Table XXIV tend therefore to be more a statement of family complaints than an accurate measure of the condition of their dwellings.

The Table shows very little change in the before and after situation for the entire survey area. Well over half of the families had at least one complaint to make about their dwelling, and a substantial minority had several complaints. The South Welsh, however, seemed to feel a good deal less contented with their rehousing than their West of England counterparts. In four of the five categories listed there were more complaints about the first dwelling after temporary accommodation than about the one before it. In contrast, although the overall level of comments from West of England families was similar for the pre-temporary accommodation dwelling, they dropped substantially afterwards.

Families were also asked about the suitability of their homes for their children—whether it was safe or unsafe. A third before the hostel and a quarter afterwards felt that their homes were unsafe.

Overall, although the vast majority of families were profoundly grateful for having a roof over their heads, they had many substantial and often serious complaints in detail about their housing conditions. On the families' own assessment of the long-term changes in their housing position, only 34 per cent felt that there had been some improvement. 19 per cent felt that their position had deteriorated and 37 per cent considered that there had been no change. The assessment of the causes of homelessness gave a high rating to some issues of housing management, but it gave rather low importance to housing conditions as such. However, whatever the causes of homelessness might be, the families who used temporary accommodation have lived, and can expect to continue to live, in some of the worst housing in South Wales and the West Country.

7

THE IMPACT OF THE SOCIAL SERVICES

The two previous chapters have looked extensively at housing issues. This chapter focuses on the family's contacts with the personal social services. It begins with a section on preventing homelessness. A survey of homeless families inevitably has a bias towards those in which preventive measures have failed, and conclusions based on material given here must be interpreted in this context. The second section provides some basic information about the use made of temporary accommodation, and the results of questions to families about their attitudes to hostels. The third section looks at the part played by social workers in the care of homeless families, and the fourth takes a similar approach to voluntary organizations. The final part of the chapter is concerned with problems of departmental boundaries.

Prevention

In practice an effective method of preventing homelessness depends on an early-warning system to all those social agencies in a position to help the family at risk. In the survey early warnings were only effective from certain types of housing, and where plenty of time was given for preventive measures to take effect. Referrals to the local authority of the families at risk in the private housing sector were infrequent. There was no obligation on the part of the landlord to notify the local authority of an impending eviction, nor were Court lists for Possession Orders always sent to appropriate social agencies. A family threatened with the loss of its home may refer the matter to the local housing authority, and then the family may be placed on the housing waiting-list. Referrals may also be made to the Welfare Department, but it seemed to be general policy to advise the family to come back again when they were actually homeless. Generally speaking the early warning system only operated for families living in council housing, where the housing manager passed on notice of impending eviction procedure to the Welfare or Children's Department.

A high proportion of families became homeless in emergency circumstances. This was particularly likely where the cause was a marital breakdown which might take the form of the wife and children leaving the home at very short notice. Under these circumstances it was quite normal for the first warning of the breakdown to come through the police. Although the police would bring in the welfare and housing authorities at the earliest possible time, it was usually too late to make any arrangement other than admitting the wife and children to the temporary accommodation hostel.

It probably has to be accepted that there will always be a substantial number of families who become homeless so rapidly that no preventive action can be taken. But commonly the family split up and the husband remained in the family home because he was the official tenant, and no emergency activity on the part of the police or any social worker could oblige the man to give up his tenancy. One preventive measure might therefore be for the landlord, whether council or private, to make the initial tenancy agreement with the wife, or jointly, or to make an immediate transfer of tenancy. In fact landlords showed a good deal of reluctance in handing over tenancies to women, because they were reckoned to be less creditworthy and less liable to be regular payers of rent than men. The transfer of a tenancy to a wife tended therefore to be the result of prolonged negotiations between the landlord and the social agency. Given an effective rent guarantee system, landlords should be less reluctant to make immediate transfers of tenancies provided the legal position was suitably clarified.

Another substantial body of emergency homelessness resulted from migration from one area to another. It was particularly easy for a family to move across the boundary of a second-tier local authority without realizing that they thereby risked having to re-qualify for the housing list.

In the main survey it was found that in 80 per cent of the cases there was no early warning, and in a large proportion of these there was no system capable of providing an early warning. Forty per cent were emergency entries. While there will always be emergencies which cannot be prevented, the scope for increasing preventive measures is still large.

Housing Authority actions. All activities of housing authorities which involve building more houses, modernizing or renovating existing dwellings or producing accommodation for groups with special needs, such as old people, will make a contribution towards preventing homelessness. There are, however, two more specific ways in which the local authority Housing Department contributes to preventing homelessness.

Firstly, the large majority of housing authorities in South Wales and the West Country have at their disposal a number of houses which can be allocated as emergency measures. Although there may be detailed methods of establishing priorities on housing waiting-lists, it was rare for the housing manager not to have discretionary power to operate the system in a flexible manner. In the smaller housing divisions of counties, individual members of the Housing Committee took a personal interest in emergency rehousing. The more fortunate families seriously threatened with homelessness might therefore be able to move immediately into another home without ever having experienced a spell in a temporary accommodation hostel. But it should not be imagined that this was a blanket coverage, and the criteria by which housing managers selected the families for whom they were prepared to make emergency provision involved a strict assessment of tenancy standards. The onus was placed on the family, or more commonly a welfare or child-care officer, to convince the housing manager not only that there was urgent need for a house but that the family 'deserved' a house. Such things as a poor tenancy record or suspicion of immorality would certainly be major impediments to immediate rehousing.

The question of direct local authority rehousing rather than admitting a family to a temporary accomodation unit had to be treated with a good deal of care by the housing manager, simply because such activity tended to bypass the usual structure of housing waiting-lists. Many homeless families were large and qualified under the prevailing allocation system for rapid rehousing, but a good deal of emergency rehousing must inevitably appear to the housing manager and to many of his potential tenants on the waiting-list as a form of queue-jumping. The effect of this was usually minimized by granting immediate tenancies for sub-standard properties only, but another solution was to hand over control of a block of tenancies to the Welfare or Children's Departments. In two authorities this had gone a stage further, and the social work agency had offered to share in the cost of building or renovating properties in exchange for some control over the tenancy. In general, however, housing managers were reluctant to accept this form of partnership.

Secondly, housing authorities operated a substantial preventive scheme as a part of their normal procedures to obtain rents from those families where the threat of homelessness stemmed from rent arrears. In only a few authorities was there a strict and rapid process of eviction following the accumulation of rent arrears. In the majority, the housing manager and his committee would go through a prolonged attempt to obtain the arrears or agree on some long-term method of payment rather than evict the family. The success of this in preventing evictions for rent arrears varied from authority to authority between 95 per cent and 100 per cent. Thus the number of requests for the payment of rent arrears or notices to quit might be very large, but the number of Possession Orders and evictions was likely to be small. (There is a slight difficulty here in defining terms. In some areas the term 'eviction' was the same as 'Possession Order'—that is, when a possession order was obtained the family was automatically evicted. For other authorities eviction referred only to those families for whom a Possession Order had been obtained and who were finally put out on the street by the bailiff. It excluded therefore any families who had paid off all their arrears since the possession order and had not been put out of their house, as well as those families who had voluntarily left the house before the time-limit of the Possession Order expired.)

An illustration from one small authority will show what was the general policy. After arrears had been accruing for four weeks the tenant was sent a letter asking for payment of rent arrears; notification was also sent to the Housing Committee, and to the Welfare and Children's Departments. If the arrears had not been paid off one month later the tenant would receive a further letter as follows:

'At an earlier meeting of the Council's Arrears of Payments Committee, I was instructed to write giving you 28 days in which to clear outstanding arrears on the above rentals. The letter was sent but does not seem to have had the required effect. This has now been reported back to the Committee who have instructed me to inform you that unless these arrears are cleared in one month from the date of this letter, the Committee are almost certain to make a decision to give you Notice to Quit.'

If payment was still not made after the 28-day period another letter was sent:

'I am instructed to inform you that if the sum of £——, being rent/loan instalments owing by you on the above property is not paid before the ——, the Council will take certain action to recover possession of the property. This period (which is normally another 28 days) is allowed for you to clear the arrears, on the understanding that you make regular weekly payments reducing the arrears each week. Failure to do this could result in further action being taken before expiry of the period. If you think there are any special circumstances which warrant a longer time being given to clear the arrears, please inform me without delay and the matter will be given due consideration.'

It was a further month before a formal note of Notice to Quit was issued and still later before any approach was made to Court for a Possession Order. Therefore the family with rent arrears could expect at least four and probably five months from the time the arrears began accruing, until the time they were faced with a court appearance for possession of their house. There were very few instances in which the local authority social work agencies and the local supplementary benefits officer were not given this period of time in which to take some action. Only rarely was there any evidence of the determination of the housing authority to go ahead with an eviction regardless of any help that might be offered in the interim. These cases were generally where the family were reckoned by the housing manager to be extremely unsatisfactory tenants, and where the existence of rent arrears was a peg on which to hang an eviction rather than the reason for the eviction. Although small in number, these cases nevertheless caused a good deal of difficulty within the social work agencies, and rehousing was a major problem. Most housing authorities, however, seemed to be prepared to accept the unsatisfactory tenants they already had on their books. Where they were much more careful was in the selection of new tenants, and a family which actually experienced homelessness might have a great deal of difficulty in being rehoused with any local authority, if there was any suggestion of the family having in the past been an unsatisfactory tenant. The term 'unsatisfactory tenant' refers to a wide range of tenancy behaviour and not particularly to rent arrears. For example, poor tenancy behaviour cited to the researchers could include such things as immoral behaviour, quarrels with neighbours, being the subject of frequent complaints from the neighbourhood, or causing damage to the house itself.

Time was crucial if the local authority was to be given the opportunity to co-ordinate and make effective its preventive services. The large majority of local housing authorities were perfectly prepared to give the Welfare or Children's Department sufficient time, but the private sector was less willing to accept voluntary delays. It would perhaps be helpful if the powers of the Courts to delay granting possession orders could be supplemented by giving the appropriate committees of each local authority the right to require a delay of up to perhaps six months in granting such orders.

Co-ordinated action. Because their needs cut across so many departmental boundaries the homeless family was often best helped through a Case Co-ordinating Committee. Unfortunately many of the Co-ordinating Committees in South Wales and the South West have fallen into disuse, and some of those remaining were not working very effectively. This is not the place for a post mortem on Co-ordinating Committees; suffice it to say that the homeless family was one of the victims of the general decline.[1]

In most arrears cases, therefore, the only formal co-ordinating machinery covered referrals of rent arrears to the Welfare Department, the Children's Department and the Supplementary Benefits Office. In the majority of instances the housing manager felt that his task was done once this notification was made, and it became the responsibility of the social agencies to do whatever they could to overcome the rent arrears, before the warning period expired. However, in some authorities there has been agreement between chief officers in the local authority that the Welfare and Children's Departments should have some say in any decision to carry through an eviction. Here, for example, is the procedure as laid down for the City and County of Bristol:

(a) The housing manager to submit names of families in danger of eviction for investigation by the children's officer, preferably at the time when Notice to Quit is about to be served,

---

[1] Co-ordinating Committees were not studied in detail, but there were a number of pointers to their ineffectiveness.

a) The Younghusband Report suggested co-ordinating committees at the policy and individual case level. The former were not set up in most of the survey area, and hence the Case Co-ordinating Committees were left without clear policy guidance.

b) Authority to convene and chair the committees was often vested in officials who were not prepared to look beyond their own departmental responsibilities. Usually they were medical officers of health.

c) Individual departments showed reluctance to delegate authority to someone from another department, for co-ordination purposes. Statutory duties (e.g. with probation orders) were commonly held to prohibit delegations.

d) Some social workers grew to feel that their clients' interests could be damaged by discussion in the Co-ordinating Committee. In particular accusations were often made that supplementary benefits officers heard confidential information in committee discussions, which subsequently prejudiced their willingness to give benefits.

e) Decisions of the Case Co-ordinating Committees were not carried out reliably.

such cases to be submitted to the medical officer of health for information;

(b) The type of family selected to be one where (i) there are dependent children, (ii) the rent arrears are such that the housing manager is seriously considering eviction proceedings, (iii) the housing manager has been unable to obtain the tenant's co-operation following interview, and, (iv) Notice to Quit is about to be served or has already been served;

(c) The housing manager to notify the children's officer of any known social factors about a family such as home conditions, financial circumstances, family relations and health problems, etc.;

(d) In carrying out his investigations the children's officer to consult his existing records and if necessary any other Department or agency involved with the family, including the Health and Housing Departments and the family itself;

(e) Before instituting Court proceedings against any family dealt with under this procedure, the housing manager will request the observations of the Children's and Health Departments as to whether they wish to oppose eviction, and in the event of an objection being received the case to be referred to this meeting;

(f) The children's officer to offer advice and guidance to the family until the expiration of the Notice to Quit and thereafter as required;

(g) At the expiration of the Notice to Quit, should the children's officer decide to cover rent payments, such arrangement to continue for a period of 5 weeks or until such time as the arrears have increased by a sum equal to 5 weeks' rent or a maximum of £20, in which event the approval of the Children's Committee to be sought for continued support; and

(h) Upon completion of his investigations the children's officer to submit appropriate cases to the Area Case Committees to ascertain the best means of obtaining the co-operation and co-ordination of services, this action, however, not to preclude a referral to such Committees by any other department or agency, pending an appropriate investigation.

Actions by the Supplementary Benefits Commission. It was common for supplementary benefits staff to be involved in evictions for rent arrears, since a large number of the families so threatened were on income levels which would qualify them for benefit. Where families are felt to be in need of support following a means test, the Supplementary Benefits Commission has considerable flexibility in the extent and method of offering it. Throughout the six local authority areas there were many examples or rent payments or lump sums to cover arrears and prevent eviction. But the exercise of discretionary powers by local supplementary benefits officers was the cause of much controversy.

There was a wide variation in the way benefits were paid. Some officers insisted that benefits must be made payable directly to the recipient family, whereas others were quite prepared to enter into agreements with a local authority to make direct rent-payments to the authority. There were many examples of supplementary benefits being paid to a family to help with rent and the money then being used on something else. This caused strong pressure from local authorities for supplementary benefits officers to be uniformly willing to enter into direct arrangements for rent-payments. It was variably estimated by housing managers that as many as a third of rent-arrears evictions would have been prevented if this had happened.

Ever since the 1963 Children and Young Persons Act made local authority grants possible there has been persistent dispute as to which source was appropriate in helping homeless families. This is particularly true of non-recurring grants where a good case can be made out for the use of supplementary benefits or local authority material aid. The treatment of Mrs Thomas illustrates the dilemma.

Mrs Thomas has five children and up till a few months ago lived in a council house. Her marriage had broken down some years ago, and although the husband made sporadic visits to the house he had not been seen in the previous four months. He had, however, retained tenancy of the house, and as far as Mrs Thomas knew had continued to pay the rent. It therefore came as a considerable surprise to her when she received a visit from the housing officer to inform her that she was substantially in arrears. She was told that, unless she was able to pay off the arrears, the Housing Department would have to go through the necessary procedure to have her evicted from the property. She was also told that she would be given plenty of time so that she could pay off the arrears slowly, and that once the arrears were paid off the Housing Committee would give sympathetic consideration to an application to have the tenancy transferred into her name. The housing manager notified the local

Supplementary Benefits Office, the Welfare Department (in this instance a joint Health and Welfare Department) and the Children's Department. It was immediately arranged that payment of supplementary benefits for rent which had previously been allocated to Mr Thomas should be transferred to Mrs Thomas, so that there would be no further difficulty over the payment of current rents. However, it was abundantly clear to the child-care officer who made inquiries about the family, and to the supplementary benefits officer, that Mrs Thomas was and would be in no position to pay the substantial arrears that had accrued. It was at this stage that a dispute arose between the local Supplementary Benefits Office and the Children's Department as to who should be responsible for paying off the arrears. After a lot of correspondence the supplementary benefits officer agreed to pay the arrears on condition that the Housing Committee would guarantee that Mrs Thomas would not be evicted and that her house would be transferred into her own name. After considering this the Housing Committee decided that it could not offer such a guarantee, since it was contrary to general policy to guarantee rehousing families who were threatened with eviction for rent arrears. The Children's Department then offered to go halfway towards the arrears with the Supplementary Benefits Commission and without any guarantee from the Housing Committee, but the Supplementary Benefits Commission refused to join unless such a guarantee was given.

Mrs Thomas was evicted and spent a brief period in a psychiatric hospital while her children were taken into care. She was eventually rehoused by the local authority with a tenancy in her own name after arrears had been paid off from a voluntary charity.

Actions of the Welfare/Children's Department. The main preventive weapon of these agencies was the rent guarantee. The term 'rent guarantee' does, however, cover a wide range of provisions, from a full guarantee of all rent arrears in council property throughout the local authority area to the occasional selective use by specific recommendation of the appropriate committee. In general the rent guarantee was better established and more widely in use in the South West than in South Wales, but in both areas there were examples of guarantees being offered by the Welfare or Children's Committee, only to be rejected by the relevant Housing Committee. The number of mortgage or private rent guarantees was insignificant.

Reluctance to operate an extensive guarantee system was based partly on fear of rising costs and partly on the expectation particularly in the minds of housing managers, that once such a system became known to the general public its use would snowball. There was very little evidence to support these fears. Gloucestershire Welfare Department increased its rent guarantees from 378 at the beginning of 1962 to 681 at the end of 1966 and felt fully justified in organizing an automatic guarantee on all council house rents in the County. The other authorities have, however, retained their more individual approach to arrears cases. Somerset County Children's Department would guarantee 100 per cent of rent arrears for specific clients. Generally the guarantee was given for six months with the possibility of extension, but it was unusual for the Children's Department to enter a rent guarantee unless a family was known or had recently been visited by a child-care officer. Whereas Gloucestershire saw the rent guarantee scheme as primarily a method of preventing homelessness, Somerset saw it in a wider context of helping a multi-problem family over some of its difficulties—as an aid to social work. All the authorities who used it also saw the rent guarantee as a tactical weapon to delay eviction procedure.

The system in Gloucestershire required that after the arrears had built up for a certain time the family was visited by a welfare officer. It has been found that in practice very many arrears of a short-term nature clear themselves up without any need for a visit. Only a minority of cases required a visit and subsequent support from a welfare officer. There was no evidence of this system leading to a general reluctance on the part of tenants to pay their rents or of a particularly heavy bill accruing to the local authority.[1] The discretionary powers of the agency operating the rent guarantee could perhaps best be exercised after the rent guarantee has been put into operation rather than before. That is, instead of waiting for an investigation of each family before a rent guarantee is offered, the agency could offer the guarantee, subsequently visit the family, and on this basis determine whether the rent guarantee should be terminated or perhaps extended to cover a larger part[2] of the rent. It may be added that, except for some complexity in its administration, there seems to be no particular reason why the rent guarantee

---

[1] The approximate annual cost for the Gloucestershire scheme was £1,000, for 900 or so guarantees.

[2] The majority of schemes began by guaranteeing a portion (usually 75 per cent) of the rent only.

should not be extended to tenants of private properties and to those who were getting into trouble through mortgage arrears.

The use of rent guarantees, payment of debts and other forms of material aid may be backed up by social work support. The amount of support given depended on local staffing situations. The 1963 Children Act and subsequent circulars from the Home Office have encouraged local authorities to take whatever preventive measures they can to avoid the need to bring children into care. But it was only a limited number of authorities who had interpreted this sufficiently widely to include the prevention of homelessness as in the long run aiding in the prevention of need to bring children into care. Very little was done in this sphere by housing welfare officers, and, with the major exception of Gloucestershire, the same can be said of welfare officers. So, generally speaking, where there was some kind of provision it was operated through the Children's Department.

In parts of the survey area an increase in the number of social workers would undoubtedly increase the amount of successful prevention. In one county borough the Children's Department received notification of rent arrears cases and other homelessness threats, but because of staffing shortages was often unable to take action. The referrals added to an already large waiting-list and eviction procedure was being carried through by the housing manager before a child-care officer had the opportunity to visit the family. This occurred in spite of a delay of several months between notices to quit and evictions. In one of the counties, intensive social work support was given to families in the temporary accommodation hostel but, again for staffing reasons, was not available either to families at risk of homelessness or families recently rehoused. In another, despite the usual complaints about staffing, there was provision to tackle the risk of homelessness, integrated with an overall programme of preventing family breakdown. Because the temporary accommodation facilities in Somerset are themselves administered through the Children's Committee there was a considerable degree of integration between preventive measures and the use of temporary accommodation. This could well result in a positive decision to transfer a family to one of the houses of which the Children's Committee was the landlord or to a rehabilitative hostel, with a view to preventing overall family breakdown.

It is perhaps appropriate at this stage to say something about the varying attitudes and priorities of social workers in different settings, because the research showed up a clear division between welfare officers and child-care officers. Welfare officers appeared to see their responsibilities as clearly and narrowly to prevent or overcome homelessness. Though in some areas they may have been rather inflexible in their use of available provisions, they were nevertheless willing to get involved directly in the details of preventing a family becoming homeless, or of helping a family to find new accommodation once it had lost its previous home. Child-care officers on the other hand saw homelessness as just one of the many threats to family breakdown. Many of them had a tendency therefore to appear less specifically focused in their supportive action, less decisive, and less prepared to involve themselves in the detailed technicalities of the problem. For some child-care officers there were obviously difficulties about their professional status with regard to work in preventing homelessness. One quotation summed up a widely held view: 'It is not our job to trudge the streets or do the rounds of housing agents on behalf of our clients.' This paragraph contains generalizations to which there were very many exceptions, but its intention is to suggest some reluctance on the part of professionally trained case workers to undertake full responsibilities towards homeless families. The reluctance was partly at taking on any addition to work-loads, but partly also stemmed from a view that housing matters should be the responsibility of the families themselves, possibly helped by volunteers or social work auxiliaries.

Self-help. Chapter 4 showed strong reluctance by families to approach the local authority when homelessness threatened. Instead, the family was likely to be diligent in making emergency arrangements, for example to lodge with relatives or friends when the day of homelessness came along. There was less evidence, however, of the family's ability to undertake measures to prevent the loss of the original home. Many families accepted a very low standard of living in order to keep up with rents or help pay off arrears, but it was common for them to have very little knowledge of their housing rights, of agencies capable of giving help, and the other measures that could be taken. There was little evidence of harassment or illegal eviction, but many families seemed to have no knowledge at all of the constitutional eviction procedures. They were sometimes lulled into a false sense of complacency by the duration of the eviction process, or were unable to distinguish between a mere warning letter, a Notice to Quit, and a Possession

Order. Too often therefore homelessness came to the family as a surprise and shock although it might have been threatened for many months, and it was only retrospectively that many of them began to work out the measures they might have taken.

The social services gave little help to the family which did wish to do everything in its power to prevent the loss of its home. There was no obvious place to which such problems could be taken: hence we found families threatened with homelessness referring themselves to a wide range of voluntary and statutory agencies, including the usual social work agencies, the Citizens' Advice Bureau, the rent officer and a number of localized voluntary groups. The section on voluntary work illustrates the willingness but rather limited scope of volunteers in this field, while there was a good deal of evidence to suggest that local authorities had the facilities but not the initiative to give a hand early enough. There might be considerable value to be gained by establishing, perhaps in conjunction with existing facilities, housing advisory and entitlement services.

One hundred and sixteen families did in fact approach the local authority social services for help to prevent homelessness, mostly contacting the Welfare Department, but using the Children's Department as well. A further 27 asked for and met the housing manager in an effort to get an eviction threat put off, and the same number appealed to their local M.P. or Councillor for support. Two-thirds of all of these felt that they received some useful help, even if it was not exactly what they wanted. The remaining third felt that it was a wasted effort.

Temporary accommodation

The survey area included examples of all the major types of temporary accommodation provided outside the large urban centres. The three county boroughs, Swansea, Cardiff, and Bristol, all had the traditional hostel type of accommodation, with a certain amount of communal living, and a regulation excluding husbands.[1] Glamorgan county has a hostel at Rhoose, at the southern end of the county, and hence distant from many of the valleys. The hostel comprises a number of utility buildings, which need a good deal of maintenance to keep them standing, and again there were no provisions for husbands. Gloucestershire County Council is closing

---

[1] Since the end of 1969 Bristol's hostel at 100 Fishponds Road has been converted into family units. In Swansea the hostel consists of a cluster of wooden huts equipped to give families some degree of independence and privacy. The family generally has a hut to itself with cooking facilities, and only toilets and baths are shared.

down its hostel at Newent and has built up over the years a number of dwellings, often new buildings, spread over the county. Somerset County Council has a hostel for genuine emergencies, a rehabilitative unit which takes entire families for long periods, and some scattered houses. Of the families in the survey sample, a very large majority, 491, had been in hostel type accommodation from which adult males were excluded.[1]

Entries varied greatly month by month, and in order to cope with the maximum intake in any one month (over the last five years), hostel capacity needed to be approximately 20 per cent of the annual intake. Except for rare short periods the hostels were not full. In part this was a policy decision, with the aim of retaining some emergency beds at all times, and staffing levels were certainly set on the assumption that the hostels would not be full up. However, the entry figures can be taken as a reasonably accurate guide to the level of urgent demand.

Table XXV shows the number of families entering temporary accommodation in the six local authorities by the month of their entry.

There were no clear-cut seasonal patterns, but some hints at factors which could influence the level of demand. Entry was

TABLE XXV

FAMILIES ENTERING TEMPORARY ACCOMMODATION BY
MONTH OF ENTRY

Month	Glamorgan	Swansea	Cardiff	Bristol	Gloucestershire	Somerset
January	14	12	10	17	3	—
February	7	13	13	4	3	2
March	9	18	4	5	3	1
April	19	10	13	5	2	—
May	13	18	5	6	7	—
June	13	12	2	11	3	—
July	23	24	2	6	5	1
August	15	13	7	10	5	1
September	13	9	6	12	3	—
October	20	11	5	7	4	2
November	15	10	3	6	6	—
December	9	10	5	4	4	

[1] See Table I

uniformly low in December, and high in January, suggesting that landlords were reluctant to see a family put out on the streets shortly before Christmas. In the coastal resort areas, noticeably Glamorgan and Swansea, hostel entry was high in the summer months. This could be related to the availability of alternative shelter; South Wales has many caravan sites, and in the summer these were filled with holiday-makers; in the winter it was easy to obtain a caravan at a relatively low rent, and this may have attracted many homeless families as preferable to applying for hostel accommodation. The most tentative suggestion of all, which really applies only to Cardiff, is that there could be some relationship between entries to temporary accommodation and seasonal unemployment. Entries to the Cardiff hostel increased at the same time as did the incidence of unemployment as a cause of homelessness.

Four of the six local authorities had regulations imposing a time-limit on the family's length of stay in temporary accommodation. From the point of view of the welfare officer or other officials involved, this might be used as a flexible rule, which could be altered to suit the individual circumstances of each family. In practice there were extensions to the time-limit in almost every case where it was required. Nevertheless these local authorities felt it necessary to place on record an official reminder to each family of the length of permitted stay, and a statement of the date by which the family should have taken itself away from the hostel. This was likely to be reinforced by verbal pressure from hostel staff, with the result that, for the families, this regulation appeared very rigid. For the minority there was intense but unnecessary fear of the risk of being thrown out, with the children having to go into care. For the majority there was pressure to obtain alternative accommodation at the earliest possible moment, so rushing many families into accepting unsuitable types of accommodation, sometimes with the connivance and encouragement of a welfare officer or a child-care officer.

Table XXVI shows the length of stay of families in temporary accommodation in the different local authorities. A third of the families stayed for no more than a week, and well over a half had left before a month had passed. Over 90 per cent had gone within six months, and in the areas imposing a time limit less than 3 per cent of families had to have an extension. The families making a long stay tended to do so in Gloucestershire and Somerset, where the county authorities had largely dispensed with the normal hostel type of shelter and were primarily interested in a programme of rehabilitation.

It was often asserted that the separation of husbands and wives, when the wife went into the hostel, could have a permanently damaging effect on family unity. This was not proven. Five per cent of the couples where the husband was not allowed into temporary accommodation separated afterwards, and 3 per cent where the husband was allowed in, but the difference is not statistically significant. In fact, for the 491 entries where there was a rule which excluded husbands, only a third (34 per cent) were separated by that rule and no other factor. For the remainder there was either no adult male in the family, or some other reason (usually a marriage split) for his not wishing to go into the hostel.

When families were interviewed they were asked about their hostel experiences, under the headings of space, personal hygiene, laundry, toilet facilities, children's play facilities, and privacy. Only one family in twelve complained of insufficient space in the hostel, although a rather larger proportion, 28·8 per cent, had to share a room. A half of the families were happy with the bathroom facilities provided for them, and most of the remainder had no complaints. One family in seven (14·7 per cent) felt that the facilities for personal hygiene were seriously deficient. There was a very similar division of opinion over facilities for washing clothes, though perhaps a little more criticism over the drying and ironing facilities. Only 7 per cent of the families had anything critical to say about lavatories, and these were evenly divided between those who were reluctant to share a lavatory and those who felt that the lavatories were too far away from their rooms.

There was much more criticism when it came to children's play facilities. Over a third of the families (38·1 per cent) felt that these were decidedly poor. Most of these felt that a serious deficiency was the amount of space available to play in, though there were an equal number of comments on the absence or shortage of toys. Many families coming into temporary accommodation, particularly those who came in emergency circumstances, were unable to bring such things as toys with them, and were inevitably dependent on what was available on the spot. Since there tended in the hostels to be a rather high proportion of children to adults, there were many views expressed to the effect that some kind of organized play or play leadership would be extremely helpful to the families. None of the hostels had such arrangements, or any formal provisions to care for

TABLE XXVI

LENGTH OF STAY IN TEMPORARY ACCOMMODATION BY AREA

Length of stay	Glamorgan	Swansea	Cardiff	Bristol	Gloucester-shire	Somerset	Total length of stay No.	Total length of stay Percentage
1 night only	22	31	10	19	4	—	86	15·7
Up to 1 week	30	43	10	16	1	—	100	18·2
1 week to 1 month	41	27	24	25	10	—	127	23·1
1–2 months	30	26	8	7	7	—	78	14·2
2–3 months	10	16	13	14	6	1	60	10·9
3–6 months	28	13	5	8	10	1	65	11·8
6–9 months	2	1	1	2	5	—	11	3·6
9–12 months	3	1	1	—	3	1	9	
12–24 months	1	1	1	—	2	3	8	
Over 24 months	—	—	—	—	1	1	2	1·8

the children while their mothers and fathers sought rehousing or employment or underwent medical treatment. Of course many of the hostel staff were willing to help out in these circumstances, but this was at the cost of still longer working hours.

Much the strongest feelings against hostel facilities concerned privacy. Well over half of the families (57·9 per cent) complained that they had no privacy whatsoever, and only a few were entirely satisfied on this score. In particular what was missed was a chance for a wife to be alone with her husband, especially if his visits were relatively infrequent, and confined to specific, limited, visiting hours. Most sets of regulations specifically forbade an adult male to go into the bedrooms, even if it was a husband wishing to go into a bedroom occupied only by his wife. So not only were the parents deprived of the opportunity to get together and talk or quarrel over their problems, but also, except in primitive circumstances outside the hostel, their sex life was impeded. The women were generally more concerned about the exclusion of their husbands from the hostel and the lack of privacy than the husbands themselves. Even women who came into temporary accommodation to escape, temporarily, from an unsatisfactory domestic set-up sometimes found themselves swinging round to the view that they had taken an unwise decision. By being in the hostel with their children, they had left their husbands free to do whatever they liked, and the fantasy, sometimes the reality, was that the husbands were being unfaithful to them. The only complaint which a significant number of husbands made concerned the cost and availability of transport to get to the hostel. Nearly a quarter commented on this, while a rather smaller group mentioned the mileage from their own residence to the hostel. Only eleven were unhappy with the regulations, two said that they were made to feel unwelcome when they visited, and one could not find the hostel at all.

The majority of families, despite all their complaints about the details of the hostel provision, were nevertheless grateful for it. 'It was a roof over our heads and we were glad of it at the time' illustrates the typical comment. A few were really happy with what they found, but these had generally not been sent to a hostel at all, but to one of the bungalows or houses which Gloucestershire and Somerset could offer. 'It was the best home we have ever had' was one such comment. Mrs Probert was contented in her hostel—'One big happy family' was how she described it. She said that the children liked it a lot and that she had a good deal of time to think over things and sort herself out. Mrs Probert needed little to make her happy. In the hostel she had one bedroom with six beds, for herself and her five children, and felt this to be plenty of space. She shared all the other domestic facilities, and was adamant that she had plenty of privacy, for, as she said, 'I can always wait in the sitting-room until everyone else has left.'

Mrs Morgan's pre-hostel experience had been of a rather higher standard of living, and she was a little snooty about the amenities. She did not like her neighbours—'I'm a very clean person, and I don't like to see all these children running around dirty with runny noses.' Nor did she like having to share some aspects of her life: 'I'm a respectable person and we always paid our rent and kept ourselves to ourselves. I am not going to wash in the same room as anybody else.' Mrs Morgan may have sounded a rather difficult woman to get on with, but despite her attitudes she spent many hours and quite a lot of her savings helping a man in the hostel whose wife had deserted, leaving him with five children.

If the majority were grateful for what was offered, a substantial minority were most vocal in expressing their dislikes. They tended not to vent their disapproval on the regulations which excluded their husbands or set an uncomfortable time-limit to their stay, regarding these as laid down from above, and beyond any chance of alteration by either the families or the hostel staff. But they were extremely critical of the course of their day-to-day lives. 'I hated it—I'd take anyone in my home before I'd see them go into the hostel.' That was Mrs Jackson's remark. The staff sometimes managed to arouse great anger, expressed with full emotion months after a woman had left the hostel. Mrs Dean said, 'She only needed a whip—she treated us like dirt—like Gestapo.' Quoting Mrs Jackson again, 'The warden was a pig, that's exactly what he was, a pig. If any of the women were willing, he was there for a bit—mind he didn't ask me as he knew what he'd get—I'd have cut it off for him—he was a pig. He used to walk around the garden with his dog and frighten everyone. They thought it would come after them if they ran away. It was all rules, you couldn't go out late.' The staff's insistence on getting the work done was similarly unpopular. 'That woman, the matron I mean, wouldn't let us get a bite of breakfast until we'd done all the cleaning,' or 'it was bloody horrible—I didn't get out of my bed before the Warden was in telling me to get on with my work. It was work work work all the time.'

It would be unfair to end this section without redressing the balance of comment on the staff. There were as many complimentary as critical remarks. Mrs Reany said, 'It was lovely. When we got there they made us a nice cup of tea, and made us sit down to drink it, while they picked up the children and played with them. I don't know what we'd have done if Mr and Mrs —— (the Warden and his wife) hadn't done all that they did for us, and helped us to find a place to go afterwards.'

Social work and material aid
'I am responsible for the casework services which are being offered in the temporary accommodation hostel, and I think probably without realizing it, this has been the most significant development of the section's work, and I think it can be said, particularly on the basis of last year's admissions-to-care figures, that the input of a very great deal of social work effort has paid dividends, and has resulted in a much happier situation in this most vulnerable area.' This confident assertion was made by the section head of a Children's Department, who had specific responsibilities for homeless families. His evidence was a substantial fall in the numbers of children taken into care from homeless families. This is indicative of the recent development of local authority policies, which gathered force when the 1963 Children and Young Persons Act became operative, and speeded up following the series of government circulars relating to the care of homeless families. Unfortunately the staffing shortage imposed continual restraints.

Earlier chapters, particularly Chapter 3, amply demonstrated the need for social work and material aid services for homeless families. This part aims to see how the services have responded to the challenge. Where the text mentions social work or casework, it is referring to the work done by the welfare officer, the child-care officer and to a lesser extent the probation officer, the mental-welfare officer and the N.S.P.C.C. officer. Reference to material aid will be very largely comment on the work of the Supplementary Benefits Commission and in a smaller way the local authorities' own material aid schemes.

Many of the families (59 per cent) had been in long-standing contact with one or more social workers, dating from well before the threat or fact of entering temporary accommodation. All families (except those in Somerset) came into contact with a welfare officer in making arrangements to enter temporary accommodation, but it is significant that so many families (36 per cent) were taken on to the case loads of other social workers for the first time when they entered temporary accommodation. This means that 95 per cent of the families were in touch with one or more social workers for reasons unconnected with the specific provision of temporary accommodation. The fact of becoming homeless was in itself obviously a significant point of referral to social work agencies whose concern ranged well beyond the immediate physical welfare of the family. Many of the referrals were channelled through the police. Table XXVII gives relevant figures.

It is difficult to calculate exactly what proportion of contacts with a welfare officer were specifically for the purpose of arranging hostel accommodation. Probably as many as four-fifths would come into this category. Except in Gloucestershire the Children's Department was the most active social work agency working in the broader context of family problems. The Table also shows the importance of supplementary benefits as a contributor towards the material welfare of the families.

Table XXVII is a measure of the extent of contacts with social agencies that were still current at the time the family entered temporary accommodation. 'Current', in this context, generally meant that the agency case file was still open, though it could occasionally (e.g. as with the Employment Exchange) refer to the frequency of contacts, or the nature of the contact (e.g. police referrals). There were wide variations in agency contacts between local authorities, but no discernible pattern, beyond confirming the differing administrative arrangements for caring for homeless families (for example the agreement that in Glamorgan the Children's Departments should be responsible for their welfare), and hinting at the confusion which servicing from a number of agencies might cause for many of the families.

Table XXVIII goes on to relate treatment to the specific difficulties found in each family. It makes no statement as to the type, quality or intensity of treatment, but provides a count of the problems for which treatment was being offered, as recorded in social workers' case records.

The Table shows that, of the major cause of homelessness, those connected with domestic difficulties were least likely to be receiving any social work attention. Some of them, such as family breakdown (marital and otherwise) and the attendant violence, may not be discovered until the family actually becomes homeless, and even

FAMILIES' FIRST CONTACT WITH SOCIAL AGENCIES
(Nos of Families from a Sample of 549)

	Mental welfare	Welfare	Education[1]	Children's	Probation	Ministry of Labour[2]	Supplementary Benefits Commission	N.S.P.C.C.	Police[3]	Other[4]
More than one year before homelessness threatened	42	70	8	116	41	36	138	51	42	29
Less than one year before homelessness threatened	9	17	8	30	15	4	26	12	15	16
Between the threat of homelessness and entry to temporary accommodation	23	455	1	114	17	8	38	16	65	32
After entry to temporary accommodation	27	—	10	66	17	13	41	9	13	33
Total No.	101	542	27	326	90	61	243	88	135	110
Total %	18.4	98.7	4.9	59.4	16.4	11.1	44.3	16.0	24.6	20.0

[1] Educational welfare officer and School Psychological Service
[2] Disablement resettlement officer and Employment Exchange
[3] Contacts on social problems only—i.e, excludes summonses and cautions for criminal activities
[4] Predominantly voluntary organizations

TABLE XXVIII

TREATMENT OF FAMILY DIFFICULTIES[1]

	Difficulties being treated before entry to temporary accommodation		*Difficulties being treated after leaving temporary accommodation*
	No.	*As % of total incidence of difficulties*	No.
Marriage breakdown	94	36·9	118
Unemployment	73	49·2	72
Poverty	72	66·7	79
Criminal conviction	71	60·7	70
Rent/Mortgage arrears	61	48·8	59
Mental Illness	51	41·8	55
Overcrowding	48	44·9	49
Domestic violence	44	37·9	52
Single parent family	41	38·0	60
Physical handicap/illness	38	50·7	41
Poor domestic management	37	54·4	46
Poor housing conditions	35	39·3	48
Sexual misbehaviour	35	50·0	36
Drunkenness	33	49·3	30
Misuse of resources	31	55·4	37
Large family	30	33·7	39
Workshy	29	54·7	29
Family dispute (non-marital)	22	24·2	32

then they may not come within the scope of treatment facilities. But such things as a large family or a single unsupported parent were easily discoverable and appropriate for supportive services. Overcrowding and poor housing conditions also received relatively little attention from social work agencies. Indeed the overall conclusion is that many families in the sample faced serious problems without social work assistance.

[1] Categories are the same as those used in Table XII. The first column shows the number of families in which the problems listed are noted in agency records as receiving treatment. The second column expresses the same figures as percentages of the total of families in which, as a result of this study, the problems were known to exist. Both columns are concerned with problems before the families entered temporary accommodation. The third column, however, gives the number of families receiving help after leaving temporary accommodation, again taken from agency records.

The third column suggests that there was little change in the numbers receiving attention after families left temporary accommodation. In practice many of the families on case loads before becoming homeless continued afterwards, while those who first came to the attention of the social work services at the time of their homelessness were often dropped when they were rehoused.

Table XXIX gives the levels of recorded contacts between families and social agencies after rehousing, expressed as a percentage of contacts which were known to be current at the time the family went into temporary accommodation. The Welfare Department dropped very largely out of the picture, once their responsibility for providing hostel accommodation had been fulfilled. The exception was Gloucestershire, where the County Welfare Department employed family caseworkers for rehabilitative work with rehoused families. Police contacts also declined radically, because the type of contact recorded here has tended to be a once-and-for-all referral of a problem to another agency.

Family contacts with the other agencies tended to break off in from about one-third to a half of their maximum level. The variations between different areas, particularly for the Children's and Probation Services, were less marked than for the original level of contacts. Both agencies tended to retain contact with about two-thirds of their clients after rehousing. There was some uniformity also in the position of the Supplementary Benefits Commission, which, as perhaps could have been anticipated, had a low drop-out rate.

The extent to which families were removed from current case loads should not be taken as an indication of policy decisions on the part of the agency. In a few instances such decisions were made, but there were two more significant reasons. The first of these was staffing shortages, particularly in the agencies employing social caseworkers. This made it difficult to mount an intensive follow-up programme, except for families where there was a person on probation, or a child on supervision, or some other reason requiring statutory visits. The second factor was the proportion of families who moved out of the area after leaving temporary accommodation, without making any effort to ensure the continuity of any help that they might have been receiving. Where the family had given a forwarding address the agency would generally refer them to the appropriate department in the family's new area, but there was little evidence of effort to trace families who had moved, even if it

TABLE XXIX

CONTACT WITH SOCIAL AGENCIES AFTER REHOUSING

(Percentages of Total known to be in Contact before or in Temporary Accommodation)

	Mental welfare	Welfare	Education[1]	Children's	Probation	Ministry of Labour[1]	Supplementary Benefits	N.S.P.C.C.	Police[1]	Other[1]
No record of contact after rehousing	54·5	76·4	51·9	30·1	29·4	20·0	11·0	45·9	71·4	49·4
Regular contact after rehousing	23·8	8·8	14·8	39·2	38·2	20·0	64·8	21·6	1·0	19·1
Sporadic contact after rehousing	15·8	9·8	18·5	23·0	22·1	48·6	20·5	25·7	21·0	23·6
Contact briefly after rehousing	5·9	5·0	14·8	7·8	10·3	11·4	3·8	6·8	6·6	7·9

[1] Components as for Table XXVII.

was thought that they remained within the same local authority area. Rather they were accepted as proving welcome relief from the overall pressure of work.

No one, for example, seemed to bother much about the unattached women who appeared from time to time and asked for hostel accommodation. As far as the local authority was concerned this was generally a problem to be passed on to someone else. Case records were thin and contacts regularly broken. Winnie was one example, 'A very confused woman' who had travelled from Glasgow where she had been lodging. It was very difficult to trace her movements. She said she felt dissatisfied with her room, had gone to London and been directed to South Wales where she had had relatives, though she admitted they had been dead for five years. She seemed to think she could get accommodation in Manchester and was advised to get help with the fare from the Supplementary Benefits Commission. When it was found she had enough money in her own savings book, a welfare officer spent it getting a ticket for her and she vanished in the direction of Manchester. Or June, aged 16, of whom the records said: 'A destitute girl needing accommodation. Was involved in an affair with a married man in whom the police were interested and had hitch-hiked from the Midlands to see him. Fare arranged through the Supplementary Benefits Commission for her return to the Midlands.' Polly, a widow well into her sixties, had been living on and off for the last ten years in London, often in temporary accommodation. On an impulse she had taken a ticket to South Wales— her only connection being that she had been born in Glamorgan and had had an aunt, long dead, in West Wales. The fare had taken most of her pension. She called at the police station for help, hoping to get a job as a resident domestic, and was admitted to the hostel for one night. The following morning she was given a warrant and persuaded to return to London. Angela, a girl on licence from Borstal, ran away from home because she was afraid of her brother's violence. She travelled firstly to Bristol, then Swindon, then Llanelly, and finally landed up in another part of South Wales where she approached the local police. She only had 2s 6d in her pocket and her parents refused to pay her fare back to her West Midlands home. After a night in the hostel she was put on a train with a ticket to take her no more than a few miles down the line and very little nearer her home. She has not been heard of since.

Only brief interest was shown in these people, and it was often tinged with regrets at the inconvenience they caused by coming along wanting accommodation in the middle of the night. Rarely was there any follow-up, rarely any referral back to the woman's town of origin for further information. There seemed to be no one who was willing to put aside the train timetable and follow the dictum of Harry S. Truman, 'The buck stops here.' Most of these women were in a desperately emotionally distressed state when they were either picked up, often by the police, or came along and asked for help. One middle-aged woman, known to the medical officer as suffering from early dementia, was found, in the words of the case records, 'wandering very confused and suffering loss of memory'. A 16-year-old girl's mother died and her father, allegedly a drunkard, pressed her immediately into taking over responsibilities for her younger brothers and sisters. Unable to face up to this, she ran away. Another girl was thrown out of her home by her father when he discovered that she was pregnant. She came to the police, who brought in a welfare officer who in turn approached a supplementary benefits officer. The girl was given a train ticket back to her home, where no one had checked that her father would be prepared to take her in again. These girls each spent only a single night in the hostel. Had they stayed there for a longer time they would undoubtedly have received some attention, and a social worker would have tried to clarify and perhaps sort out some of their problems.

There were instances where the local authority took the trouble to contact the homeless person's family, often with successful results. Jean, for example, followed a couple of boys from the North of England, and lived with them for a week in South Wales. She wanted to go back home, but her parents refused to have her. The police and a welfare officer contacted her parents on her behalf, and they eventually agreed to take her back. Another girl, again from the north, came down with a boy and spent three weeks hitch-hiking around with him and sleeping rough. She was picked up on suspicion of being drunk and disorderly. Her parents were contacted and were keen to have her back, so she was put on a train to them with a food parcel.

These women mostly seemed to be running away or were with someone who was running away. They may have been trying to escape from a terrible personal upset, like Pauline, of whom the records said: 'Evicted from a bed-sitter for being drunk and befriended by a neighbour. The neighbour had been a friend of her daughter's, who had died in tragic circumstances eighteen months ago.' Or getting away from an intolerable family situation, as with a 16 year-old girl, whom the case file described as having 'had a baby last year, now adopted. She says her father is very authoritarian and after the birth of the child just did not want to know her.' Sometimes they were trying to avoid the police. Comments such as these were common in the files: 'She would not reveal the name of her boyfriend as he was wanted by the police,' or 'She is with a man, Mr ——, who is thought to be wanted by the police.' Sometimes, on the other hand, nomadic existence would itself bring about contact with the police. Sheila, for example, came down with a boy from the Midlands, lived with him in a boarding-house for a week, and then found herself on a charge of breaking into a gas meter and non-payment of rent. The police agreed not to press the charge provided she would go back to her parents, which she did.

The statistics of agency contacts give no impression of the nature or quality of the social work services provided, or indeed any comment on their effectiveness. The only clear fact to emerge about effectiveness was a close link between the extent and usefulness of social work treatment and the length of stay in temporary accommodation. This is illustrated at one end of the scale by the treatment of many of the unattached women, discussed in the preceding paragraphs, and at the other end by the rate of successful rehousing and rehabilitation in Gloucestershire and Somerset, where stay in temporary accommodation was longest.

Some more case histories might, however, illustrate other aspects of social work. Activities were on two levels, trying to cope with the immediate difficulties of the family's threatened loss of its home or need of a new one, and tackling the underlying causes. Helping the homeless mainly involved the Welfare and Children's Departments, with some support from voluntary agencies. Beyond the straightforward provision of temporary accommodation, however, this task did present officers with some difficult decisions, specifically in relation to how far they should go in trying to help. Some officers, particularly professionally qualified child-care officers, felt that it was an improper use of their time to get involved in the mechanics of homelessness—that is in trying to stop the family's loss of its home or find an alternative.[1]

In practice many of them did take on this sort of work, but with some reluctance, feeling that it was an administrative chore rather

[1] For further discussion of this point see p. 136-7.

than casework. The job involved such things as negotiating with landlords to have evictions delayed or postponed, trying to persuade a housing manager to give a family priority on a waiting list, or perhaps taking the family from the hostel to look at a new house. Regardless of the rights or wrongs of professional attitudes, what was noticeable was the effectiveness of social workers if they did throw themselves fully into this particular task. As a housing manager said: 'If someone comes along applying for a house he gets routine treatment, which may not mean much, but if an application comes from a councillor or from some other department then it gets special and immediate attention.' The Shehan family's recent history provides an example. Mr and Mrs Shehan and her children are Irish, though they had lived for several years in London, until Mr Shehan had lost his job through illness, had been unable to keep up the rent of their rooms and had been evicted. The family arrived in South Wales (not in the survey area) and applied for temporary accommodation while Mr Shehan looked for a job and a home. They were accommodated with a good deal of reluctance, for one night, and told that this was because the hostel was full (which it was not), and that it was reserved for families from that local authority only (a subsequent investigation could not unearth any such regulation). The next morning the family were told to take a bus into the next local authority area (inside the survey area) where they were told they would find some help. With this level of support from the social services, the family had little hope of being able to help themselves, so they duly took the bus. The director of welfare services at the family's new destination was extremely angry at the way the family had been shuffled across his boundary, and eventually extracted a written apology from his neighbouring chief officer. But he also felt the family had been given a raw deal, and instructed a welfare officer to do all in his power to resettle the family. Within two weeks the family had a flat, and Mr Shehan a job. The welfare officer felt that his work was done, though just before withdrawing he referred the family to the Children's Department as possibly in need of material aid.

The next sequence of events illustrates a frequently observed inconsistency in social work practice. The child-care officer recorded in the case history after her first visit, that in her view the welfare officer had committed the social services beyond the level of help which they are usually prepared to offer, and had given the Shehans the impression that they could sit back and wait for help to come to them rather than helping themselves. It seems that Mr Shehan had welcomed the child-care officer in the expectation that she would furnish the flat for him. The officer felt that at this point it was in the family's long-term interest for help to be refused, although she did mention the name of a voluntary organization which might be able to provide some second-hand furniture. A couple of days later the hot-tempered Mr Shehan made a clumsy and unsuccessful attempt to steal some furniture and found himself with a three-month prison sentence. After coming out of prison Mr Shehan flatly refused to have any more contact with the local authority services, but with a lot of encouragement from a local Irish Catholic priest was able, after a long struggle, to improve the family fortunes.

A more serious deterrent to social work help for families threatened with homelessness was the wish to avoid too much conflict with other agencies, particularly with the local authority Housing Department. Social workers were generally prepared to try influencing landlords, public or private, but not necessarily to go beyond that. One children's officer explained his attitudes as follows: 'I wouldn't expect the housing manager to find houses for unsatisfactory tenants just because they had been requested by the Welfare or Children's Departments. It all depends on the causes of homelessness, and who is to blame. You can't let these people jump the queue ahead of deserving tenants. Public opinion wouldn't stand for it. It's the length of time people have been on the waiting list and the standard of their previous tenancies that matters.' This opinion would have delighted many housing managers, but it pinpoints the dilemma which social work agencies felt over the implications of the 1963 Children and Young Persons Act. The Act places on local authorities the responsibility for preventing such disruptions to family unity as might lead to children having to be taken into care. The threat of homelessness, or the urgent need for rehousing is clearly risking such unity. How far should social workers go in an attempt to see that this responsibility is carried out? None of the local authorities in the survey area had laid down a clear set of priorities on this matter, and much was left to the discretion of individual social workers.

Generally speaking, social workers were prepared to represent their clients in Court in a case for eviction brought by a private landlord, if the worker felt that the tenant was not receiving a fair deal. But instances of opposing a request for a possession order brought by a local authority housing manager were rare. In one instance a child-care officer reported his intention of appearing in such a case on his client's behalf, and was instructed not to do so by his children's officer, on the grounds that it would prejudice the general relationship with the Housing Department. In another instance, where a psychiatric social worker (in a private capacity) did appear to speak for a family, she was rebuked by the magistrates for 'trying to interfere with the course of justice'.

There was similar reluctance to get involved in other formal procedures, such as appeals against Supplementary Benefits assessments. One example illustrated the confusion of priorities within a single agency. A child-care officer felt that a family on his case load had been very unfairly assessed by the supplementary benefits officer, and had persuaded the family to appeal against the assessment. The social worker appeared on the family's behalf at the appeal to present the family's case, and the grant was increased. The manager of the local supplementary benefits office promptly wrote a strongly worded letter of complaint to the social worker's immediate superior, who in turn rebuked the social worker for his action. The rebuke was not accepted, and the whole matter was referred to the children's officer, who decided that it was in order for staff to represent clients in Court or at Tribunals, but not as a matter of routine.

It was often not sufficient to rely on the voluntary co-operation of housing managers. This was particularly true in the smaller housing authorities which did not have properly trained managers. Mrs Dale's troubles provided an example. She lived with her husband and five children in a council house where there was a chronic record of rent arrears. The Housing Committee issued a notice to quit, but agreed not to go ahead with a claim for a possession order after the Children's Department had agreed to pay off the rent arrears and offer a rent guarantee. Shortly afterwards Mr Dale left his wife and went to live with another woman in the same town. This event was placed in a rather unsavoury context as the woman concerned had been widowed less than a week previously, and the housing manager promptly reacted by reversing his decision and going to Court for an order to evict Mrs Dale and her children. Since the rent arrears had been paid off, and it seemed most unlikely that a Court would evict Mrs Dale on the grounds of her separated husband's behaviour, there were strong grounds for opposing Court action. However, a compromise was reached, and the Housing Committee agreed to delay going to Court, and gave written assurances to the director of welfare services, the children's officer, and the medical officer of health that the proceedings would be dropped altogether, if Mrs Dale would take out a formal separation from her husband. Mrs Dale went to Court, and was denied a separation order on the grounds that her husband was still living in the town, albeit with another woman, and that there was still chance of a reconciliation. Although Mrs Dale had expressed her own intentions clearly enough, the Housing Committee preferred to believe that there was no separation, and proceeded to have the family evicted.

Such examples show very much the negative side of relationships between social work agencies and the landlords. The norm was for friendly and useful co-operation, though both sides were perfectly open in expressing their disagreement with each other's thinking. The point to make, however, is that housing authorities asserted their authority sufficiently frequently to force social workers on to the defensive in their aims to do what they thought right for their clients.

In the broader context of social work with families, it has to be borne in mind that the objective of the social worker, depending on the agency from which he comes, will be to treat problems arising from mental illness, or delinquency, or family instabilty, etc. There is no social work agency with specific responsibility for treating the causes of homelessness as such. In general this disparity of objectives did not much affect the type of service which was provided to families, although the method and language of agency records sometimes gave a false impression of variations. Differences of opinion were sometimes apparent, as with the Shehan family, in assessing the appropriate level of support which should be offered, including the use of temporary accommodation facilities; but the overall impression of social work in the field was of a broad basis of agreement backed up by mutual support. Perhaps the only regular and predictable clash was between the child-care officer, who saw her responsibility as keeping the children with their families in the community, and the N.S.P.C.C. officer, who sometimes appeared more anxious to remove the children from a setting in which they were at risk of cruelty or neglect. In one example, Mrs Drew and her three children came into temporary accommodation a few months after her husband had deserted. Mrs Drew was seven months pregnant by another man, and also was thought to be in urgent need of psychiatric treatment. She went from the hostel to a maternity unit for her confinement (the baby was placed for adoption), and from there to a psychiatric hospital. Her children were taken into care, and at this point the N.S.P.C.C. officer wrote expressing his view that this was in their long-term interests, as the parents were 'a bad lot'. When Mrs Drew came out of hospital the Children's Department, supported by the medical officer of health, helped to rehouse her, and her children rejoined her under very close supervision from the child-care officer. The N.S.P.C.C. officer wrote expressing his disapproval, but did not interfere. A few months later Mrs Drew announced her ability in future to cope on her own, and the child-care officer, perhaps a little reluctantly, agreed to reduce her visits to about one a month, though making it perfectly clear that she would willingly return for any emergency or whenever Mrs Drew wanted. Two months afterwards the N.S.P.C.C. officer telephoned the Children's Department to say that he was unable to tolerate any further the risk of ill-treatment to the Drew children, had removed them from the family, and was about to bring them to the local authority Reception Unit. After the inevitable furore, the children were returned home once again, and treatment reverted to close supervision. The N.S.P.C.C. officer was strongly criticized for his actions, but there was evidence of ill-treatment of the children.

Instances of this sort were uncommon, and the effect of having no agency specifically designated and with power to tackle the root causes of homelessness was more keenly felt in the clash of interests between, on the one hand, social work agencies, and on the other local authority housing managers, supplementary benefits officers, and occasionally the local hospitals. Samples of these clashes have been given earlier in this section and elsewhere.[1] Another potential risk lay in the possibility of multi-visiting by social workers, or more commonly, in view of the staff shortages in most agencies, of passing a family from agency to agency without any decision as to who should be chiefly responsible.

The history of the Charles family is an example of this situation. This was a matriarchal family in which Mrs Charles, an arthritic, ruled from her bed or a wheel-chair. With her husband and three children she came into the survey area several years ago, and immediately went into temporary accommodation. From there the family was rehoused in sub-standard property, and contact with the Welfare Department continued when Mrs Charles was registered handicapped. The welfare officer dropped out of the picture after

[1] See the section on *Illness* in Chapter 3 and on *Prevention* in Chapter 7.

he had arranged for Mrs Charles to enter hospital for treatment, and referred her case to a medical social worker. The treatment was unsuccessful; Mrs Charles returned home to her bed and, from the viewpoint of the social services, there were no further developments for several months. At this stage one of the children died in hospital, and a pathologist's report suggested that the illness from which she died could well have been aggravated by cruelty. This sufficiently interested the police to cause them to call in a consultant psychiatrist for an opinion, as a result of which the police decided not to prosecute. The psychiatrist felt that Mrs Charles was mentally ill, but would not benefit from hospital treatment, and ought to be referred to the Children's Department and the senior mental welfare officer. Mrs Charles did not welcome visiting social workers, and after a couple of attempts the child-care officer reported back that nothing could be achieved, and the Children's Department file was closed. Two grounds were given for this; firstly that Mrs Charles's problem was that of mental illness, and therefore outside the scope of the Children's Department, and secondly that she 'is difficult'. There was no record of the Children's Department's concern for the remaining two children, and when the medical social worker attempted to reopen the case she was first of all discouraged by the family's G.P. in her attempt to gain information, and later told by the Children's Department that they were not prepared to take further action. The children's officer stated that the mental welfare officer was undertaking full responsibility for the family. The mental welfare officer visited for a further six months, reported no sign of mental illness, and so closed her file. She notified the children's officer that she was doing this on the grounds that Mrs Charles did not like several social workers visiting, and the health visitor was perfectly competent to cope with the family. She also wrote to the Welfare Department reminding him of Mrs Charles's handicap, and a welfare officer took up sporadic visiting. This came to an end when Mrs Charles claimed a cure by 'faith healing' and stated that she no longer wanted to be visited by representatives of the local authority.

The part played by the police in many of these situations was to be the point of contact with the family, and then to refer on to the appropriate agency. In one Children's Department 60 per cent of the total family caseload had been referred by the police. For example, Mr Harrington rang the police when his wife left him. He explained that when they had been living in the Midlands his wife had been having regular outpatient treatment at a psychiatric clinic, but since moving to the West Country she had not been to hospital and had run out of her pills. Mr Harrington suspected that his wife had caught a particular train, wanted the police to waylay her and return her to him. An officer met the train, took Mrs Harrington to a day-care centre, and arranged for a welfare officer to stay with her for a while. The police then arranged transport for Mrs Harrington back to her home town, contacted her husband, and with his agreement got in touch with the hospital in Mrs Harrington's local authority.

Much of the problem of caring for homeless families stemmed from the fact that, when such referrals were made by the police or the Housing Department, there were insufficient staff in the social work agencies to cope with them. While most local authorities were able to provide some kind of emergency attention, there were few who could offer much continuous follow-up with new cases. What was suggested by the statistics of Table XXIX was reinforced by many of the case histories. June Gordon, a single girl, had run away from home rather than face her parents' reaction to the news of her pregnancy. She had wandered around the country with her young baby for a couple of years before arriving in the survey area eight months pregnant with a second child. She went first into temporary accommodation, but later into hospital for her confinement, and the welfare officer arranged, through the Children's Department, for short-term fostering for the toddler. The new baby was placed for adoption, and the moment she was free June literally snatched her other child from the foster parent in the park and vanished.

Meanwhile the hospital had reported their concern at Miss Gordon's emotional state, and hinted that she might possibly have been an alcoholic. The local authority senior welfare officer wrote across this file, 'please make every effort to find Miss Gordon'. Neither the Welfare Department nor the Children's Department had the facilities or staff to follow-up, particularly for someone who might have left the area, and the file came to an end.

In another instance, Mrs Cook and her six children came into temporary accommodation when her own mother died and left her unable to look after the children and an ailing grandfather. Mr Cook had died several years before. Mrs Cook went through a long period of depression in the hostel, and when she was rehoused four of her children came with her, but the two elder ones were taken into care. As soon as it became clear that she was able to look after the four children, her other two were returned to her, and the housing manager transferred her from substandard property to a new council house. By all outward signs Mrs Cook was a model tenant: she paid her rent regularly and, within the limits of her poverty, kept the house in good condition. The child-care officer soon decided that she could not really justify continuing with visits, because Mrs Cook's difficulties were very much less than those of other clients needing attention. This was undoubtedly a fair assessment of the social worker's caseload, but it left Mrs Cook unsupported, badly needing some advice and encouragement, and deprived of essential material aid. These needs could well have been met by a voluntary organization, but on the new housing estate none had yet been established.

Given the need to deploy her working time carefully amongst a large caseload, a social worker may well give primary attention to the most urgent and difficult situations that her clients have to face. But on the evidence of this survey she will be equally influenced by the attitude of the client. As in the case of Mrs Charles, unfriendliness, or a request to stop visiting, often seemed to be taken as an excuse to close the case, regardless of the social worker's own assessment of continuing family problems.

Rather than produce some more negative samples, it might be as well to end this section with an instance in which a very co-operative and friendly client received a lot of attention and support. Mr and Mrs Telling with their two children came into temporary accommodation when they were evicted from their own privately owned flat for chronic rent arrears. Despite the low standard of the hostel conditions, the family kept their room absolutely spotless, and received favourable reports from the warden on the way they cared for the children. Mr Telling and the welfare officer spent a lot of time looking for alternative housing, but were unsuccessful, in the welfare officer's view because of Mr Telling's origin (West Indian). The welfare officer discussed the situation with the housing manager, who agreed to find a house for the Tellings the moment a vacancy cropped up. Two months later the family were rehoused as promised, and there followed nearly a year of intensive support to make sure that the chronic rent arrears did not continue. When this seemed to have been achieved the file was closed, but the welfare officer retained informal friendly contact with the family and was able to report a continuing improvement.

L

Voluntary services

In South Wales and the West Country the help given to homeless families and individuals by voluntary organizations was not as great as it might have been, in the sense that many of the requests for help had not been met. There was some suggestion that this represented a failure to understand fully the severity of the problem. For example, the report of a Samaritan group on the subject of emergency hostel accommodation said: 'During the last four years speakers have addressed something like 400 different organizations ... the majority have been church organizations of one sort or another, a fair number of business organizations for both men and women, a few Humanist groups, a few political groups. ... At the majority of these meetings the problem of hostel accommodation was put fairly forcefully, admittedly as only one of a dozen or more major problems. The reactions have been frustrating and disappointing. Amongst the churches one might summarize the local attitude as being merely "Oh dear, how dreadful." It is evident that the churches have lost any sense of initiative in local affairs, whilst a political group, some two years ago, reacted by telling the director that the problem did not exist, and that anyway it was under control.'

Some of the frustrations expressed here stemmed from the widespread feeling, following the spate of publicity on television and in the newspapers, that homelessness was a problem for London and the other big cities with large slum areas, but not for the rest of the country. Many voluntary workers who did show concern for homelessness in the survey area held that it was a problem which should rest squarely on the shoulders of the local authority. The basis of this viewpoint was practical, that the costs of getting involved in rehousing families or providing emergency accommodation were so high that only a small percentage of voluntary organizations were in a position to take any action.

There was no doubt of the demand for help. For example, speaking in the autumn of 1969, the chairman of the Cardiff Catholic Housing Aid Society estimated that 58 homeless families had sought assistance in the previous twelve months. The captain of a Salvation Army Hostel estimated that during the winter months, 12 to 15 unattached men, commonly alcoholics, were turned away daily because the hostel was full. During 1968 the Bristol Samaritans were approached by 50 men wanting immediate accommodation, and 33 were helped. There were also requests for help from 20 homeless women (6 with children) and 9 couples (2 with children). To quote the Samaritan Report, for the couples, 'There is no hostel accommodation in Bristol for these people. In the case of one family with children the problem was solved by obtaining permission for them to spend the night in the waiting-room at Temple Meads Station. Five families would not be separated, indeed, being somewhat inadequate, they could not stand being separated, and we failed totally to find accommodation. This is a disgraceful and heartbreaking state of affairs.'[1]

People using voluntary organizations tended to go to the nearest, or to one with which they had had satisfactory dealings in the past, regardless of whether that particular agency was equipped to deal with problems of homelessness. A number of locally based organizations have therefore taken on as part of their work the job of referring such inquiries to more appropriate groups. Specialized advisory and referral services have emerged in a few areas, particularly in Cardiff and the West of England. For example, St Paul's, Montpelier and Totterdown (all Bristol) present considerable problems of overcrowding and poor housing standards, and it was in an attempt to have a closer look at these that the St Paul's Residents Advisory Service was formed. It has weekly meetings, and the voluntary workers act as a sounding-board for complaints, grievances and general inquiries. In the early stages of its development the service found an advantage in establishing links with the local authority Housing Department and the Supplementary Benefits Office, and through accurate referrals were able to see that many clients gained their entitlements without undue delay. This was an unusual development, in that some areas showed rather tenuous links between voluntary and statutory organizations. It was possible to see two clear channels through which the homeless families could go, the first involving voluntary advisory services and temporary hostel accommodation, perhaps ending up with rehousing help from a Housing Association, the second involving the usual local authority facilities.

The voluntary services met resistance when the advice they offered involved referring clients to a statutory official, particularly to the rent officer. This was not because of any reluctance to contact the rent officer as such, but merely through a fear of eviction from private lodgings if a complaint was known by the landlord to have been taken to an official body. Agencies prepared to act as

[1] This position has changed. See p. 138 footnote.

intermediaries and to carry out preliminary inquiries on behalf of the client were in considerable demand.

Relationships between voluntary bodies and the local authority were often tense, particularly when volunteers made a point of investigating complaints made by clients against the local authority. These might be about such things as housing conditions, continual delays and lack of interest shown by local authority officials, buck-passing between departments, or the non-payment of benefit to which the complainant felt convinced he was entitled. There appeared to be an increasing willingness to take issue on such matters, and few of the qualms of the sort which restricted the involvement of many professional social workers. The St Paul's Advisory Service, for example, was prepared to investigate carefully all complaints concerning housing problems, to assess their validity and what efforts could appropriately be made to deal with them either by the tenant, the landlord or the local authority. The service was particularly concerned that the inadequate or inarticulate client should be helped to prepare and present his case. On a slightly different tack, Bristol's Dockland Settlement would attempt to involve the appropriate local authority official in an on-the-spot investigation of complaints. Claimants' Unions are a more recent development, but, as with the new Swansea Union,[1] are extending this type of service into the field of social security benefits and so helping families with rent arrears. There was some reluctance on the part of the older-established groups to get themselves involved in grievances over monetary benefits, on the grounds that the claimant had too much scope for fabricating his case when so many confidential issues were involved. There was no evidence, however, of a group being deceived into offering its support for a false but successful claim.

When an agency was approached specifically for accommodation, the chances of finding anything depended largely on whether the inquiry came from an unattached person or a family. For single men there were the usual range of long-established institutions, such as the hostels run by the Church Army and the Salvation Army, as well as a thin network of reception centres run by the Supplementary Benefits Commission. Voluntary organizations commonly referred men to these reception centres, although some of them (such as the one at Stormy Down in mid-Glamorgan) were completely isolated from the main centres of the population. Unattached

---

[1] An entitlements campaign run by people who receive social security benefits.

women could, as a last resort, be referred to the Welfare Department temporary accommodation hostels, but many voluntary organizations were reluctant to use them. Instead, they would try to arrange lodgings or bed-sitters—a difficult enough task throughout the survey area, but especially so in the three county boroughs, all of which had a substantial student population. Except for the statutory provisions in Bristol, Gloucestershire and Somerset, there were no facilities, statutory or voluntary, for families needing urgent shelter. Particularly in the county boroughs, a number of voluntary groups were faced with a steady trickle of homeless families who were reluctant to approach the local authority, in the knowledge that going into temporary accommodation would involve the separation of husband and wife.

Faced with such demands, there was little that most voluntary groups could do, except try to convince the family that there was no alternative to the local authority hostel. A few groups, such as the Bristol Council of Social Service, kept a register of addresses where accommodation might be found. Others, such as the Family Welfare Association, or Moral Welfare Association, tried to keep a similar register, but more specifically for unsupported mothers or pregnant women. Although in theory the housing which went on to such registers was checked for quality, in practice many of the groups were forced to admit that a register could only be effective if it was made up of the very poorest standard of accommodation—rooms, basement flats and so forth, which no other section of the population wanted. The warden of Bristol's Dockland Settlement, for instance, said that he was generally only able to place families in extremely poor and cramped conditions, as a further temporary measure, and their only hope of adequate housing was their advancement up the local authority housing waiting-list.

Some minorities in the community could expect virtually no help at all. The 'dossers' made up a seasonally varying number in the survey area, roughly estimated at an average of 300. Their attitude to a more permanent form of shelter was not at all clear, but efforts to check the need by offering facilities were either very limited (such as opening a church over the Christmas period and offering some food as well), or risking a good deal of local opposition. An effort by a group of young people in Cardiff to provide a more lasting form of shelter was seriously hampered when the premises were set on fire.

Ex-prisoners were equally unwelcome in many local communities and were forced to live rough. A newspaper report of the opening of a hostel for ex-prisoners (Rowton House) in Cheltenham included the following: 'Lord Stonham was shown a derelict car in the car park opposite where, Alderman Irvine explained, three men had spent the previous night because all the hostel beds had been taken. Commenting on such situations Lord Stonham said: "As we go into the seventies, I feel it is appalling that men are still having to live under such terrible conditions because they have nowhere else to go."'[1]

The county boroughs in the survey area all had hostels for unattached ex-prisoners, though in some instances they were unpopular amongst the men, who did not wish to be so singled out within the community. The alternatives were investigated in Bristol in 1969 by the National Association for the Care and Resettlement of Offenders, who advertised for people prepared to take ex-prisoners as lodgers. There was no response. This difficulty was not confined to unattached ex-prisoners. Some of the families in the main survey sample had become homeless when the adult male had gone into prison, and had not been able to re-establish themselves after the sentence was completed. There was some evidence that, where the official tenant of property went into prison or was sentenced for a criminal offence, he was deprived of his tenancy, and any offer to transfer it to his wife was conditional upon her obtaining a separation from her husband. A number of voluntary organizations were concerned at the way landlords, both private and local authority, could use the offer of a tenancy as a lever to separate a mother and children from a criminal father, but none was able to take any effective action against it.

There were other examples of minorities for whom it was difficult to find accommodation, either temporary or permanent. These included coloured immigrants and the mentally ill, particularly individuals with no local family attachments. The mentally sick formed an especially large group which has grown substantially since the Mental Health Act of 1959 and its emphasis on transferring mentally ill patients from hospitals to community care. There appeared to have been little improvement in community facilities. A few years ago the medical officer of health for Swansea wrote: 'The need for hostels and sheltered workshops is still a matter for much concern ... suitable lodgings are found with difficulty for a

[1] *Gloucestershire Echo*, October, 1969.

small number of patients, but some are using hospital accommodation as a hostel, because there is no alternative. Many too are attending the industrial therapy unit at the hospital, because of the lack of sheltered workshops in the community.'[1] Virtually identical views were expressed by voluntary organizations in 1969. In one borough, for example, the Industrial Therapy Organization has been obliged to take over some houses, as an interim measure, to provide temporary shelter for the growing body of clients who were waiting for a job and a home within the community. In Bristol a shelter for single women has closed, partly because it was no longer able to cope with the increasing number of referrals from the mental health services.

While the concern of many voluntary organizations was with the immediate and urgent need of families and individuals for temporary shelter, there were a growing number of Housing Associations concerned with longer-term housing. There were more of these in the West Country than in South Wales, and their work involved building new properties as well as buying and converting older ones. They were non-profit-making groups, and rents were linked to the cost of repaying the loan which was needed to build or convert the property, together with an assessment of future maintenance. Rents were therefore very competitive, but because of the narrow margins permitted in balancing the Associations' budgets, tenants had to be picked with great care, with a view to eliminating any family at risk of building up rent arrears. In practice therefore the Housing Associations tended not to concentrate on the areas of most desperate need, but on other groups within the community who were not particularly well serviced by either the local authority housing provisions or the private sector. One Housing Association, for example, concentrated on older families, who were not acceptable for a mortgage, but who nevertheless had an adequate income to maintain rentals. The Catholic Housing Aid Societies were concerned for large and fatherless families, but again needed the guarantee of regular rent payments.

A small group of voluntary organizations were concerned with providing social work help for, amongst others, homeless families, or raising funds which could eventually be used to obtain and renovate properties. For example, the Moral Welfare Associations throughout the survey area were basically aiming to provide

[1] County Borough of Swansea Medical Officer of Health Report, 1964, p. 68. By 1970 over 120 ex-patients had been found suitable lodgings, but this number of placements was only made and maintained with tremendous effort.

case-work services for the unmarried mother or pregnant girl, but were inevitably involved in a great deal of practical work trying to find lodgings.

Raising funds to build new houses or modify old ones for the purpose of helping homeless families was seen by most voluntary organizations as beyond their scope, and something in which they could not afford to become involved. Those groups which offered advisory or referral services needing limited funds tended to use the traditional methods of flag days, door-to-door collections, jumble sales and so forth. However, in recent years the Shelter organization has come along with new ideas on fund-raising, the yields from which were specifically intended for providing houses for homeless families. Throughout South Wales and the West Country, Shelter activities have received a good deal of publicity, and in some areas large sums of money have been raised. However, the money raised by Shelter was mostly sent to the London head-quarters, and there was little evidence of its use to help cope with homelessness in the survey area. In view of the extent of homeless-ness in South Wales and the West Country there appeared to be a strong case for diverting Shelter funds to deal with the local situation, but this was not a viewpoint shared by Shelter head-quarters. Local Shelter groups seemed somewhat dispirited by the narrowness of their terms of reference and by the fact that they saw so little of the results of their activities in tangible form. There was also some resentment that the suggestions for local initiative outside the range of fund-raising were given insufficient encouragement. In short, it was disturbing that the activities of volunteers and the sums of money raised locally were not being clearly directed towards tackling local needs.

Problems of administrative boundaries
One clear fact to emerge from this study is that a family which is threatened with homelessness or has already become homeless may find themselves in contact with a number of different social agencies. A comprehensive programme for coping with the homeless must, therefore, depend on close co-operation between these agencies. The previous section included comments on relations between voluntary and statutory bodies. This section focuses on the statutory bodies. It begins by looking at relationships between agencies in different local authority areas, bearing in mind the Poor Law tradi-tion that each area should be responsible for its own destitute

families. The section then moves to interdepartmental working within a single administrative unit.

In looking at types of homelessness it becomes clear that there were several groups who received little help. One such group included any family newly arrived in the neighbourhood without employment, and it was policy everywhere to send families back— or perhaps officials would prefer to say encourage them to go back —to areas where they might have connections. Young and sometimes large families were sent back to such places as London, Plymouth and Hereford, all with the same advice—to seek help wherever their nearest connections might be. In one unusual case two large related families had been evicted from tied cottages in North West England and guided by the Children's Department to a South Wales county borough because the husbands had lived and worked in Pembrokeshire. In the angry exchange of letters that followed, the officer admitted that he had sent them to what he believed to be the nearest town. The fares had cost nearly £30, and he agreed to pay whatever extra costs might be involved in moving them or in resettling them. Of the families, one, because it had a supporting husband, stayed in South Wales for a time, while the other, where the husband was in prison, travelled on to the South of England where the wife's family had been contacted and with some reluctance had agreed to take them in.

Another example of the dangers of crossing over the boundary concerned a family with four young children evicted from a tied cottage. They decided to move into a nearby county borough where there was more industry, in the hope of getting work and a settled home, but after one night in temporary accommodation were turned out by the local authority. The police advised the family to make for the nearest Reception Centre, forty-five miles away in the neighbouring county, insisting, whether deliberately or in ignorance, that it would take in families. When the family arrived there in the evening they were turned away, but by this time the distress and exhaustion of the children was so great that they were given transport to the county's hostel, though they were then separated, as husbands were not admitted. In this case two counties were involved and, in fact, made formal protest to the county borough about the treatment this family had received.

It was informative, too, to contrast the treatment given by one authority to two families made homeless by fire. The first, a large family established in the district and buying its own modest house, was rehoused at once with the Welfare Department providing basic furniture and the housing manager ceremoniously handing over the key. The second was a young couple with two very small children. Following eviction from a bedsitter in London, where they had gone in the hope of finding work, they had returned to their home town. Unable to find a flat or to afford the cost of living in a boarding-house, they had made their home in a tent. When it and all their possessions were destroyed by fire they were given temporary accommodation, but having the multiple disadvantage of being new arrivals to the area, unemployed, and of no fixed abode, the question of rehousing never arose. They quickly discharged themselves from the hostel and there was no record of their further movements or of any help they may have received.

The first of the examples in the previous paragraph illustrates the scope local authorities have to allocate houses in an emergency without going through the usual qualification procedures. But their unwillingness to allow the waiting-list to be bypassed frequently has already been noted,[1] and most families crossing into the area of a different housing authority must expect to find their efforts to obtain public housing hampered by the need for a residential qualification, even if the points system gives them a high priority.

Unattached people coming into the area also had difficulties. Men were expected to look after themselves, but when an authority provided shelter for single women, girls did get some measure of protection. Mostly they were picked up off the streets by the police and referred to the Welfare Department. There were few such girls in the survey, and in nearly every case the police tried to contact their families and make sure they would take the girls back. Generally the local authority tried to get the parents to pay the girl's fare, or part of it, and then the girls were escorted to the train. Whether they were met by a policeman or welfare officer at the other end was not recorded, but at least some agency was made aware that a problem existed.

Elderly women were not so fortunate, for though often described as 'confused', 'evasive and lying', or 'a Care and Attention case', they often either wandered or were sent away. Some of them were widowed and without living relatives, and while some seemed to have moved impulsively from a settled address, others had come from temporary accommodation in London, or travelled regularly between hostels in the whole area under study.

---

[1] See p. 103 for a further discussion of this point.

Geographical boundaries were strictly observed in the provision of aid. As described, it was common practice to press families to go back to the area where they belonged. If they could casually drift back the expense would fall on the receiving authority; if the distance was too far for anything but a deliberate sending, the details of cost were scrupulously worked out between authorities. Some families who had been in temporary accommodation more than once would arrange to stay with friends in the area they favoured in order to qualify by residence for the local hostel.

Counties have special problems in respect of administrative boundaries in that police areas, Supplementary Benefits Commission areas and second-tier local authority areas may all be quite different, and county Welfare and Children's Departments had some difficulty in working with them all.[1] Clients could find themselves dealing with several offices that were many miles apart and, as rural bus services were infrequent and costly, could waste their time and money. One family interviewed, with insufficient knowledge of the area and living on a caravan site, found themselves dealing with the Supplementary Benefits office in one town, the Employment Exchange in a second, and the Housing Authority in a third, while the school their children went to and their postal address, were in a fourth.

The difficulties for homeless families in terms of relations between departments within a single authority have their basis in the legislative position. There is no legislation specifying homelessness as a social need for which provision should be made. Hence there is no obligation placed on local authorities to provide housing or to retain a person in a tenancy once certain tenancy conditions, such as regular payment of rent, are broken. The provision of temporary accommodation, required by the National Assistance Act of 1948, for 'persons who are in urgent need thereof',[2] is open to a wide range of interpretation, as the survey of six local authorities has shown. The provision of social work support by the Welfare Department was generally seen as authorized under the same Act, which instructs local authorities to 'have regard to the welfare of all persons for whom accommodation is provided, and in particular to the need for providing accommodation of different descriptions suited to the different descriptions of such persons as are mentioned

---

[1] See the first section of Chapter 5 for comment on relationships between county council agencies and local Housing Departments.
[2] National Assistance Act, 1948, Section 21.

in the last foregoing sub-section'.[1] Comparable provision by the Children's Department, the other main agency involved, is based on paragraph 1 of the 1963 Children and Young Persons' Act. Although both pieces of legislation are directed at local authorities as a whole, the majority of housing managers did not feel that the welfare of homeless families could be considered a part of their terms of reference. Indeed, one of the difficulties facing homeless families is that legislation which is directed at the local authority is in practice interpreted as of relevance to one specific department only. One housing manager, for example, boasted of never having looked at the 1963 Children and Young Persons' Act.

The apparent conflict between different pieces of legislation, and the resulting confusion of priorities, have been sufficient to deprive any single department of the necessary authority to provide a comprehensive service for homeless people. An illustration might clarify some aspects of the situation. Mr and Mrs Christopher had lived for eight years in a council house. Mr Christopher had never held a regular job, and had served three short prison sentences for larceny. There were four children, all under 10. The housing manager decided that the time had come to evict the family, and went to the County Court for a Possession Order, after giving the family due warning of his intentions. His case was perfectly straightforward. There was a record of rent arrears stretching back to the early days of the tenancy, and these had been continuous for two years. Arrears currently stood at over £100. The family had received numerous written warnings from the Housing Committee, and several personal visits from the housing manager, but there was no improvement. Other agencies were approached to check on the possibility of a rent guarantee. An allowance for rent was already being made by the Supplementary Benefits Commission, but the local manager was not willing to make the payment direct to the Housing Department. The Children's Department refused a guarantee on the grounds that rent payments were being handled by the Supplementary Benefits Commission. The housing manager felt he had no alternative to eviction.

The children's officer saw the matter in a different light. He saw Mr Christopher as a thoroughly feckless character, whose gambling used up much of the supplementary benefits. For much of the time Mrs Christopher looked after the children well, but she was liable to periods of depression during which she could only cope with

[1] Ibid.

intensive support from a child-care officer and a voluntary home help organization. The children's officer concluded that eviction would 'tip the scales' in the family's struggle for survival, and he would have no alternative but to receive the children into care.

The children's officer wanted to oppose the eviction case in Court, but was deterred by his Committee's reluctance to agree. In the event possession was granted to the housing manager, the family evicted, and the children went into care. The Citizen's Advice Bureau was approached by a social worker in a private capacity for a legal opinion as to what defence a children's officer could make in such circumstances, and the solicitor stated that there would be a prima facie case under paragraph 1 of the 1963 Children and Young Persons' Act for opposing an eviction for rent arrears. The solicitor added, however, that, because of the absence of precedent, attempts to sort out these aspects of local authority legislation would involve numerous appeals and be very expensive. In the case of the Christophers the housing manager was acting perfectly within his legal rights, and clearly fulfilling his responsibility to his own Committee. The children's officer was equally within his rights and responsibilities in wishing to keep the family housed, offer comprehensive supportive services, and prevent the need for the children to come into care.

These difficulties could be ironed out by more effective policy control at the local authority level. The co-ordinating committee, described the Younghusband Report as 'composed of chief officers together with other senior staff', was envisaged as fulfilling this task.[1] In practice, in the survey area, senior officers rarely, sometimes never, attended co-ordinating committee meetings, whose subject matter was more suited to what the Younghusband Report described as the objectives of a case conference—'A means of assessing the total situation in individual cases, of enabling the workers concerned to make a plan, and to assign responsibility for carrying out the action required.'[2] There was even a growing tendency for this kind of meeting to cease to have a regular basis, and to be called only when emergencies arose which required a united front on the part of several interested agencies. Meetings between the relevant heads of departments to discuss policy were uncommon, and in one authority at least there had been none since the passage of the

---

[1] Report of the Working Party on Social Workers in the Local Authority Health and Welfare Services, 1959 (Younghusband Report), paragraph 1085.
[2] Ibid.

National Assistance Act. Many local authority officials, when interviewed, argued that co-ordination at all levels was a matter of informal personal contacts, and the half-hearted attempt to put it on a formal and more comprehensive basis was clearly making little progress.

Not all agencies involved with homelessness come under the control of the local council. The role of the Supplementary Benefits Commission was crucial, as the main provider of material aid, and the only agency likely to know the full extent of a client's financial resources. The strict confidentiality with which this information was treated often led to misunderstanding with other agencies, who felt that it was being used to conceal a less than generous provision. The separation in control of the three basic components of help to the homeless family—housing, financial aid and social work support—led to disputes between senior officers and between field workers, and a lot of inefficiency where one component failed because the others were not available at the appropriate moment. Given the kinds of difficulties facing homeless families in the survey area, it was clear that rehousing by itself, or financial aid alone, or social work without anything else was most unlikely to meet the full range of family needs.

Particular difficulties arose with the supplementary benefits officers when the pattern of a family's earning was very irregular, or when the husband had worked too recently to qualify for help with debts or other special needs. There were records of many grants for working clothes and boots, and a sympathetic consideration for an extra allowance for fares in order to get a man used to working again. But whenever a man got a reputation for being workshy, the supplementary benefits officer felt justified in taking a tough line, including cutting down benefits, to persuade the man to go to work. There were instances where the unexpected lowering of benefits or refusal of a grant disrupted the long-term treatment of family problems, as well as an instance where the officer's pressure resulted in the man getting a job.

There were other agencies involved in a similar way. For example, most low-income families faced the difficulty of meeting gas and electricity bills, with the attendant arguments as to who should pay them. Gas and electricity boards often refused to install slot-meters in working-class areas, on the grounds that the cost of installation and collection was too high, and the risk of theft too great. Consequently there were examples of large bills accumulating, some of them between £50 and £100, before any warning was available to the welfare officer, child-care officer, or even the housing manager. And there were examples of fuel being cut off equally unexpectedly, with large families being left to cook on open fires or primus stoves and to rely on candles for lighting. Sometimes a social worker would intervene, but not always successfully, as in the case of a family which included a handicapped child, half blind and very lame. In this instance the electricity board made a promise to postpone cutting off the light, but did not keep it. Another family, a mother with five children, was rehoused by her local authority, but because she had a bad record with both electricity and gas boards from her previous tenancy, the two got together and decided that as a warning they would not switch on the supply in the new house for three days. The particular difficulty of these large bills was that, if they were paid off by small instalments, new bills would begin to arrive well before the old debt had been paid.

Where there was conflict between agencies it commonly involved money, and if the homelessness emergency was the result of a large debt, there often seemed to be reluctance on the part of departments to take responsibility for the family. Other kinds of situations which involved a number of agencies were generally less likely to provoke disputes. Often the responsibility which brought in a number of agencies was a statutory one, as, for example, when a member of the family was on a probation order. In these cases there was usually good co-operation between the agencies because responsibility had been accepted on a sound legislative position. There were a small number of examples of a family disrupted by too many visiting officers, predominantly in circumstances involving mental illness. If there were no legal duties to be carried out, the risk was much more of agencies opting out of a situation than of multi-visiting.

8

———————

SUMMARY AND CONCLUSIONS

The summary and conclusions fall into several interlocking sections. Firstly come the findings about homelessness as a social need, focusing on the causes and context of the loss of a home, as it was experienced by the people in the survey. The next sections summarize and comment on the study's findings about the extent, type, suitability, and quality of the services available to help the people threatened with homelessness or actually homeless. The summary of findings ends with an estimate of the numbers of homeless in the survey area. The chapter continues with a review of the hypotheses made at the beginning of the work and concludes with some recommendations for central government and local authorities on the treatment of the problem.

Summary of findings:
(a) *The families and their problems.* Families in the survey were larger than average for England and Wales, and a substantial minority of them were the remnant of broken marriages. There were a number of unattached people, some of whom were of pensionable age, but the majority of adults were young parents, with young children. Half of the children were of pre-school age, and few mothers had all their children at school so that they were free to take up employment. Furthermore, there was only a small number of children who had left school and were contributing to the family budget. Looked at over a number of years the families were characterized by instability, in housing, in levels of income, and in the relationships between family members.

The employment picture showed a lot of chronically unemployed men, and many of those who did have jobs worked sporadically. Almost all the work was unskilled. Families were therefore dependent, many of them for years at a time, on social security benefits, or supplementary benefits, or low unstable wages.

Housing conditions were also inadequate. Over a quarter of the sample had no housing of their own, and either shared with others, lived entirely in institutions, or in a few cases lived rough. Most of the remainder were dependent on the private housing sector, and rents were high in relation to the average level of earnings or benefits. The lack of, or need to share, kitchen, bathroom and lavatory showed up further the low standard of dwellings—a picture that was reinforced by complaints about decorative and structural conditions.

These conditions seemed to follow families in their frequent changes of house, and most families spent many years in substandard properties. Although a third of the families felt that there was some improvement in housing conditions over the years, few attained the level which most people in the community would expect for themselves. Indeed for the majority of the sample there was no improvement or even a deterioration.

The three factors mentioned so far—(1) handicaps in family structure, particularly women left unsupported to care for children, (2) unemployment and poverty, and (3) the prolonged burden of poor housing—were important and interrelated causes of homelessness. But numerically more significant were the various behavioural and relationship problems within the families. Difficulties connected with the management of the household and various forms of pathological behaviour featured extensively, but domestic upsets, mainly marriage breakdown, dominated the overall picture.

Illness, particularly mental illness, did appear as an important factor, but perhaps not as great as might have been anticipated.[1] Difficulties connected with children were not important as a cause of homelessness, but where an unsupported mother had a lot of children to look after there could be problems. In particular, the large family was one of the groups (old people who could not be self-dependent were another) for which there was a shortage of housing in the literal sense of insufficient buildings of the necessary size and with the required amenities.

The emphasis so far has been on homelessness as the result of a wide range of other social problems. The study was also concerned to discover to what extent homelessness, or the provision made to cope with it, could be seen as a causal factor for family breakdown. Clearly there was no precise distinction between causes and effects,

---

[1] For example a large majority of the families studied by Philp in *Family Failure* were handicapped by both physical and mental illness.

but there was very little evidence of homelessness acting as a catalyst for other social upsets, and chronologically it tended to be a sequel to other family difficulties rather than a starting-off point. However, although the separation of husbands from wives in temporary accommodation did not appear to lead to prolonged family breakdown, some of the wider housing issues did. In particular, a poor tenancy record could condemn a family to a pattern of frequent moves through sub-standard properties, and despite the shortage of hard evidence, many families and social workers were convinced that this did contribute to family breakdown.

(b) *Housing services.* The part played by landlords in the survey area, whether private or local authority, was limited. In theory everyone has the chance to get a house, yet to a considerable extent the homeless are those who have been deprived of the chance—in small degree because of the shortage of specific types of property in some areas, but mainly because they have not maintained required standards of tenancy behaviour, or have gained reputations in other ways which make them unattractive prospects for landlords, or are outsiders to the area. In the circumstances the contribution of the housing services to preventing or coping with homelessness has to be measured not by bricks and mortar, but by the willingness of landlords to discriminate in favour of (instead of sometimes against) particularly needy groups, and accept a minority of tenants who have difficulty in paying rent or keeping up with other standards.

There is no reason why the private commercial housing sector should concern itself with potentially bad risks, and many of the local authority housing managers in the study did indeed argue that they were taking the full burden of unwanted or unsatisfactory tenants. The survey results showed, however, that no more than 42 per cent of the sample were rehoused from temporary accommodation to the local authority sector. There was a persistent and growing reluctance to take on potential problems, partly balanced by an equal firmness in keeping those difficult families who were already tenants. The majority of the homeless were forced on to the private market. A few who could demonstrate their creditworthiness might expect help from a voluntary housing association, while the remainder had to pay high rents for poor conditions.

In addition to the unhelpful attitudes to rehousing of many of the housing managers, there were other difficulties for the homeless family in search of a council house. One was the profusion of housing authorities (over seventy in the survey area). It was extremely easy for a family to wander over a boundary to look for a house, only to find that they had thereby forfeited a place on the housing list in the area they had left, and needed a residential qualification before going on to the list in their new area. The twenty-three housing districts in Glamorgan showed a great variety in methods of establishing the waiting-list and priorities on it, but almost all demanded a period in residence in the area as a first step. Another difficulty was the range and complexity of systems of housing allocation, some dependent on an elaborate points calculation, others on the patronage of the local councillors, and others having rules discriminating against such people, for example, as caravan dwellers. Above all, the ordinary member of the public had no easy way of comparing the regulations for different areas, the length of waiting-list, the total store of housing, or the level of rents. Often the areas with short waiting-lists charged high rents or had vacant tenancies well away from places of employment, and there was little advice to be had about the pros and cons of such situations.

Where landlords, private or local authority, did rehouse people with problems there was a tendency to hold the view that a favour was being done to the family, and that this justified pressing the family into accepting sub-standard housing. The survey showed this to be one of the major reasons for keeping such families in the worst available housing over a prolonged period. Although there was an overall improvement in conditions on rehousing from temporary accommodation, many families continued in a chronically unsettled state, hoping for something better to come along.

The law imposes certain conditions and procedures on landlords wishing to evict tenants, and this gives the tenant or the local authority a short time, usually twenty-eight days, in which to prevent homelessness occurring. The survey unearthed very few illegal evictions, but a large number of instances where there was no early warning to the local authority, or where nothing was done to try to prevent the eviction. Staff shortages for preventive work were mentioned time and time again. Local authority Housing Departments gave a much longer period of warning of eviction procedure, and most took a direct interest in trying to avoid the necessity of going through with the eviction. The willingness to allow time to pay off arrears was perhaps the most effective method used, and had reduced the number of evictions significantly. Housing managers did, however, have other means of helping, which they tended to use selectively, sometimes according to their own distinction between the deserving and undeserving. Occasionally a tenancy was taken out of one person's name and passed to another in the household, particularly if it avoided making children homeless. Occasionally also housing managers would make emergency allocations of housing to prevent homelessness, though this measure was strongly tempered by a reluctance to bypass the waiting list. On a more formal basis, blocks of sub-standard properties were leased to the Welfare and Children's Departments, for allocation to families on their caseloads, and in Gloucestershire the housing authorities were invited by the County Welfare Committee to participate in a building programme for tenants with special needs. Few had accepted.

(c) *Personal social services.* In the survey area the Welfare Department and/or Children's Departments also had a major responsibility for preventing homelessness. They were limited by the shortage of early warnings from the private sector, and the homelessness which occurred in emergency circumstances where evasive action was impossible. Nevertheless over a third of the families entering temporary accommodation did so in circumstances where there was no emergency and no early warning, or a warning but no action. Three preventive measures were in common use by the Welfare or Children's Department—a rent guarantee, usually selectively employed; payment of all or part of accumulated arrears; and persuasion, working to get the eviction process delayed and the tenant to do whatever was possible to remove the reasons for the eviction. It was noticeable that prevention was almost always seen in the context of homelessness stemming from formal eviction procedure, and had little impact on other ways of becoming homeless.

Once a family became homeless the direct responsibility for providing shelter rested with Welfare Departments (Children's Department in Somerset), but on the basis of the estimated total number of homeless in the survey area, only a minority made use of it. In part this indicated many people's reluctance to call on a government (as opposed to voluntary) agency for help, and in part it also reflected the deterrent reputation of some of the hostels. Primarily, however, the small numbers going through hostels resulted directly from local authority regulations, which generally prohibited taking in all but mothers with children, who had to be demonstrably without a possible alternative roof.

The National Assistance Act specified the provision of accommodation and concern for the welfare of the homeless, and this was interpreted by most of the local authorities as a hostel and a casework service to deal with attendant social problems. The Act did not specify a rehousing service, and although there was a great deal of activity by welfare officers and other social workers, there was only a little organized rehabilitation and rehousing provision.

The three South Wales authorities in the survey area continued with hostel arrangements which excluded husbands and imposed time-limits. The West of England authorities were more in line with the policy of the Department of Health and Social Security,[1] though Bristol and Gloucestershire had conventional hostel provisions during the period covered by the survey. The survey did not offer any evidence that the separation of husbands from their wives had any long-term effect on family unity. Most of the families in the sample were subject to such separation, but for two-thirds of them there were no husbands, or other reasons why the husband would not move into the hostel. However, amongst those couples who were kept apart by local authority regulations there was a good deal of inconvenience and distress. This was exacerbated by the lack of privacy in the hostels, about which many families complained. It did not prove easy to give a precise measure of the effects of a time-limit. Almost all families had left the hostels before their time-limit expired, but there was some evidence that they did so through pressure built up from continual reminders about the time-limit. There was also evidence that both the families and social workers were hurried into unsatisfactory rehousing arrangements.

Casework services were provided for the large majority of the sample whilst they were in temporary accommodation. But before and after the family used temporary accommodation the services were much thinner, and the entry to temporary accommodation was a point for establishing contact with many of the families, just as rehousing was considered a suitable occasion for ending contact. Many families with severe problems were not known to the personal social services until they became homeless. The reasons given for the lack of continuity were staff shortages, particularly for follow-up, and the high proportion of families moving to another area on rehousing. The survey suggested that some caseworkers were reluctant to get involved in the practicalities of rehousing.

Although much of the social work took place while the family

[1] Circulars 20/66 and 19/67 (Wales) Welsh Board of Health.

was in temporary accommodation, there was only a little use of the hostel, or other forms of temporary accommodation, as a social work aid. In the West of England county council areas there was some rehabilitative work; in South Wales the hostels were used as a base for marriage guidance, and in a small number of instances throughout the survey area temporary accommodation was used as a means of putting pressure on the local authority for rehousing. But generally the hostels were seen as no more than a temporary shelter.

There were a number of community services involved in helping the homeless. The local authority mental welfare services could have played a larger part than they did, but were hampered by a lack of facilities, especially sheltered housing. Voluntary groups contributed in several ways, running hostels, mainly for single men, keeping housing lists, offering advice and information about housing, helping clients in their dealings with local authority and government officials and, more recently, developing campaigns to ensure that clients received their rights in the housing and social security fields. There was also a good deal of informal help given to families threatened with homelessness by their relatives, friends and neighbours, all to be added to the efforts of the families themselves. Indeed the principle of self-help was one which the local authorities pressed hard on to families at risk of losing their homes, and many of the families coped on their own for years in most difficult conditions. Nevertheless the survey showed up the limitations of self-help, particularly in rehousing.

(d) *Material aid.* Housing and social work services were reinforced by material aid provisions, mainly operated through the Supplementary Benefits Commission, but also using local authority grants and some voluntary support. A large proportion of families in the survey were partly or wholly dependent on social security or supplementary benefits, and the low level of benefits left many of the families in serious poverty. In particular there was dissatisfaction, often felt by social workers, at the inadequacy of some of the non-recurring grants, over which the supplementary benefits officers were able to exercise some discretion. The survey showed a few instances where the wage stop was used, but the biggest problems for the homeless came with the difficulty of getting money when they had no address to give, and overcoming the suspicion with which many of their claims were treated.

Throughout the period covered by the study the local authorities in the survey area were expanding their own material aid schemes, a large part of which were devoted to preventing homelessness by paying off rent arrears. There was evidence of local authority aid effectively preventing homelessness, or contributing to a family's rehabilitation, but also a few examples of money having no noticeable impact. Some social workers argued that more care and discrimination was needed in offering material aid, and that it would be bad if caseworkers became known as sources of charity.

Taking an overall look at the services provided for the homeless, the survey emphasized some of the effects of the separate control of the three main components, housing, personal social service and material aid. There were few attempts at policy co-ordination between the agencies involved, and although there was a general pattern of sound co-operation in the field, there were many examples of disputes, from some of which the clients emerged as the losers. The survey uncovered very few instances of homelessness where just one of the components—a house, or some money, or social work support—were sufficient in themselves, but it did suggest that where (e.g. as in Gloucestershire) one agency had taken over as much responsibility as it was allowed, both preventive and rehabiliative services were more effective.

How many homeless?

What was the overall size of homelessness in the survey area? How many people were homeless? It would be convenient if it were possible to give a straightforward figure in answer to this question. It raises, however, a number of complex issues, not least of which is a definition of homelessness. The Department of Health and Social Security stated that for England and Wales as a whole there were in September, 1970, 24,274 people living in temporary accommodation hostels. This represented 4,933 families. There are few who could claim that the total population of temporary accommodation hostels could be closely equated with the total numbers of homeless, even using the Department's own rather narrow definition of homelessness.

By extending the definition for homelessness to include people living in grossly unsatisfactory housing—housing which is temporary in the sense of being condemned—Shelter estimates that there may be as many as three million homeless in this country.[1] What is the real figure for homeless in South Wales and the West of England,

[1] Shelter pamphlet *Face the Facts*.

if a relatively tight definition of homelessness is taken, as people without a roof?

During the six-year period from the beginning of 1963 until the end of 1968 approximately 1,100 families passed through temporary accommodation in the survey area. This is given as an approximation because the recording of some of the local authorities is not altogether clear on this point, and it has proved difficult to be exact in eliminating all multiple entries to temporary accommodation, particularly where a family entered hostels in several local authorities.

However, families did not commonly move direct from their last permanent home into a temporary accommodation hostel without first trying some alternative method of housing, either by themselves, or staying for a short while with friends or relatives, generally in overcrowded conditions. In many instances this was not a solitary incident but numerous stays. Occasionally the family was prepared to split up temporarily and be lodged with several families. Other emergency measures included renting caravans outside the holiday season when rents were low, moving into derelict or condemned housing scheduled for demolition, or using voluntary institutions such as Salvation Army hostels.

Although it has not proved possible to produce an exact figure, it could be reasonably estimated that on average a family entered temporary accommodation once for every five times that it made some alternative arrangement. This would suggest that over any given period the number of families who were homeless was about five or six times the number using hostels.[1] Information about homeless people who have not passed through temporary accommodation is less reliable, but by using such sources as referrals to the Rent Officer, to the Citizens' Advice Bureau and other voluntary groups, Court lists of Eviction Orders, etc., a tentative figure can be suggested.

This calculation is not a simple matter of adding up the numbers of homeless who become known to voluntary and statutory organizations. Allowance has to be made, in particular, for three substantial variables. Firstly, agencies keeping a note of homelessness referrals rarely distinguished in their records between clients seeking to overcome a threat of losing their homes, and those who had actually lost or were to lose them. Differences between threat and reality covered a wide range. At one extreme less that 1 per cent

[1] See Chapter 4, Table XIII and its explanatory comment.

of notices to quit issued by housing managers in the survey area led ultimately to eviction. At the other end of the scale a substantial majority of families referred for other reasons were already homeless; for example, those migrating from another area, people just released from penal custody, or those discharged from long-term stays in hospital.

Secondly there was the question of overlapping referrals, of homeless people who got their names on to the lists of a number of organizations. The overlap between families receiving Court Orders for Possession and families entering temporary accommodation appeared to be small.[1] On the other hand many families who used temporary accommodation had also been in touch with voluntary organizations. Five per cent of families in the survey acknowledged voluntary help in trying to prevent the loss of their homes,[2] and 11 per cent in rehousing.[3] Overlapping between different voluntary groups was thought by voluntary workers to be limited, because clients generally confined their approaches to organizations in particular localities;[4] but there is no clear evidence on this, since some groups did not record the names of referrals.

Thirdly, the extent of homelessness varied greatly month by month,[5] and there was no indication that low months for entry to temporary accommodation were balanced by high referrals elsewhere, although the tendency was noted for homeless families to use vacant holiday caravans during winter months as an alternative to the hostel.

In coming to a figure for the number of homeless in the survey area it is possible to combat short-term variations in overall levels by making an estimate over a period of a year, rather than at one point of the calendar.[6] Taking an average year between 1963 and 1968, but bearing in mind that the long-term trend in homelessness has been upwards, a little under 200 families passed through temporary accommodation (about 900 persons). This would indicate about 1,000 families (*circa* 5,000 persons, or 900 multiple family units and 100 individuals) experiencing homelessness during the

[1] See p. 210.
[2] See p. 94.
[3] Table XVI, p. 109.
[4] The section on Voluntary Services in Chapter 7, especially p. 163 gives some light on this.
[5] Table XXV, p. 139.
[6] Ministry of Health figures relate to persons in temporary accommodation on a specific night in each year.

year, based on local authority figures. To this should be added a
further number, taken predominantly from estimates from voluntary
sources. This number was calculated by adding up the totals of
referrals and then removing two-thirds to allow for overlapping
and those who were threatened but never actually became homeless.
As has already been suggested, the removal of two-thirds has only
slight derivation from the limited and varied empirical evidence
available. Rather it is based on the opinions and experience of the
research team and voluntary workers who have come into contact
with the homeless. On this estimate the numbers of homeless in an
average year who had no record of contact with Welfare Departments in the survey area were 1,200 multiple family units (about
7,000 people) and a little over 3,000 unattached individuals.

This would indicate that an average annual figure for all homelessness in the survey area between 1963 and 1968 was approximately
15,000 persons, comprising about 2,000 multiple units and over
3,000 individuals.

Testing the hypotheses. The summary of findings has included much
direct comment on the hypotheses which the study set out to
investigate. The next few pages take a more systematic look at the
hypotheses, and the reader must accept some repetition of what has
gone before. The study started with the central hypothesis that
homelessness would vary between areas with severe housing shortages and those with an adequate supply of housing. Further hypotheses were taken from a pilot study in Glamorgan, and from the
recommendations of the Seebohm Committee.

There were no parts of the survey area in which there was an
entirely adequate supply of housing. Generally there were enough
conventional family dwellings, but there were pockets of shortages,
especially in Cardiff and Bristol, places where housing was not
reasonably close to jobs, and other places where rents were high in
relation to average earnings. Throughout the area there was a
shortage of dwellings for groups with special needs, particularly
large families and handicapped people needing special facilities and
services. Single persons were also badly served in some places.
However, housing conditions were much more favourable than
those in some of the very large urban areas elsewhere in the country,
and the problems of finding homes for everyone in the survey area
centred more on renovating old properties and on overcoming many
irregularities in housing allocation.

The Glamorgan pilot study suggested a number of findings, most of which were validated in the larger survey.[1] One concerned the variation between the national pattern of reasons for entering temporary accommodation and the underlying cause of homelessness. Causes connected with housing conditions featured more prominently in the major than in the pilot study, but the importance of marriage breakdown and of multi-problem situations was established, along with the assertion that the loss of a home was not always central to the origin of families' problems. The weakness of preventive and follow-up social services, and the extent to which help for families was confined to the time of their stay in the hostel, were also confirmed, though the pilot study over-estimated the use of temporary accommodation as a social work aid. The pilot survey hinted at the difficulties caused by administrative fragmentation, and at the importance of other services as well as housing in overcoming homelessness.

The bulk of hypotheses, however, were those contained in the Seebohm Report.[2] The Report makes a number of recommendations about avoiding homelessness. It comments on the extent to which local authorities have already taken measures to reduce the evictions from council property, and this was certainly evident in the survey area. 'A basic element,' says the Report, 'must be an efficient system of early warning which will enable families in difficulty or potential difficulty to be identified, so that measures can be taken to prevent arrears accumulating to an extent which makes eviction a serious possibility.' In the context of arrears there was evidence of a very high success rate in preventing evictions through rent guarantee and lump sum payments, where local authorities were willing to make such provision. However, many families did not receive such help, partly because of the selectiveness of local authorities in applying preventive measures, and partly because of the limited level of early warnings. While a wider acceptance of this Seebohm Report proposal in the survey area would certainly have reduced the volume of homelessness, there remained the task of coping with situations in which help with the rent was not needed. This included families with a wide range of social problems, but more importantly those who became homeless in genuinely emergency circumstances, mainly through marital and other domestic upheavals. Although the use of housing and material

[1] pp. 18–20 above.
[2] pp. 20–22 above.

aid services has been effective and could be more so, the survey suggested that a comprehensive preventive service would also need a large expansion of social work effort both to uncover families at risk and to help stop their difficulties leading to homelessness. This would involve an investigation of the possible value of marriage guidance services.

The Seebohm Report goes on to identify the importance of the private sector, and the survey confirmed the large extent to which the homeless were and continued to come from private housing. The Seebohm Report makes three recommendations. The first concerns closer liaison and negotiations with private landlords, and there was evidence in the survey area that local authorities either did not have or were unwilling to deploy many resources for this purpose. Families threatened with homelessness in the private sector were largely left to their own devices to take whatever preventive action they could, although volunteers sometimes helped. The Seebohm Report suggests an advice service for such people, and if it included in its functions some direct assistance in house-finding, it would serve a very useful purpose. An extension of the rent guarantee to the private sector might also be a useful measure, and there was nothing in the survey findings to suggest that such a development would be unworkable or too expensive.

Secondly, the Seebohm Report argues that local authorities should take a greater responsibility for 'the most vulnerable families'—a view which this survey would support, though without much optimism that it will come to pass, unless it is made a requirement in legislation. Housing managers in the survey area were prepared to keep the bulk of the vulnerable families already in public housing, but few were willing to take on additional families without feeling assured that they would reach the required standards of tenancy.

The third proposal is that courts and rent tribunals should work closely with local authorities, and that courts should have a duty to report eviction proceedings. Time was important in successful preventive measures, and there was evidence that the time given was often insufficient for preventing private evictions, even when there was an early warning. The Seebohm proposal could be extended to give local authorities the right to require a longer pause before a Possession Order became operative.

In a final paragraph on avoiding homelessness the Seebohm Committee refers to the value of 'early identification and notification

... of families at risk of eviction ... [which] should be regarded everywhere as the immediate and urgent responsibility of any social agency which is in contact with them'. Over a third of the families in the survey came into temporary accommodation in circumstances that did not involve an emergency, but where there had been no early warning. This problem could be met more effectively with the help of a register of families at risk of homelessness. It could be drawn up by including families experiencing those difficulties, or combinations of difficulties, which are shown in Chapter 3 as major causes of homelessness, alongside the family's previous housing record. The concentration of several problems or the sudden emergence of a problem in a severe form might be taken by the Social Service Department as a warning sign that homelessness could be approaching.

For families who become homeless and enter temporary accommodation the Seebohm Report endorses the suggestions made in a government circular,[1] and emphasizes two points. The Report strongly opposes splitting up families on entry to hostels, arguing that 'we should not by public policy help to make this a permanent separation of husband and wife'. This survey suggested that splitting up did not have this effect, but nevertheless found other difficulties stemming from the same policy. In the short run there was often friction between husband and wife when they were kept apart, especially where the hostels offered no privacy. This did not have any lasting effects on the state of the marriage (as compared with the control group of homeless families who were not split up), but it did sometimes hinder the task of rehousing and resulted in unsuitable rehousing or a continuation of temporary conditions. The second point concerned privacy and other conditions of life in the hostels. The survey showed that families were critical of the lack of privacy and of children's play facilities, rather than of hostel life in general.

The Seebohm Report draws a distinction between 'accommodation for homeless families and special residential care', and says that some families, who may also be homeless, could benefit from a period of training in a recuperative unit. Some homeless families might also 'need social work help and assistance which falls short of admission to a recuperative unit'. The relevant finding of this survey was that a high proportion of the homeless families needed social work help, and that all of them needed close attention from a social

[1] 20/66 (Wales).

worker before deciding that further care was not necessary. The extent of social problems was larger than the Seebohm Committee envisaged, and this could well be a particular characteristic of homelessness outside the big urban centres.

Only Somerset had a recuperative unit in the sense envisaged by the Seebohm Committee, though other authorities in the survey area had intermediate accommodation. In Somerset the primary emphasis was on preventing homelessness through a programme of social work support for families threatened with losing their home, and the recuperative unit took a small number of those who, the children's officer thought, could benefit from a period of residential training. Families who showed some positive response to the training were helped to find a new home and job afterwards, and the results were encouraging.

The survey indicated a wide variation in type and quality of provision to combat homelessness, with the result that some authorities felt that their services were exploited by other authorities which did not make proper provision. There was some evidence of families gravitating to the more helpful authorities, and some of the families being given a push in that direction. In the words of the Seebohm Report, 'the more "helpful" authorities require protection from their less "helpful" neighbours'. The Report suggests the need for 'co-ordinated policy and action between neighbouring local authorities, particularly in the conurbations'. The problem was possibly greater in the administrative counties with their multiplicity of second-tier housing divisions. In the survey area there was some agreed policy between county council departments and local housing departments, but for the most part any family crossing over boundaries was likely to become the subject of prolonged negotiation and bickering, almost always about who should pay for hostel and other costs. Some standardization of policies at the regional level and, as suggested by the Seebohm Report, the advice of a central government inspectorate could be useful. But for the homeless migrant the problem is not who pays hostel charges, but how to get round the discrimination most housing authorities have against newcomers. A form of co-ordination which included a method for transferring families from the waiting-list in one local authority to a comparable point on that of another authority would certainly prevent some homelessness, but given the attitudes expressed by housing managers in the survey area, such a measure would have to be imposed from above.

Weaknesses in co-ordination were equally apparent between departments within a local authority. In particular there was a clash of interests between social work and large-scale housing management. The need for a clear-cut designation of legislative responsibility for the homeless, both as a means of overcoming these clashes of interest, and to permit a more effective and comprehensive service, is a major recommendation from this study. The Seebohm Committee held similar views, and recommended that 'the responsibility for accommodating homeless families, as distinct from providing limited overnight accommodation, should be placed squarely on housing departments. We suggest that the social workers from the Social Service Department might be attached for all or part of their time to housing departments in order to deal with the more difficult social problems among council tenants or people in need of housing'. Recuperative units would come under the auspices of the Social Service Department.

On the question of 'limited overnight accommodation' the survey indicated the need for better co-ordinated control, under the Social Service Department. In view of the extent of homelessness amongst single persons the provision ought to be less limited than at present, and worked out in close collaboration with the voluntary sector, which has long-standing interests in this field. Also the changing pattern and increasing volume of homelessness made the Supplementary Benefits Commission hostels something of an isolated anomaly, and these could usefully be passed to the local authority.

Recuperative units have a place in a personal social service department, though survey evidence suggested that these should be treated with some care. Many homeless families needed rehabilitative care as well as shelter, but it did not always follow that the appropriate provision was a residential recuperative unit. The effectiveness of rehousing within the community accompanied by a programme of rehabilitation was comparable with that of residential care, and offered the families involved a greater sense of long-term stability.

Should housing departments have responsibility for homelessness? The answer to this question depends on how far the causes of homelessness can be seen in terms of housing problems, and how far the cure for homelessness is rehousing. What part do or can housing departments play in preventing, coping with, and overcoming homelessness?

In prevention, housing departments in the survey area were

making a contribution by modifying their eviction policies, but this often depended on the willingness of some other agency to offer a rent guarantee or pay off accumulated arrears. Housing managers almost unanimously presented an actuarial reason for needing such guarantees. Housing budgets were made up predominantly of rent payments from tenants, with a small variable contribution from rates. If the Housing Account has to take the burden of chronic rent arrears, then that burden falls on the remaining council tenants, not on the local authority as a whole. A rent guarantee in effect transfers the liability from a part of the local population to the general rates or taxes. No doubt housing managers could operate a rent guarantee or its equivalent for local authority tenants, and possibly extend the guarantee to the private sector, but only if a separate budget from tax or rate sources was made available for the purpose. Housing managers in the survey area showed reluctance to take on such a task, and no arguments were advanced in terms of administrative convenience or other reasons for moving this function out of the hands of the local authority personal social services and the Supplementary Benefits Commission, although better co-operation between these two latter groups was certainly needed.

There were examples of rent guarantees being used in effective collaboration with preventive social work. Furthermore, the assessment of the causes of homelessness showed that although there was a lot of homelessness caused by housing conditions and shortages, as well as unhelpful attitudes in housing management, the major causes were social issues which would most appropriately be tackled by social workers. In short, although the assistance of housing departments was important, the task of prevention rested primarily on the personal social services.

It was sometimes argued that if housing departments were given greater responsibilities for dealing with homelessness, fewer families would need an interim stay in temporary accommodation because they would be immediately rehoused. While this argument might not hold in areas of acute housing shortage, it could be applicable to large parts of the survey area. However, the survey suggested another factor which was very important to housing managers—the extent to which the special demands made by the homeless could be allowed to supersede the needs of those families waiting patiently on the list for a house or a transfer, but not actually homeless. In districts where there was enough housing to go round, and the task was one of allocation, many housing managers were adamant that their good tenants should have the opportunity to transfer to better-quality or more desirably sited dwellings if they wished, and that those who had qualified for housing through routine channels should be housed before new arrivals or the homeless 'riff-raff'. Some housing managers argued that a spell in low-standard temporary accommodation or a period of housing instability was the price for the privilege of special consideration in rehousing.

To make Housing Departments responsible for rehousing homeless families would therefore not necessarily speed up their rehousing, unless it was at the expense of other valid claims. The managers' view, which was the consensus of opinion in the survey area, was that it would be contrary to the just practice of housing management to pick out one of a range of misfortunes for preferential treatment. Who, then, should have responsibility for housing the homeless? The Seebohm Report is clear on one possibility. 'We are against any division of the responsibility for housing—by, for example, giving the Social Service Department responsibility for letting and managing specific groups of houses for groups of people in special need.' Yet departments other than housing have long had just such responsibilities for special groups, such as the elderly and the mentally ill, on the grounds that it was necessary to combine housing with personal service.

Four of the six authorities covered in the survey had some intermediate housing, where follow-up servicing was possible. There were two schemes under which this was, in practice, a more permanent form of rehousing. In Cardiff, for example, a block of housing had been made available to the personal social services. This was a more acceptable procedure to the housing manager than handing out tenancies to individual applications on behalf of homeless problem families. Representatives of the agencies involved in Cardiff expressed satisfaction with the scheme. In Gloucestershire the County Welfare Committee had bought, built and renovated a number of houses throughout the county, as a contribution to temporary accommodation and a base for rehabilitation. In these and other schemes in the survey area there was no evidence of serious difficulties, provided the families could be moved into other housing when the process of rehabilitation was complete. There was certainly nothing to justify the Seebohm Committee's assumption that such schemes were unworkable; rather the reverse, for the schemes appeared to work well, Gloucestershire's having the added value of offering good-standard instead of sub-standard properties. In view of the extensive need for social work care amongst homeless and rehoused families, this study recommends that, in the survey area and other similar places, specialized housing provision by the Social Service Department should be encouraged.

The study of homelessness in South Wales and the West of England has, therefore, provided evidence to support the Seebohm Committee's view that one agency should be given specific responsibility for the homeless, but has suggested that on balance the personal social services have a larger stake in meeting the needs of the homeless, and should be given overall responsibility, in close co-operation with Housing Departments. There were several examples of effective co-operation in the survey area, characterized by joint consultation at policy and field level, flexibility over eviction policy, and, generally, the hand-over of a number of tenancies to the personal social services. In exchange for transferring these tenancies the Housing Departments found themselves relieved of the task of collecting rent and supervising a hard core of unsatisfactory tenants.

If further evidence is needed it could be found in the attitudes of different officers to taking on this task. None was keen to handle the job. Social workers often resented the amount of drudgery involved in helping the homeless find somewhere to live, and heads of social work departments were conscious of the intractability of many of the problems the homeless presented. On the other hand the housing managers whose views were sought had a still stronger antipathy to coping with the homeless. There was a big element of moral condemnation in their attitudes, and a firm belief that the bulk of the homeless in the survey area were guilty of some kind of culpable behaviour, or were 'deadlegs' who did not deserve any help. The small minority of homeless families with multiple social problems were already felt to cause great difficulties to the smooth running of housing estates. Rather than contemplate their departments playing a wider role, most housing managers argued that such families, even those who were former council tenants, had passed out of the range of housing responsibilities. Asking a housing manager to cope with them was greeted with the sort of mixture of reluctance and disbelief which might, for example, greet the suggestion that universities should be responsible for the educational future of students who have left after failing examinations.

Summary of recommendations

Already many recommendations have been made about ways of trying to deal with homelessness, but for the sake of greater clarity the rest of this chapter draws together the major ones. The reader must, however, look in earlier sections for the arguments on which the recommendations are based.

1. The administrative recommendation is for a flexible national policy to allow the Social Service Department to be made responsible for dealing with homelessness in areas where housing shortages are not a dominant issue. When the study was being carried out this would have included all six local authorities in the survey area.

2. Recalling that there were three basic components to the needs of the homeless—housing, material aid and social work—a government directive would be necessary to ensure full co-ordination with housing and social security services in areas where the Social Service Department is responsible to the homeless. This is suggested because on the evidence of the survey there was insufficient voluntary co-operation, on three points in particular. Firstly, local authorities should be required to make a block of housing available to the Social Service Department, sufficient to meet the emergency needs of the homeless and the longer-term programme of rehabilitation. The two other points affect the Supplementary Benefits Commission. One is that the scale of supplementary benefit available in different circumstances (non-recurring grants) should be notified to the head of the Social Service Department. This would end a frequent source of misunderstanding. The other is that rent payments should be paid through the Social Service Department, at the request of the director of social services, for families with a record of misappropriating benefits. These two might be considered an unprecedented local authority intrusion into the social security services, and an alternative would be to make funds available so that all such grants could be paid by the Social Service Department. This would involve an extension of most local authority material aid schemes as currently practised.

This would leave a great deal to be done through continued voluntary collaboration at the local level, particularly in housing families who have received or are felt not to need rehabilitative treatment.

3. In working towards better co-ordination between different authorities, the use of a central government inspectorate, as

recommended in the Seebohm Report, is an important measure to ensure greater uniformity of provision.

4. To help with the problems of people migrating across local authority boundaries, two measures are suggested; the first, that each local authority should provide, on request, information on the housing situation for people planning to move into that area. This could form part of advice centre activities.[1] The second is that active consideration should be given to a scheme for transferability between housing waiting-lists.

5. The services provided by the local authorities to prevent homelessness could be extended, particularly in the private housing sector. With this in view the rent guarantee schemes which most local authorities now operate should be widened to include tenants of private housing, with an automatic guarantee for a proportion of the level of rent. The wish of local authorities to retain some selectivity over offering guarantees could be met by a subsequent decision in each individual case to extend or terminate the arrangement, but the value of a short-term automatic guarantee in preventing more serious arrears was abundantly clear in those areas where it was employed.

6. A much wider use of social workers to combat the non-material threats to the loss of a family's home is also needed. This, like the rent guarantee, relies for success on an effective early warning system, and the Seebohm recommendation to place on statutory and voluntary agencies the responsibility for referring all people at risk of homelessness to the appropriate department would serve a useful purpose. This could well be structured into a risk register, which would help to keep the large number of chronically homeless people in continuous view. The task of prevention is not, after all, simply to prevent the occurrence of a single isolated incidence of homelessness; a big part of the job is to prevent homelessness recurring and establishing itself as a regular feature in the histories of many families.

7. An effective preventive service would require time to allow the various measures to bite. The time available, even with an early warning, was often not sufficient, particularly in evictions from private housing. It would help if the Social Services Department was given the power in certain circumstances to require a delay in eviction procedure. The problem remains of families becoming homeless in emergency circumstances. A really broadly based early

[1] See p. 188.

warning network, including referrals from one local authority to another where appropriate, would reduce this number, but there is likely to be a continuing number for whom preventive measures are not possible.

8. Turning to people actually homeless, none of the local authorities in the survey area accepted full responsibility for them. The various restrictions imposed on the use of temporary accommodation have resulted in the majority of the homeless not qualifying to receive help. A more comprehensive provision to meet a more realistic view of homelessness would require additional facilities, in the form of both family units and places for unattached men and women. The conventional hostels do not properly meet the needs of either group, and after more than two decades of running temporary accommodation, local authorities should begin to give serious thought to purpose-built facilities, providing, as the National Assistance Act suggested, particular types of accommodation to meet particular needs. The Supplementary Benefits Commission Reception Centres should also pass under the control of the Social Services Department, so that 'casuals' are brought together with the rest of the homeless, and can, if they wish, share in rehabilitation and rehousing facilities.

9. Generous help could also be given to voluntary organizations working within each locality, both to those running residential accommodation and to the newly formed entitlements campaigns. The latter, by the nature of their work, often come into conflict with the local authority and the Supplementary Benefits Commission local offices, but there was evidence that they could have an impact on relieving situations that lead to homelessness.[1]

The value of an advisory service dealing with housing and other social issues has been mentioned. Although this is a function that might best be co-ordinated under the Social Service Department, there are many areas where considerable voluntary experience already exists, and should be used.

10. At present the bulk of the homeless have to cope themselves with their problems, aided a good deal by relatives, friends and neighbours. Without undermining the importance of self-help, local authorities should evaluate carefully how far to push people on to their own devices, particularly when they have asked for help. There

---

[1] This is a recent development, and none of the families in the survey sample had been in touch with an entitlements group. The 'evidence' refers to a few instances noted in the survey area in the first three months of 1970.

was evidence that for many families self-help could do no more than prolong a family's chronic housing instability, where intervention by the local authority could lead to lasting improvements.

11. The task of preventing and coping with homelessness would present the Social Service Department with a variety of jobs. Four in particular can be identified. Firstly, from the time a person or family is threatened with losing their home until they are securely rehoused and in control of their difficulties, there may be a need for social casework services. Secondly, and closely related, there was an abundance of evidence that much prevention and rehabilitation could be undertaken through the assistance of home help facilities of the kind currently in use for the old and handicapped. Large and fatherless families especially could benefit from this. Thirdly, the Social Service Department would need to take on many of the functions of a housing agency, partly to maintain close links with local authority Housing Departments, and partly to ensure a detailed and up-to-date knowledge of the private sector. Only in this way could families be quickly rehoused with a minimum of stay in temporary shelter. Fourthly, there needs to be special attention paid to some small groups who might otherwise be forgotten. In particular this refers to people for whom homelessness or highly unsatisfactory living arrangements have become accepted as routine; for example, children who remain in care because their parents are not sufficiently well housed to look after them, or people like 'dossers' and ex-prisoners who are often assumed not to want a more settled way of life.

Estimating the staffing needs for such services is not easy, but there is no doubt that for many years to come the demand would emerge to make use of any new resources that are provided. Based on the overall assessment of the numbers of homeless, their likely needs, and the average size of social work case loads in the survey area, the six local authorities in South Wales and the West of England could usefully absorb an additional 40 to 50 social work staff. This step would need to be augmented by a substantial increase in material aid in some areas (one or two already have a large budget for this purpose). This assessment is made on the assumption that the social workers would themselves run many of the housing agency functions, but it might be considered appropriate to take on a different designation of staff to cope with this. Working along the same general lines of estimating, the six authorities could usefully absorb 150 home helps for work with homeless families immediately, and the need would be likely to increase as the full extent of homelessness is uncovered.

12. The major change needed from Housing Departments is in policy and attitude towards the allocation of tenancies. The continued preoccupation with discovering who is to blame for homelessness has led to some families appearing to receive privileged treatment, while for others there were refusals to house, or unnecessary delays, when there were empty properties available. A minority of Housing Departments did not warrant this criticism, and showed concern for housing difficult families, provided support was forthcoming from the personal social services. Nevertheless, local authorities should be prepared to house a higher proportion of the homeless more speedily, and at rents which are suited to the low incomes of families such as those in the survey.

13. There were localized housing shortages in the survey area, mainly in parts of Cardiff and Bristol. Generally the supply of housing was adequate, however, except for large families. There were also shortages for groups with special needs, such as the physically handicapped and unmarried mothers. Some building is therefore needed to help combat homelessness.

14. The conditions of housing occupied by families both before and after homelessness were generally poor and lacking basic amenities. This formed part of a wider need to combat bad conditions, particularly in South Wales.

15. Higher wage-levels (particularly in unskilled occupations for both men and women) and higher social security benefits could reduce the importance of poverty as a cause of homelessness. The frequent occurrence of temporary poverty leading to homelessness could be tackled by a more rapid and widespread use of material aids such as the rent guarantee.

This is the cost of recognizing homelessness as a social need and a focus for social service. Whether such changes are made will depend on all the other demands made on government and local authority resources, but tradition has always placed the homeless near the bottom of the list of priorities. The task is larger and more pressing than many officials in the survey area were prepared to admit; and, unlike some other forms of social breakdown, there was still a tendency to think of homeless people in terms of 'deserving' and 'undeserving', and a great deal of pressure was imposed, particularly on the 'undeserving', to devise their own means of getting out of the mess which they themselves had got into. At best the work being done by local authorities at the end of the 1960s offered real opportunities of improvement for a limited number of families, and temporary relief for many more. But there remained many homeless people, needing help, asking for help, and being turned away.

APPENDIX I

SOME SPECIAL PROBLEMS

A phrase which has been bandied about very frequently in recent years is 'hidden homelessness'. Although the main body of the survey was intended to probe the circumstances of families who were known to be homeless, it was clear that some attempt should be made to discover how far homelessness was hidden from the view of the social services, and how much of it existed. For present purposes hidden homelessness is defined in terms of homeless individuals or families for whom there are no effective statutory provisions, as well as those about whom little is known.

The first part of the appendix concerns a section of the population, predominantly old people, who come on to the periphery of both the local authority community health and welfare services and the hospital services. The second section focuses specifically on children who have been separated from their parents as a result of homelessness, or who cannot be reunited with their parents because there is no suitable parental home for them. The final section takes a more general look at possible areas of homelessness in the community which need further investigation and the provision of services.

Homeless old people

A number of assertions were made by social workers and medical staff[1] in hospitals that homeless people, mostly elderly, were filling scarce hospital beds, because there was nowhere else for them to live. This was felt to be a serious problem in view of the growing proportion of old and dependent people in the population.

Social factors are important when considering illness and physical disabilities, especially for the older age-group. Whereas a relatively

---

[1] Unless stated otherwise the medical opinions given here are based on interviews and not published material.

short attack of, for example, bronchitis might be treated at home by the G.P. in a younger person, with an active family around to help, the older person living alone, who has no surviving friends or relatives nearby to help, must be admitted to hospital. To take another example, a severely arthritic wife may have depended for years on her husband, but if he falls ill or perhaps even dies, she cannot be left alone and usually she will be referred to hospital, at first for assessment and, later, for possible transfer to more appropriate accommodation.

Geriatric medicine today aims to restore the older patient as far as possible to a normal community life. However, this is not always an easy task, as, for example, with Mrs Collins. She was an elderly widow who had lived in an upstairs flat for some years until she fell, injured her legs, and had to go into hospital. Once in hospital Mrs Collins was found to be diabetic, with the result that her leg injuries did not respond quickly to treatment, and for many months she remained bed-ridden. Meanwhile, Mrs Collins's niece, who had previously looked after her, married and moved away from the area, so that Mrs Collins was unable to return to her upstairs flat to live alone and unsupported. She went to a residential home for the elderly where she could have a downstairs room and thus remain mobile within the limits of her disability. Mrs Collins herself was happy with this outcome, but had she perhaps not wished to make such a move, there was no alternative to offer her. She needed more care than could be provided in the community, and her only relative had made it quite clear that she could no longer devote the larger part of her time to caring for her aunt.

As with Mrs Collins, there were many occasions when a medical emergency resulted in an elderly person coming into hospital and thereby ending an arrangement for her care by friends or relatives. Once freed from the task, many friends and relatives were reluctant to take it up again, so that the patient became effectively homeless.

Medically, the pattern for many elderly people was of recurrent breakdown and thus a need for immediate short-term admission and similarly fairly quick discharge from hospital back to the community, where they would require varying degrees of regular support. In 1968 the Geriatric Unit in Cardiff, for example, admitted 3,273 patients through 380 beds. The rate of admission has increased despite a recent fall in the number of beds available, but the flow could only be maintained by constantly increasing pressure on the community services. If it was found that there might be difficulties in getting the patient rehoused from hospital, then there was reluctance to admit to hospital in the first place.

A difficulty in this particular unit was that other types of long-stay hospitals in the area had ceased admitting patients, with the result that beds originally designated for those in need of long-term specialist medical care were being increasingly occupied by those in need of limited medical or nursing care who were, in addition, mentally frail and confused in their behaviour. So unacceptable were these patients to the community that they were taking priority over those in need of medical care alone, as it was easier to maintain the chronic physically sick by using other resources. Expressed another way, the community was much more prepared to tolerate and support physically sick old people than those with dementia or any other mental illness.

Families were under a lot of pressure from both hospital and local authority workers to keep a home for elderly dependent relatives, and the Geriatric Day Hospital was often used as a palliative in such cases, offering the much-strained family a day or two a week 'off duty'. None the less, if the patient is resented at home, and finds himself being packed off into an ambulance to hospital twice a week against his will, and without understanding, just how much of a home does he have? Hospital staff might offer some comfort, but their priorities must be to offer medical services, and the hospital resources were increasingly called upon to meet social needs far in excess of their capacity.

There is no easy division of the social and medical needs of the elderly, and hospital and local authority officials often could not agree on the allocation of responsibility for a particular case. Perhaps the most vulnerable elderly person was one who had no urgent medical need, but whose difficulties were mental frailty and/or behaviour which was unacceptable to the community. Some were lucky, like Miss Randall. She had been known to the mental health services for years and as a result of constant support had been maintained in a home of her own, with the co-operation of a tolerant landlady. It is unlikely that such a solution could be provided for the increasing number of elderly mentally frail and confused in this manner. They fall between several services, probably needing something from all of them. They may not be in need of either an acute psychiatric or acute geriatric hospital bed. Nor were there places in the psychiatric hostels, as these were under pressure constantly from the psychiatric hospitals, and were usually full of long-stay residents.

Take as an example the case of Mrs Twinning. A subnormal woman, she was discharged from institutional care after a period of more than twenty years to live with relatives. However, difficulties soon began and for a period of about eight years Mrs Twinning was homeless. She stayed for a while with friends and relatives in turn, all of whom found her behaviour unacceptable. She was referred back on several occasions for psychiatric reports and was deemed, according to records, to require a 'niche' in society, 'not a hospital bed' as she was a 'social' not 'medical' problem.[1] On at least four occasions temporary accommodation was used as a last resort; but it was not until Mrs Twinning's physical health finally broke down after these years of having no home that she was admitted to hospital alongside other subnormal or demented patients, and stayed for the rest of her life.

A case with a different ending concerned Mrs Endean. She had three broken marriages behind her, and her last entry into temporary accommodation left her finally homeless when her husband refused to have her back. Mrs Endean was at this time well past her 60th birthday, her behaviour was described as 'confused and her general demeanour rather muddled although not grossly so'. The Health Department suggested that Mrs Endean was quite able to maintain herself in 'suitable lodgings'. Extensive psychiatric tests confirmed this opinion. However, in a city with a large student population, lodgings available for anyone who might be in the slightest way a liability were of such a poor standard that it was not surprising that nothing was found for Mrs Endean. Eventually she went to a voluntary institution, where she earned her keep by helping to care for the children resident there. Such voluntary institutions, or a hospital, can generally offer some sort of attention twenty-four hours a day, seven days a week. Until welfare services can do this, thereby offering support both for clients and potential landladies, the scope of community services is limited.

Building special accommodation to overcome homelessness amongst such people has made progress in the survey area. A recent report of a housing and estates manager notes that 'the problems of the elderly are very different, and an adequately housed elderly person may suffer hardships and discomforts arising from ill-health and financial difficulties which require special consideration'. This

---

[1] Quotations are from case records.

indicated appreciation that a roof over the old person's head did not necessarily mean that he was living in suitable accommodation. Particularly when infilling new housing developments, a good proportion was of one-bedroom type accommodation, and where possible applicants for retired persons' dwellings were housed 'within the area of their association'. This represented a practical effort to tackle the actual physical housing needs of the elderly, but none the less the waiting-list figures (in Cardiff alone over 1000) indicate only a portion of those in need of suitable housing. Many suffered unnecessary hardships in old properties with no indoor lavatories, unclimbable stairs, etc; and many lived, perforce, in one room while their former home literally crumbled around them, through their inability to look after it.

There was only a small amount of sheltered housing, and demand for it was far in excess of its resources. Throughout the survey area waiting-lists were long and entry was in reality only in an emergency. Glamorgan in particular had the added difficulty of being a large administrative area in which an elderly person might be forced to remain in his own unsuitable accommodation or move some distance to a welfare home, suited to his needs, but perhaps too far removed from his home for his elderly friends to visit him. The other county councils shared this problem, though their resources tended to be more evenly spread.

In Cardiff alone there were (at August 1, 1969) 187 people (147 women and 40 men) on the official waiting-list for residential accommodation. Of these at least 40 needed urgent admission, and there were many others who were not put on the list, as the welfare officers knew there was little chance of them ever being offered a place. Cardiff had 552 places, with an annual turnover of 30 per cent, so about four vacancies occurred each week, usually by the death of a resident or such extreme physical and/or mental deterioration that permanent hospitalization was sought.

Homelessness in its extreme form was clearly seen in the 50 or so elderly persons referred every year to the medical officer of health in Cardiff as actually having nowhere to go. Though not so visibly obvious, other forms of homelessness were spread widely through the elderly population.

Homeless children
The problem of homeless children in care may not be a large one for any single authority—for example they made up 15 of 268 children

admitted to care in Cardiff, 20 of 364 in Somerset and 35 of 542 in Bristol in the year ending March 31, 1969. Yet the cumulative problem of children remaining in care was more serious, and the figures given by local authorities did not really cover all children admitted because of homelessness. There were a number admitted because of unsuitable home conditions, such as condemned caravans or cramped rooms in old houses, and others who were officially admitted after their parents' desertion or sickness, but who remained in care when the parent subsequently lost the home.

It was frequently difficult to evaluate the importance of homelessness as a cause of children coming into care. The example of Mrs Pady is an illustration. Mrs Pady had cohabited with one man and married another and had seven children of these associations. Both fathers were violent and had criminal records. She was unable to set up a stable home with either although she was twice given local authority housing. Apart from these homes, she and the children had lived in private rooms and caravans. During this time she was given support from the Children's Department and the Supplementary Benefits Commission, and twice went into temporary accommodation. On both occasions she was admitted because of disputes with her husband, not technically because of lack of housing.

The regime in the temporary accommodation hostel at this time was restrictive and punitive, and it was disliked by many who went there. On the second occasion Mrs Pady ran away from the hostel, and her children were admitted to care, where they have remained, together with one born since. As the family was so large the children were split between a number of foster homes and children's homes, and only saw each other on rare occasions. Their mother disappeared for some time and eventually contacted the Children's Department from an address in the Midlands, but there was no prospect of her having the children back again. One of the 'husbands' made sporadic contact with the children, but again there was no prospect of him offering a permanent home. The long-term result was that the family was wholly split up. Whether the main cause was homelessness, the fecklessness of the parents, or inadequate or incorrect treatment by the social agencies involved, the fact remains that there were eight children in care with little hope of returning to their parents or being together as a family.

A few children were also admitted to care from temporary accommodation when the time allowed for a stay had expired and the family had failed to find a home. In addition to this children were admitted from temporary accommodation because their mothers became ill, and were unable to set up home again afterwards.

Two separate case histories could illustrate this point. In one case a boy was taken into care after his mother had gone to hospital from temporary accommodation. Both parents were under the supervision of a mental welfare officer, as the mother was diagnosed mentally subnormal and the father as psychopathic. The boy had already been in care previously and was back home on a supervision order. He and his mother were admitted to temporary accommodation after a marriage dispute, and the mother was taken to hospital shortly after this. Two years later the child was still in care, and the local authority had assumed parental rights. It would be possible to argue that, in this case, the child was admitted to care because the parents were incapable of providing a stable home, not because of homelessness; but the line between these two was often very difficult to draw. A child who came into care because of 'homelessness' often, though not invariably, came from a highly unstable family background.

Another case was that of a mother and children admitted to temporary accommodation through eviction. Mother was a drug addict and had to be taken into hospital, so the children went into care. After the mother's discharge from hospital she wanted the children back but was unable to establish a proper home. She slept rough before eventually obtaining a flat in what was described by local social workers as 'the most infamous street in South Wales'. She eventually found a better flat, and with support from the Children's Department the children were returned home. She was later granted a local authority tenancy and the family appeared to be settling down, with intensive social work support.

The position of the unmarried and unsupported mother often caused concern. She was at serious risk of being insecurely housed, and was frequently obliged to live in furnished accommodation or with relatives who regarded her as a 'black sheep'. This often led to her admission to temporary accommodation, and the survey showed up a large number of the admissions of unsupported mothers. In one example a girl was admitted to temporary accommodation from the home of her boy friend and his family, following a family dispute about the paternity of her child. This girl had a long history of unsettled behaviour, being rejected by her adoptive parents and sent to an Approved School. She went to temporary accommodation while the baby was only a few months old and ran away, leaving the child to be received into care. She later set up home in another part of the country with a married man whose child she had just had. She felt that she could not take the older child back, and the only course was for him to remain in care. This child was placed with foster parents, but if his mother could have found reasonable accommodation for herself and had had a better standard of living earlier, there was no reason to suppose that she would not have kept him.

Another story was that of a young woman separated from her husband and unable to set up a secure home for herself. After quarrelling with relatives she was asked to leave their home and went to temporary accommodation. She and her two young children stayed there for five months and were then issued with a notice to leave. The mother disliked temporary accommodation, stating that her period there was 'the most miserable time of my life'. She ran away, and the children were taken into care. After some time she was contacted again and the eldest child was returned to her. She went back to her relatives, and there was a repetition of the family quarrel and admission to the hostel. On this occasion she was given a good deal more support and help, and the Children's Department found accommodation for her in an old but sound terraced house. Her other child was returned from care, and she has established a stable home over the past two years, again with intensive support from the Children's Department. Why could this not have been done after the first admission to temporary accommodation?

There were further situations where children were admitted to care as a result of housing conditions but not recorded as such in official statistics. One concerned a couple with a young family and living with grandparents. The grandparents still had their own children at home and were well known to local social agencies. The home conditions were grossly overcrowded. Father had served several prison sentences. The mother was trying her best to cope in these difficult circumstances, but could not obtain local authority housing (this from an authority which claimed that twelve months was the present maximum wait for a family with 'difficulties'). Eventually the mother's health broke down and she was admitted to a psychiatric hospital and the children into care. She eventually went from hospital to temporary accommodation, where she was reunited with her children while the Children's Department tried to obtain housing for her.

The work of the Children's Department has been stressed in several of these cases, and it might be anticipated that the provisions of the 1963 Children's Act have caused a decrease in the admission of children into care because of homelessness. This appeared to be the case in Glamorgan and Cardiff, but not in Somerset and Bristol.

CHILDREN RECORDED AS ADMITTED TO CARE BECAUSE
OF HOMELESSNESS

	Glamorgan	Cardiff	Somerset
1964/5	19	71	15
1965/6	30	62	8
1966/7	11	43	7
1967/8	0	12	24
1968/9	Not known	15	20

Figures in Bristol have remained around the 35–45 level.

While entries to care as a result of homelessness remain a cause for concern, a child's length of stay in care should not be ignored. In an effort to keep families together, the Children's Department would accept extremely bad housing conditions and frequent experiences of homelessness, rather than take the children away. But if something occurred which made it unavoidable for the children to go into care—and the spark was often, as earlier illustrations showed, an emergency illness, desertion, etc. rather than homelessness as such—then the standard of housing and domestic conditions needed before the family was reunited was generally very much higher. As a result, children came into care for reasons other than homelessness or poor housing conditions, but these factors came to the forefront when discharge from care was considered.

Hidden homelessness
Hidden homelessness exists in our community to a much greater extent than many would be prepared to admit. The use of the description 'hidden' does not imply that it is altogether concealed from view. Rather, it contains two implicit assertions. Firstly that there are known sectors of homelessness which remain hidden in the sense that they have not yet been quantified. Secondly there is

homelessness which is fully identified, but hidden in the sense that the social services choose not to see and provide for it.

It is some measure of the extent of hidden homelessness, and of the difficulty in tracking it down, that over 200 families from the survey had left the area, had discharged themselves from temporary accommodation leaving no address, or had moved, no one knew where, from the last address obtained by the social services, and could not be found. In addition there were areas where single women were not admitted to temporary accommodation, where requests for temporary accommodation were a lot higher than admissions, and instances where families asking for a second spell were refused because they had used up the allotted time—usually three or six months—granted by the authority. In one county borough families evicted from council housing were not admitted to temporary accommodation.

The rent officer and the Citizens' Advice Bureau both reported a steady rate of inquiries from families in private housing threatened with eviction, but few ever came back, and they had no idea what finally happened to them. In one area, annual figures of County Court proceedings in 1968 showed 112 claims for possession, 54 Possession Orders granted, and 18 evictions by bailiffs, mostly by local authorities. In another, of 42 evictions, 22 were from council housing, but none at all had entered temporary accommodation or could be traced. Although only one of the survey families had 'flitted', most local authorities mentioned 'moonlight flits' as a serious and growing problem to them, and it is understandable, perhaps, that many families with rent arrears preferred not to bring themselves to official notice.

There were a large number of families known to be living in overcrowded conditions, temporarily sharing with relatives or friends, perhaps because they still owed a debt to the council or had not raised their standards of management and cleanliness high enough to be considered potential satisfactory tenants; or those who were too newly arrived in the neighbourhood to qualify for council housing.

One city had a growing problem of unmarried expectant mothers who sought the anonymity the area could give them. Yet the local council's policy was to close down all the accommodation it had for single women and girls, arguing that a single 'unit' could easily find a place to live. This left exposed a particularly vulnerable section of the community. If the mother decided to have her baby adopted, she would come out of hospital alone and with minimum support when she perhaps needed some protection. In a few areas there was some prejudice still against housing unmarried mothers, and they might be allocated 'suitable accommodation' which would mean sub-standard housing in less popular districts.

Another large group of people whose problems often remained concealed until it was too late for effective help were people in private housing and regular employment who had no contact with a social agency. Rural families in tied cottages and caravans were an example. The dwellings themselves were often of a low standard, and the families' eviction almost without warning. Such families were in some cases the equivalent of the town problem family; poor and badly paid, with too many children and often records of sickness and unemployment. Their frequent evictions, interspersed with stays in the homes of relatives, meant that it was difficult for agencies to keep track of them. They might not stay in one district long enough to register with a doctor, visit a clinic or be visited by a health visitor, and chronic problems could remain hidden for long periods. Most of the tied properties were farm cottages, but a few were public houses, and some were National Coal Board properties.

Others escaped notice by their very adequacy. They never presented symptoms to bring them to the notice of any agency. Their children were clean, adequately dressed, and neither delinquents nor truants, and would never come to the notice of the health visitors or educational welfare officers. However the struggle to keep up appearances could prove disastrous. Often no one from the social services was warned when a family was getting into serious rent arrears in private housing or falling behind with the mortgage, and there were a number of cases, sometimes of large families, where income from regular employment had only with the greatest struggle covered expenditure, and the growing needs for such things as shoes and school uniforms had finally tipped the scales. Employed families, however low their income, did not qualify for any help with lunches or for the Educational Welfare Grant, which in any case might be as little as £4 every two years. Extra expenses when, for example, a boy might be a member of the school rugby team could be quite high—boots, kit and fares for away matches having to be met from the family's pocket. Providing materials for cookery and needlework for girls could be also a continual drain on its resources, and 23 families in the survey mentioned this. School uniform was a formidable expense, and 35 families complained about it. One local authority school even demanded a regulation swimming costume. The cost of school outings, where spending-money had to be provided as well as the fare, was noted by 28 families, school fares by 24, and school dinners by 15.

The problems of a family like this could be completely hidden. One such had fallen behind with mortgage payments. When eviction was threatened they had been able to borrow the necessary money, but the Order for Possession had already been granted. It cost an extra £31 in solicitor's fees to get their house back. Although the eviction had taken place over three years earlier, no agency had since visited the family to make a sympathetic inquiry to find out if there were any further difficulties. The experience had left scars on the marriage, which the wife doubted would ever heal. Her first reaction to the survey was that she would not be interviewed, but she finally agreed because of her bitterness at the total lack of help she had received.

In another young family the husband, also regularly employed, became ill with peritonitis. Before he had recovered the baby developed meningitis and was then found to have a serious heart defect and transferred to a specialist hospital over forty miles away, where he remained for several months. The cost of visiting the child was high, and the couple were young and inexperienced enough, in the worry and extra expense they were involved in, to neglect the rent in order to pay the costs they felt more pressing. Again their house was privately rented, and though they too were able to offer the full amount of the arrears, possession had already been given to the landlord.

Chronic illnesses like asthma, bronchitis or ulcers, which could cause long spells of unemployment without the obvious disablement that excited immediate sympathy, sometimes tended to get short shrift from officials, who obviously thought there was an element of malingering about them. There was evidence, too, that G.P.s became impatient with the demands made on them by chronically sick or neurotic families, and there were several examples where the doctor stated that he no longer wished the family to remain on his list.

A similar reaction sometimes followed temporary marriage breaks. In the survey there were accounts of wives admitted to temporary accommodation at their doctor's request to recover from quite severe beatings; there were husbands who threw their dinner at the wall or the furniture out of the window; there was an attempted strangling and a knife fight in which the husband was stabbed in the stomach. This suggested the occasional need of a temporary refuge for families for a few days, but the problem was an unpopular one for official or police interference, and at least one authority had responded to a growing demand by deciding that ill-treated wives no longer qualified for admission. They said that the wife in almost every case returned home voluntarily after one or two nights in hostel, and that therefore such women were not technically homeless.

The sincerity of marriage breaks, with or without a separation order, was often questioned. Sometimes the separation did not last for more than a few months, or even weeks, and the Supplementary Benefits Commission felt that occasionally it had been used with definite intention to defraud, and has investigated some of its clients on this suspicion. Some probation officers involved in separation procedure took a similarly cynical view and could quote examples of couples who separated whenever rent arrears became too pressing. They were also concerned about the increasing number of husbands who sought their advice because they were threatened with eviction by their wives.

Generally, if a marriage break seemed permanent, some effort was made to transfer the tenancy of the house to the wife, if she was looking after the children. But there were several cases where the magistrates decided against giving a separation order, contrary to the advice of both Probation and Welfare Departments. In consequence the Housing Department declared itself unable to transfer the tenancy. In one instance the husband had installed a mistress and continued to live with her in the council house while his wife and three children, when their time in temporary accommodation came to an end, had to take a service tenancy looking after an invalid. It was only when the husband decided on a divorce and obtained it that his family were housed again.

Another wife had taken temporary refuge in the hostel with seven of her nine children, and at the last moment refused to take out a summons for cruelty against her husband. She was granted a separation, but the Housing Department refused to acknowledge it as the terms of one shilling per year per child maintenance were so strange. The Welfare Department relaxed its time-limit in favour of so large a family, and the Children's Department pointed out the expense of keeping them if they should come into care, but the Housing Department felt that the husband had always been a satisfactory tenant and that they had no real case for evicting him. While there was a remote chance of reconciliation they did not wish to prejudice it, and so he remained in a large council house while his family stayed in the hostel.

Any family that has proved inadequate with the support of Welfare or Children's Departments and been evicted with their agreement has really lost almost any chance of climbing back to the comparative security of local authority housing. It was very unlikely that any agency would continually pay their debts, and where case-loads were generally so heavy that it was barely possible to keep up with new cases, support might be withdrawn.

The extent of chronic homelessness, and the limitations on services for the kind of families who have formed the core of this study, should not detract from the amount of hidden homelessness amongst small minorities. Since the gradual closing down of casual wards and the much longer distances between Reception Centres,[1] old-fashioned vagrants have become rare, but every town and city had a number of men, some in regular employment, who preferred to sleep rough. The police estimated a hard core group of regular 'dossers' of about a dozen in Swansea, and from ten to twenty in Cardiff. But estimates of voluntary social workers put the figures much higher—up to 80 around the furnace industries of Swansea during the winter, and 120 in Cardiff. From time to time these men might present themselves at the local hospital when their health broke down. Usually they were fed and given some clothing, and a short admission of twenty-four hours for observation might be enough to improve their condition. Others needed longer treatment but often would not stay long enough to get it. The high incidence of mental illness—many of the dossers were ex-psychiatric patients —tended to go completely untreated. Only one of the six local authorities had lodging-houses for some of the older men, who were persuaded to accept this form of housing, when they were beginning to feel the strain of years of living rough.

A great many ex-prisoners joined the hidden homeless. They

---

[1] A survey made by the Ministry of Social Security in 1965 estimated 13,500 people throughout England and Wales using hostels or sleeping rough from time to time. They were mostly labourers or factory workers, with a few professional men. 'The same person might be at one time categorized as an ex-prisoner, at another as an unemployed man, yet again as an ex-hospital patient, and so on. Homelessness or social instability appears to be frequently a manifestation of a deep-rooted and long standing situation or difficulty.' (Homeless Single Persons. A Survey carried out between October 1965 and March 1966. H. M. Stationery Office.)

generally preferred a bedsitter to a hostel because they liked the anonymity it gave, and they wanted to believe they could fend for themselves. Their tragedy in fact was that at their most weak and helpless they often felt or were obliged to feel that they could stand alone. Local prison welfare officers estimated that about half the men released had no interest in finding a home and settling. Many of them would not return to their wives and families but were likely to make brief and changing cohabitations. A few returned regularly to prison after living rough for several months. Those were sometimes alcoholics or meths-drinkers.

Voluntary organizations also found a number of rootless men among their clientele, irregular workers, moving from one area to another. Not all the areas had a Salvation Army hostel, but where they did it was found that a high proportion of the men using it were 'regulars', and it was home to them as long as they stayed in the area. There is evidence that a proportion of cases appearing on every magistrate's list were registered 'no fixed abode' and may have committed an offence as a way of seeking temporary shelter.

Other problems of homelessness that became apparent were those of migrants, both immigrants and families moving from other parts of the U.K. There was evidence too from both prisons and hospitals of growing numbers of drug-takers, and, like alcoholics, they were a group especially vulnerable to becoming homeless.

APPENDIX II

HOMELESSNESS IN LONDON

A research team under the direction of Professor John Greve did a study of homelessness in greater London at the same time as the study in South Wales and the West of England. Although the objectives and the methods of study varied, there was regular consultation, and a good deal of direct comparison is possible between the results of the two projects.[1] This appendix follows the structure of the main report of the South Wales and West of England study (W & W), giving the relevant similarities and contrasts with the London study. All quotations are from the London study.

Introduction and background to homelessness
The London study does not use a single definition of homelessness, because 'one of our aims was to find out what the thirty-three London Boroughs ... meant by "homelessness" in the exercise of their various policies'. It shares, however, with W & W, concern about the weakness of official definitions—' "Homeless" in this context refers to persons in local authority temporary accommodation. This usually means a parent or parents accompanied by children under 16 years of age.'—and notes the variety in working definitions used by different local authorities. It concludes that *'Official statistics of "homelessness" are extremely unsatisfactory as a measure of the problem.'* The reasons for official figures not being a true representation of homelessness are partly related to the extent of exclusions from local authority provisions, and partly to the pressure on temporary accommodation. '. . . if it were accepted that accommodation should be given to all those [families] who have lost their own home and all those with Court Orders against them

---

[1] Statistics and quotations are taken from a preliminary draft of Professor Greve's work, and will not necessarily correspond to the published version. Any *underlining* is Professor Greve's.

... the admission rate would have to be more than doubled and possibly twice as much temporary accommodation would be needed.' This contrasts with W & W where temporary accommodation is rarely full, and there is no evidence of applications from genuinely homeless families being turned down for lack of space.

The problem of homeless people who are unsuccessful applicants for local authority help is a major concern of the London study, as are the difficulties of Commonwealth immigrants. Neither featured significantly in the W &W picture of homelessness.

People using temporary accommodation
Some direct statistical comparisons are possible

Family size—number of children[1]	London	W & W
	%	%
one child	24	19·5
two children	30	24·3
three children	21	17·6
four children	15	18·7
five or more children per family	10	19·9
Average number of children per family	2·8	2·8
Families with a father and mother present[1]	57	61
Age of children[1]		
Under (pre-school)	54	50
Over 10 (secondary school or over)	less than 10%	18

There is considerable similarity in family size and structure, and both studies noted the young age of parents and children, and the high level of single-parent families. In contrast there were many more families with children in care in W & W than in London.

Men admitted to temporary accommodation in London came, on average, from a higher social class than the fathers of homeless families in W & W.[2] 85 per cent of the W & W sample came from

[1] In the London study the figures refer to admissions to temporary accommodation in eight boroughs in 1966–9. In W & W the figures are taken from Chapter 2.
[2] Note the different terms. Few men entered W & W temporary accommodation.

the Registrar General's social class 4 or 5, as compared with just over a half in London. Poverty and unemployment, however, feature extensively in both groups.

Figures are not exactly comparable for levels of unemployment, wages and social security benefits, since the London study looked at the position at the time of applying for temporary accommodation while in W & W the assessment covered the year before the family entered temporary accommodation. Both, however, showed unemployment in about a third of the samples, and stressed the importance of social security (mostly supplementary) benefits for a still higher proportion of the families. Both also noted the link of unemployment and illness.

In London a third of the employed men (about whom there was information) entering temporary accommodation earned less than £15 a week, compared with over 60 per cent in W & W. This disparity was largely balanced by different costs of living, especially rent, but both studies emphasize the extent of poverty. '... Well over a quarter of the larger families admitted to temporary accommodation were dependent on earnings below the Supplementary Benefits scale.'

Causes of homelessness
Both studies distinguish between the immediate and underlying causes of homelessness, and both show a substantially different pattern of causes.[1]

'Immediate' causes for entering temporary accommodation	London[2] %	W & W[3] %
Domestic friction	18	33·6
New to area	9	15·5
Landlord required accommodation	7	10·7
Rent arrears	10	42·8
Unauthorized occupants	40	15·2

The source of data for the underlying causes of homelessness in W & W was the case history of each family in the sample, while for London it was primarily information and opinion from local

---

[1] The London study uses H41 returns, while W & W is based on an assessment by the research team.
[2] Figures for 1968 for London boroughs.
[3] More than one 'cause' per family was possible.

authorities, backed by work relating homelessness to housing deficiency areas. The overall conclusion is that in London '*it is the lack of adequate and secure accommodation at rents that can be paid out of average and below-average earnings that renders most people homeless*. . . . In a housing market characterized by growing scarcity, the stringency of tenancy requirements imposed by the landlord and the rent he charges can both be increased steadily.'

Twenty-two of 32 London boroughs thought the main cause of homelessness to be the housing shortage or a related housing issue (insecurity of tenure or overcrowding), while 6 were primarily concerned with family weaknesses; 21 saw family problems as a contributory cause. Many authorities distinguished two sorts of homeless families, those who were victims of the housing shortage and problem families. The London report says, however, that 'the distinction between the two groups of homeless seems unhelpful except in so far as it underlines the need for adequate casework support. This is not to say that the difficulties are in any way reduced; it is quite clear that the problems of homelessness are some of the most intractable which local authorities have to face. It must be recognized, however, that they are intractable because housing is in such short supply.'

The W & W position has broad similarities with London. There were many families who lost their homes because of poor housing conditions or the high cost of housing in relation to income. There were a few for whom there was a housing shortage, particularly large families. However, in general there was sufficient housing to go round in W & W, and the major housing problem was one of allocation to needy families. In one or two localized areas empty houses were distant from places of work. The biggest group of causes of homelessness in W & W was family problems, with marriage breakdown as the dominant one. Thus the difference between London and W & W was one of degree, not of kind. Nevertheless the implications are important for the type of services provided, and in considering who should exercise overall control of them.

Becoming homeless
The London study does not give parallel information to that given in Chapter 4, except to give general support to one of the important findings. '. . . We have a record of the quite unexceptional but

frequently unnoticed fact that people in trouble turn to their relations before they go to the authorities.'

Rehousing

A point made in the W & W study was that, although local authorities were becoming more willing to retain their existing unsatisfactory tenants, there appeared to be a growing reluctance to take on additional problem families. Indeed, none of the second-tier housing authorities in Glamorgan viewed a family's entry to the county council temporary accommodation as involving a commitment to rehouse,[1] and very few families had considered that by becoming homeless they might jump the queue for council housing. In contrast, many of the London boroughs acknowledged a rehousing commitment for families in temporary accommodation, though it could not always be met. As far as possible the problems of intentional queue-jumping were met by making families spend a long period in temporary accommodation (i.e. on a waiting-list for housing), and some housing authorities complained that pressure on hostel accommodation made them rehouse sooner than they thought suitable.

The problem of rehousing, either directly a family became homeless or after a stay in temporary accommodation, was a much easier one for W & W authorities to overcome, simply because of the greater supply of private and council properties. This is indicated by the shorter length of stay in temporary accommodation (see the later section on *Temporary Accommodation*). In both study areas, however, there were strict regulations and moral attitudes affecting council rehousing. Generally all rent arrears must have been paid, or strong evidence given that they would be paid, and standards of housekeeping, neighbourliness and conduct were taken into account. The distinction between 'deserving' and 'non-deserving' families, based on an assessment of the families' blameworthiness for the loss of their previous homes, affected a majority of housing authorities.

Housing standards

The London study gives information on housing before the families became homeless, but not after they left temporary accommodation. 'The kinds of people who became homeless . . . came overwhelmingly from privately rented accommodation and a disproportionate

---

[1] There was some commitment for families in 'half-way housing' by those authorities which had such a provision.

number from furnished tenancies.' In the London study 10 per cent of families admitted to temporary accommodation between 1966 and 1969 came from local authority tenancies, and 3 per cent were owner occupiers. The corresponding figures for W & W were 28 per cent and 10 per cent. The total numbers coming from furnished tenancies in London is not precisely known because there was no information for 30 per cent of the families, but at least a half of the families from the private sector came from furnished rooms, mostly only one or two rooms each. A precise figure is also not known for W & W, where most of the flats and rooms (27 per cent of the total sample) were furnished.

Professor Greve interprets the extent of furnished tenancies as a comment on the overcrowding many families have to endure. 'Unfurnished lettings were generally larger, at least a third consisting of three rooms or more.' Sharing with relatives and friends was also seen as an indication of overcrowding. About 30 per cent of entrants to temporary accommodation in the London study shared. 'The significance of the sharing of dwellings in terms of homelessness and potential homelessness is considerable. Shared dwellings are amongst those with the worst record of available amenities and standards of repair, they often suffer from overcrowding. . . .' Overcrowding in London is described as 'severe', particularly for larger families. '*Of those with five or more children . . . no less than two-fifths were living in only one or two rooms.*' In W & W 26 per cent of the families entered temporary accommodation from dwellings shared with relatives and friends, and overcrowding was mentioned as a problem for 20 per cent of the sample, though not always as a cause of homelessness. W & W had few examples of the gross overcrowding found in London, except for large families living in caravans.

Both studies looked at the availability of bathrooms and kitchens.

	London[1]	*W & W*
	%	%
Sole use of bathroom	36	44
Shared bathroom	47	23
No bathroom	17	33
Sole use of kitchen	65	56
Shared kitchen	28	30
No kitchen	7	14

[1] London figures are given for a survey of applications for temporary accommodation in 1969, and have been adjusted to remove the proportion about whom there was no information.

Comparisons are also possible for rents:

	London[1]	W & W
	%	%
Weekly rent up to £2 (inc. no rent)	11	29
Weekly rent from £2 to £3	13	33·5
Weekly rent from £3 to £4	19	22
Weekly rent from £4 to £5	21	11
Over £5	36	4

[1] *See note on previous page.*

In London rents were much higher and overcrowding more severe. In W & W there were more dwellings without basic amenities, and, seemingly, more derelict accommodation such as old railway carriages in use. Broadly, however, the conclusion of both studies is that most families have endured very poor housing conditions, and 'families who have achieved a satisfactory standard of housing were in the minority'.

The impact of the social services

Both studies mention the limited scope for *preventive measures*, although the reasons differ. In W & W the emphasis was on the problem of emergencies and on getting adequate warning of eviction risks (e.g. rent arrears), particularly from the private sector. The London study is also concerned with the private sector—'A great deal of homelessness in London is the result of private landlords evicting for reasons which appear to have little to do with any failure on the part of the tenants. This is clearly much less true of areas where housing is not in such short supply . . .' Both studies nevertheless stressed the value of giving social workers the time and opportunity to try to prevent families losing their homes.

The range of preventive measures used in both areas and the attitudes of local authority officials to them were similar. The rent guarantee was used extensively for tenants of council houses, though a minority of London boroughs rejected it because 'It is felt that this tends to discourage regular rent payments and encourage irresponsibility.' This attitude was common amongst housing managers in W & W. Few rents to private landlords or mortgages were guaranteed.

There was little enthusiasm for contacting private landlords; 'in cases of alleged harassment [this] appeared to be standard procedure, but this sometimes only involved letters being sent through the

Town Clerk's Department'. Private landlords were, however, seen to have a responsibility towards the tenants they wish to evict. 'It has been suggested that where landlords intend to seek possession through the Courts they could be required to register this intention with the local authority before proceedings are started.' In both study areas it was noted that few authorities had direct arrangements with the Courts for notification of pending evictions.

'Most boroughs had occasionally been able to arrange for Social Security help with rent arrears', but 'Very few boroughs (nine) have been able to arrange for Social Security rent allowances to be paid direct to private landlords ... [and] ... several boroughs said that local social security managers were reluctant to arrange direct payment' for council tenants. The inconsistency of social security officials in such matters and (in the view of many local authority social workers) their occasional unco-operativeness was noted in both survey areas.

Qualifications for entry to *temporary accommodation* in London were stricter than in W & W—'it is only in exceptional circumstances that single people, childless couples and people with older children are given accommodation'. Generally only the childless couples would be excluded in W & W. In contrast the London boroughs had adapted their properties more rapidly to accommodate husbands—'With the virtual disappearance of communal accommodation and its replacement by "family units", it is now rare for husbands not to be admitted with their families.'

Getting into temporary accommodation in London is difficult. '... there is little evidence that *clearly* urgent cases are being refused help ... [but they] are being refused help *until the emergency has been proved*.' A bailiff's order is taken as acceptable proof, but a story of harassment or marriage breakdown is often not. As in W & W, applicants for temporary accommodation are frequently sent away because they are not yet 'actually homeless', but examples are given in the London study of applicants who were turned away, who would almost certainly have been accepted in W & W. Reasons for refusing entry in W & W usually took one of three forms: (a) the applicant has already used up the allotted accommodation time during a previous stay; (b) the case was a marriage breakdown where the applicant was expected to return very soon to the family home; and (c) the applicant was reckoned to be the responsibility of another area. In London there was the more pressing problem of full temporary accommodation. In both areas, however, there was the feeling that 'provision must not be "over-generous". Such as it is, this is possibly the major guiding principle in decisions affecting the provision of temporary accommodation. It stems from a widespread conviction that if admission were made too easy the service would not only be wide open to abuse but also it would be used by people who could solve their problems by their own efforts.'

There was a big contrast in length of stay in temporary accommodation:

	London[1]	W & W
	%	%
Under 1 month	28·2	57·0
1 to 6 months	20·0	36·9
6 months and over	51·8	5·5

Although there were time-limits in two-thirds of the W & W survey area, and they did have some impact in forcing families out of temporary accommodation, these figures can still be taken as a clear indication of the greater scope for rapid rehousing in W & W.

The families spending the shortest period in temporary accommodation in London were, as in W & W, those suffering from marriage breakdown, and a substantial proportion return to their previous homes. However, the generally longer stay in temporary accommodation in London creates the possibility 'that for some if not the majority of families *it may be the experience of homelessness (and temporary accommodation) which turns them into "problem" families*'. This contrasts with the position in W & W, where there was evidence that separating husbands from wives in temporary accommodation might cause distress, but not marriage breakdown, and where the emergence of problem family characteristics usually ante-dated the experience of homelessness.

The standard of temporary accommodation has improved in London in recent years (as, note, the conversion of old hostels to 'family units'), but some unhelpful attitudes remain. In a system in which, as in W & W, rehousing goes first to the 'deserving' families, Professor Greve mentions the risk that 'personal prejudice can introduce considerations beyond the proper province of a public service. Regular inspections and investigations are inevitable

[1] Inner London for the year ending September 30 ,1969.

consequences of the way rehousing is organized, but the kinds of considerations which are sometimes brought to bear suggest a degree of interference and moral judgement which in other situations would be regarded as intolerable.' The W & W study gives examples of such judgements made by housing managers, while the London study offers some from social workers. The London study is also critical of the continuing use of regulations for the conduct of temporary accommodation which do 'not suggest an atmosphere conducive to co-operation'.

In W & W 59 per cent of families entering temporary accommodation were already on the caseloads of *social work agencies*; 12 London boroughs claimed that for them the proportion was around or above that figure, and 15 said it was below. While London may have more families whose needs are entirely connected with housing, both areas were concerned with how to cope with the large number of problem families passing through temporary accommodation, and both felt 'their [social workers'] supportive work to be generally successful'. Yet despite the assertion of the value of social work, only 3 per cent of temporary accommodation in London is established for rehabilitation work, and 'the general impression is that very little in the way of constructive rehabilitation is taking place, partly due to the shortage of suitable qualified staff but mainly because authorities are unwilling to divert sufficient resources or attention to work which rarely brings quick or obvious results'. This closely echoes the W & W position, though on one point there is disagreement. The London report talks of 'a growing proportion of [problem] families occupying temporary accommodation . . . being ineligible for rehousing in the normal way because of their various inadequacies. *It seems quite wrong to use Part III accommodation in this way.*' Certainly W & W housing officials shared the reluctance to accept that such families had to be rehoused eventually, and that the longer they had to wait the greater the risk of 'their demoralization and further dependence'; yet there was evidence in W & W of temporary accommodation being used consciously as part of the residential arm of a family casework service.

While acknowledging the handicap of staff shortages, the London report goes on to question 'the adequacy of casework techniques and procedures'. It ponders whether social workers have an effective method of treating multi-problem situations which are thrown out of balance by the emphasis given to specific components, such as rent

P

arrears and housing issues. This finds a parallel in the concern and reluctance expressed by some social workers in W & W to accept the homeless on to caseloads.

The London report devotes five chapters to *voluntary services* and housing associations, a sign of their importance in combating homelessness. Only the advisory services in Cardiff and Bristol offer a comparable level of involvement in W & W.

One of the characteristics of homelessness in W & W was the extent of 'dumping' or encouraging homeless families to return to their place of origin, or to some other area where they have contacts. In some instances W & W authorities were obliged to give temporary accommodation to families from London, and the London study of unsuccessful applicants for shelter reports that 7 per cent were assisted to return to their place of origin. 'Families who have come to London from other parts of the U.K. are invariably advised to go back, and they are often given travel warrants to enable them to do so.' As the W & W survey showed, such suggestions are also made to families whose roots are in London.

The London study has further comments on the *problems of departmental boundaries*. 'Fragmentation of local authority services; failure to work out joint policies in the light of social needs; and departmental interests; all combined to produce conflicting policies or time-consuming negotiations between Children's Departments and others controlling social resources . . . *Housing, Welfare and Children's Departments often have different criteria of "social responsibility"*. . . . While the statutory criteria covering Children's and Welfare Departments remain different, disputes over departmental responsibility will continue.'

Two points are made about relations between local authority social workers and other agencies. Both are criticisms which also appear in the W & W survey. First, commenting on rent payments by the Supplementary Benefits Commission, the report says that 'where husbands are apt to jeopardize the family home by spending the rent money their [Supplementary Benefits Commission] present attitude is to regard the man as the reliable head of the household . . . there is evidence that [this] policy is not as effective as it might be. . . .' Secondly an 'area in which administrative and co-ordination problems occur is in providing early warning of impending evictions, or social difficulties where breakdown of the family and homelessness are likely'.

The broad conclusion from a comparison of homelessness in

London and W & W is that there is a substantial amount of similarity, in the circumstances leading to homelessness, the type of families needing temporary shelter and rehousing, the range and quality of services offered to them, and the sort of improvements which are required. Both studies emphasizing that homelessness is a bigger problem than many officials will admit; both see in the plight of the homeless a good deal of official prejudice and traditional Poor Law attitudes; both show the large extent of problem behaviour in homeless families, and the difficulties this presents to the social services; both stress the impact of poverty, illness and family breakdown; both show the dismal standards of housing that the homeless families have experienced. The major difference, which is crucial in deciding the placing of responsibility for an effective service, is that London is dogged by a chronic and acute housing shortage. In W & W the housing shortage is much less severe, but there is a higher level of social breakdown amongst the families becoming homeless, and a need for improved housing conditions and allocation of the existing supply.

INDEX

GEORGE ALLEN & UNWIN LTD

Head office:
40 Museum Street, London, W.C.1
Telephone: 01–405 8577

Sales, Distribution and Accounts Departments
Park Lane, Hemel Hempstead, Herts.
Telephone: 0442 3244

Athens: 7 Stadiou Street, Athens 125
Auckland: P.O. Box 36013, Northcote, Auckland 9
Barbados: P.O. Box 222, Bridgetown
Beirut: Deeb Building, Jeanne d'Arc Street
Bombay: 103/5 Fort Street, Bombay I
Calcutta: 285J Bepin Behari Ganguli Street, Calcutta 12
P.O. Box 2314 Joubert Park, Johannesburg, South Africa
Dacca: Alico Building, 18 Motijheel, Dacca 2
Delhi: B 1/18 Asaf Ali Road, New Delhi 1
Ibadan: P.O. Box 62
Karachi: Karachi Chambers, McLeod Road
Lahore: 22 Falettis' Hotel, Egerton Road
Madras: 2/18 Mount Road, Madras 2
Manila: P.O. Box 157, Quezon City D-502
Mexico: Liberia Britanica, S.A. Separos Rendor 125, Mexico 4DF
Nairobi: P.O. Box 30583
Ontario: 2330 Midland Avenue, Agincourt
Rio de Janeiro: Caixa Postal 2537-Zc-00
Singapore: 248c-6 Orchard Road, Singapore 9
Sydney: N.S.W.: Bradbury House, 55 York Street
Tokyo: C.P.O. Box 1728, Tokyo 100–91